The L⌒ ⸺ ⸺ ⸺ ⸺ ⸺

One Hundred Years
with the *Library of Congress*
Subject Headings System

The LCSH Century: One Hundred Years with the Library of Congress Subject Headings System has been co-published simultaneously as *Cataloging & Classification Quarterly*, Volume 29, Numbers 1/2 2000.

The *Cataloging & Classification Quarterly* Monographic "Separates"

Below is a list of "separates," which in serials librarianship means a special issue simultaneously published as a special journal issue or double-issue *and* as a "separate" hardbound monograph. (This is a format which we also call a "DocuSerial.")

"Separates" are published because specialized libraries or professionals may wish to purchase a specific thematic issue by itself in a format which can be separately cataloged and shelved, as opposed to purchasing the journal on an on-going basis. Faculty members may also more easily consider a "separate" for classroom adoption.

"Separates" are carefully classified separately with the major book jobbers so that the journal tie-in can be noted on new book order slips to avoid duplicate purchasing.

You may wish to visit Haworth's website at . . .

http://www.haworthpressinc.com

. . . to search our online catalog for complete tables of contents of these separates and related publications.

You may also call 1-800-HAWORTH (outside US/Canada: 607-722-5857), or Fax 1-800-895-0582 (outside US/Canada: 607-771-0012), or e-mail at:

getinfo@haworthpressinc.com

The LCSH Century: One Hundred Years with the Library of Congress Subject Headings System, edited by Alva T. Stone, MLS (Vol. 29, No. 1/2, 2000). *Traces the 100-year history of the Library of Congress Subject Headings, from its beginning with the implementation of a dictionary catalog in 1898 to the present day, exploring the most significant changes in LCSH policies and practices, including a summary of other contributions celebrating the centennial of the world's most popular library subject heading language.*

Maps and Related Cartographic Materials: Cataloging, Classification, and Bibliographic Control, edited by Paige G. Andrew, MLS and Mary Lynette Larsgaard, BA, MA (Vol. 27, No. 1/2/3/4, 1999) *Discover how to catalog the major formats of cartographic materials, including sheet maps, early and contemporary atlases, remote-sensed images (i.e., aerial photographs and satellite images), globes, geologic sections, digital material, and items on CD-ROM.*

Portraits in Cataloging and Classification: Theorists, Educators, and Practitioners of the Late Twentieth Century, edited by Carolynne Myall, MS, CAS, and Ruth C. Carter, PhD. (Vol. 25, No. 2/3/4, 1998) *"This delightful tome introduces us to a side of our profession that we rarely see: the human beings behind the philosophy, rules, and interpretations that have guided our professional lives over the past half century. No collection on cataloging would be complete without a copy of this work." (Walter M. High, PhD, Automation Librarian, North Carolina Supreme Court Library; Assistant Law Librarian for Technical Services, North Carolina University, Chapel Hill)*

Cataloging and Classification: Trends, Transformations, Teaching, and Training, edited by James R. Shearer, MA, ALA and Alan R. Thomas, MA, FLA (Vol. 24, No. 1/2, 1997) *"Offers a comprehensive retrospective and innovative projection for the future." (The Catholic Library Association)*

Electric Resources: Selection and Bibliographic Control, edited by Ling-yuh W. (Miko) Pattie, MSLS, and Bonnie Jean Cox, MSLS (Vol. 22, No. 3/4, 1996) *"Recommended for any reader who is searching for a thorough, well-rounded, inclusive compendium on the subject." (The Journal of Academic Librarianship)*

Cataloging and Classification Standards and Rules, edited by John J. Reimer, MLS (Vol. 21, No. 3/4, 1996). *"Includes chapters by a number of experts on many of our best loved library standards. . . . Recommended to those who want to understand the history and development of our library standards and to understand the issues at play in the development of new standards." (LASIE)*

Classification: Options and Opportunities, edited by Alan R. Thomas, MA, FLA (Vol. 19, No. 3/4, 1995). *"There is much new and valuable insight to be found in all the chapters. . . . Timely in refreshing our confidence in the value of well-designed and applied classification in providing the best of service to the end-users." (Catalogue and Index)*

Cataloging Government Publications Online, edited by Carolyn C. Sherayko, MLS (Vol. 18, No. 3/4, 1994). *"Presents a wealth of detailed information in a clear and digestible form, and reveals many of the practicalities involved in getting government publications collections onto online cataloging systems." (The Law Librarian)*

Cooperative Cataloging: Past, Present and Future, edited by Barry B. Baker, MLS (Vol. 17, No. 3/4, 1994). *"The value of this collection lies in its historical perspective and analysis of past and present approaches to shared cataloging. . . . Recommended to library schools and large general collections needing materials on the history of library and information science." (Library Journal)*

Languages of the World: Cataloging Issues and Problems, edited by Martin D. Joachim (Vol. 17, No. 1/2, 1994). *"An excellent introduction to the problems libraries must face when cataloging materials not written in English. . . . should be read by every cataloger having to work with international materials, and it is recommended for all library schools. Nicely indexed." (Academic Library Book Review)*

Retrospective Conversion Now in Paperback: History, Approaches, Considerations, edited by Brian Schottlaender, MLS (Vol. 17, No. 1/2, 1992). *"Fascinating insight into the ways and means of converting and updating manual catalogs to machine-readable format." (Library Association Record)*

Enhancing Access to Information: Designing Catalogs for the 21st Century, edited by David A. Tyckoson (Vol. 13, No. 3/4, 1992 *"Its down-to-earth, nontechnical orientation should appeal to practitioners including administrators and public service librarians." (Library Resources & Technical Services)*

Describing Archival Materials: The Use of the MARC AMC Format, edited by Richard P. Smiraglia, MLS (Vol. 11, No. 3/4, 1991). *"A valuable introduction to the use of the MARC AMC format and the principles of archival cataloging itself." (Library Resources & Technical Services)*

Subject Control in Online Catalogs, edited by Robert P. Holley, PhD, MLS (Vol. 10, No. 1/2, 1990). *"The authors demonstrate the reasons underlying some of the problems and how solutions may be sought. . . . Also included are some fine research studies where the researches have sought to test the interaction of users with the catalogue, as well as looking at use by library practitioners." (Library Association Record)*

Library of Congress Subject Headings: Philosophy, Practice, and Prospects, edited by William E. Studwell, MSLS (Supp. #2, 1990). *"Plays an important role in any debate on subject cataloging and succeeds in focusing the reader on the possibilities and problems of using Library of Congress Subject Headings and of subject cataloging in the future." (Australian Academic & Research Libraries)*

Authority Control in the Online Enviroment: Considerations and Practices, edited by Barbara B. Tillett, PhD (Vol. 9, No. 3, 1989). *"Marks an excellent addition to the field. . . . [It] is intended, as stated in the introduction, to 'offer background and inspiration for future thinking.' In achieving this goal, it has certainly succeeded." (Information Technology & Libraries)*

National and International Bibliographic Databases: Trends and Prospects, edited by Michael Carpenter, PhD, MBA, MLS (Vol. 8, No. 3/4, 1988). *"A fascinating work, containing much of concern both to the general cataloger and to the language or area specialist as well. It is also highly recommended reading for all those interested in bibliographic databases, their development, or their history." (Library Resources & Technical Services)*

Cataloging Sound Recordings: A Manual with Examples, Deanne Holzberlein, PhD, MLS (Supp. #1, 1988). *"A valuable, easy to read working tool which should be part of the standard equipment of all catalogers who handle sound recordings." (ALR)*

Education and Training for Catalogers and Classifiers, edited by Ruth C. Carter, PhD (Vol. 7, No. 4, 1987). *"Recommended for all students and members of the profession who possess an interest in cataloging." (RQ-Reference and Adult Services Division)*

The United States Newspaper Program: Cataloging Aspects, edited by Ruth C. Carter, PhD (Vol. 6, No. 4, 1986). *"Required reading for all who use newspapers for research (historians and librarians in particular), newspaper cataloguers, administrators of newspaper collections, and–most important– those who control the preservation pursestrings." (Australian Academic & Research Libraries)*

Computer Software Cataloging: Techniques and Examples, edited by Deanne Holzberlein, PhD, MLS (Vol. 6, No. 2, 1986). *"Detailed explanations of each of the essential fields in a cataloging record. Will help any librarian who is grappling with the complicated responsibility of cataloging computer software." (Public Libraries)*

The Future of the Union Catalogue: Proceedings of the International Symposium on the Future of the Union Catalogue, edited by C. Donald Cook (Vol. 2, No. 1/2, 1982). *Experts explore the current concepts and future prospects of the union catalogue.*

The *LCSH* Century:
One Hundred Years
with the *Library of Congress Subject Headings* System

Alva T. Stone, MLS
Editor

The LCSH Century: One Hundred Years with the Library of Congress Subject Headings System has been co-published simultaneously as *Cataloging & Classification Quarterly*, Volume 29, Numbers 1/2 2000.

The Haworth Information Press
An Imprint of
The Haworth Press, Inc.
New York • London • Oxford

Published by

The Haworth Information Press, 10 Alice Street, Binghamton, NY 13904-1580 USA

The Haworth Information Press is an imprint of The Haworth Press, Inc., 10 Alice Street, Binghamton, NY 13904-1580 USA.

The LCSH Century: One Hundred Years with the Library of Congress Subject Headings System has been co-published simultaneously as *Cataloging & Classification Quarterly,* Volume 29, Numbers 1/2 2000.

Cover design by Thomas J. Mayshock Jr.

Library of Congress Cataloging-in-Publication Data

The LCSH century : one hundred years with the Library of Congress subject headings system / Alva T. Stone, editor.
    p. cm.
    Published also as v. 29, no. 1/2 2000 of Cataloging & classification quarterly.
    Includes bibliographical references and index.
    ISBN 0-7890-1168-9 (alk. paper)–ISBN 0-7890-1169-7 (pbk. : alk. paper)
    1. Subject headings, Library of Congress. I. Stone, Alva T. II. Cataloging & classification quarterly.
Z695.Z8 L5238 2000
025.4′9–dc21
                                                    00-039568

Indexing, Abstracting & Website/Internet Coverage

This section provides you with a *chronological list* of major indexing & abstracting services. That is to say, each service began covering this periodical during the year noted in the right column. Most Websites which are listed below have indicated that they will either post, disseminate, compile, archive, cite or alert their own Website users with research-based content from this work. (This list is as current as the copyright date of this publication.)

Abstracting, Website/Indexing Coverage .... Year When Coverage Began

- *INDEX TO PERIODICAL ARTICLES RELATED TO LAW* .. 1992

- *INFORMATION SCIENCE ABSTRACTS* 1992

- *INSPEC* 1992

- *LIBRARY & INFORMATION SCIENCE*
    ABSTRACTS (LISA) 1992

- *LIBRARY LITERATURE* 1992

- *REFERATIVNYI ZHURNAL (Abstracts Journal of the*
    All-Russian Institute of Scientific and Technical Information) ... 1992

- *INFORMED LIBRARIAN, THE* 1993

- *NEWSLETTER OF LIBRARY AND*
    INFORMATION SERVICES 1993

(continued)

(continued)

Special Bibliographic Notes related to special journal issues (separates) and indexing/abstracting:

- indexing/abstracting services in this list will also cover material in any "separate" that is co-published simultaneously with Haworth's special thematic journal issue or DocuSerial. Indexing/abstracting usually covers material at the article/chapter level.
- monographic co-editions are intended for either non-subscribers or libraries which intend to purchase a second copy for their circulating collections.
- monographic co-editions are reported to all jobbers/wholesalers/approval plans. The source journal is listed as the "series" to assist the prevention of duplicate purchasing in the same manner utilized for books-in-series.
- to facilitate user/access services all indexing/abstracting services are encouraged to utilize the co-indexing entry note indicated at the bottom of the first page of each article/chapter/contribution.
- this is intended to assist a library user of any reference tool (whether print, electronic, online, or CD-ROM) to locate the monographic version if the library has purchased this version but not a subscription to the source journal.
- individual articles/chapters in any Haworth publication are also available through the Haworth Document Delivery Service (HDDS).

ABOUT THE EDITOR

Alva T. Stone, MLS, has practiced cataloging at Florida State University for 25 years–first at the Main Library and later at the Law Library, except for a two-year hiatus as Librarian of the FSU Study Center in Florence, Italy. She served for four years on the Subject Analysis Committee (SAC) of the American Library Association's ALCTS Cataloging & Classification Section, and authored the 1992 "year's work in subject analysis" survey for *Library Resources & Technical Services*. Other publications of Ms. Stone have appeared in *Cataloging & Classification Quarterly, Law Library Journal,* and *American Libraries*. She has also served as Chair of two sections and one committee of the American Association of Law Libraries, and on advisory committees of the Florida Center for Library Automation (FCLA). She has taught Bibliographic Organization as an adjunct professor at the FSU School of Information Studies, and since 1987 has been contributing editor for the "Subject Headings" column in *Technical Services Law Librarian*.

The *LCSH* Century:
One Hundred Years
with the *Library of Congress*
Subject Headings System

CONTENTS

FUTURE PROSPECTS

BACKGROUND

The *LCSH* Century:
A Brief History
of the *Library of Congress Subject Headings,*
and Introduction to the Centennial Essays

SUMMARY. The history of the *Library of Congress Subject Headings* is traced, from its beginnings with the implementation of a dictionary catalog at the Library of Congress in 1898 to the present day. The author describes the most significant changes which have occurred in *LCSH* policies and practices during the 100-year period. Events noted near the end of the century indicate an increased willingness on the part of the Library of Congress to involve the larger library community in the creation or revision of subject headings and other decision-making

Alva T. Stone MLS, is Head of Cataloging, College of Law Library, Florida State University, Tallahassee, FL 32306-1600 (E-mail: atstone@law.fsu.edu).

The author wishes to acknowledge Lynn El-Hoshy, Senior Cataloging Policy Specialist, The Library of Congress, for her assistance in verifying certain facts and dates.

[Haworth co-indexing entry note]: "The *LCSH* Century: A Brief History of the *Library of Congress Subject Headings,* and Introduction to the Centennial Essays." Stone, Alva T. Co-published simultaneously in *Cataloging & Classification Quarterly* (The Haworth Information Press, an imprint of The Haworth Press, Inc.) Vol. 29, No. 1/2, 2000, pp. 1-15; and: *The LCSH Century: One Hundred Years with the Library of Congress Subject Headings System* (ed: Alva T. Stone) The Haworth Information Press, an imprint of The Haworth Press, Inc., 2000, pp. 1-15. Single or multiple copies of this article are available for a fee from The Haworth Document Delivery Service [1-800-342-9678, 9:00 a.m. - 5:00 p.m. (EST). E-mail address: getinfo@haworthpressinc.com].

regarding the *LCSH* system. Finally, the author provides a summary of
the other contributions to this collection of essays, a collection which
celebrates the "centennial" of the world's most popular library subject
heading language. *[Article copies available for a fee from The Haworth Document Delivery Service: 1-800-342-9678. E-mail address: <getinfo@haworthpress
inc.com> Website: <http://www.haworthpressinc.com>]*

KEYWORDS. *Library of Congress Subject Headings,* subject heading
languages, subject access

The summer of 1998 witnessed a different sort of celebration in Washington, DC than the usual Fourth of July fireworks on "The Mall." At the
Library of Congress speeches were made, awards presented, and a cake
designed to look like a big red book was ceremoniously sliced and consumed
by invited guests.[1] It was the 100th birthday of one of LC's perennial best-
sellers, the *Library of Congress Subject Headings (LCSH).*

Technically speaking, LC's publication of its subject headings list did not
really begin in 1898. That was instead the year in which the Library of
Congress converted from an author–plus a classed–catalog to a **dictionary
catalog**, which incorporated author, title, and subject entries into a single file.
For its first subject headings, LC used the American Library Association's
List of Subject Headings for Use in Dictionary Catalogs (1st ed., 1895; 2nd
ed., 1898), to which the LC catalogers added new headings as they were
needed. Meanwhile, with the ALA community clamoring for greater standardization as well as more cooperative cataloging, there arose a ready and
appreciative market for the LC catalog Card Distribution Service, which
began in 1902. To the larger and "outside" library world, then, that was when
subject headings formulated and assigned by LC began to be noticed and
utilized; hence, the year 2002 might be a reasonable candidate for the centennial of *LCSH*. The first actual printing of *Subject Headings Used in the
Dictionary Catalogues of the Library of Congress* (later to be titled *Library of
Congress Subject* Headings) began in the summer of 1909, was issued in
parts, and was completed in March 1914. Based strictly on first-edition data,
therefore, one could argue that the 100th year of the *LCSH* will not occur
until 2009, or even 2014. However, there was some publication history prior
to 1909. As shown in the **Chronology of Official *LCSH*-Related Publications** appended to this essay, in 1906 the Library of Congress published a
preliminary list of subject subdivisions for place names and of subjects that
could be subdivided by place. With all of these different dates to mark a
beginning, perhaps it is the most sensible thing to choose 1898, assuming this
to have been the year that the very first modification to the ALA *List* was
made for LC use, and hence, the evolution of the *Library of Congress Subject*

Headings was begun. At any rate, the span of dates certainly coincides closely enough to those belonging to the 20th century, and that is why we have chosen for the present collection the title, **The *LCSH* Century**.

In this collection of papers there are frequent references to the guidelines for subject access delineated by Charles Ammi Cutter. This is remarkable because his *Rules for a Dictionary Catalogue* was originally published in 1876. A textbook on cataloging published in 1963 attested that "nothing has been written since that is any clearer than Mr. Cutter's explanation of this aspect of cataloging."[2] Certainly, we are indebted to Cutter for the concepts of **direct entry**, the use of **natural language**, and the syndetic structure (**cross-references**) meant to compensate for the "scattering" of related topics in the dictionary catalog. And yet, the influence of Cutter on the *LCSH* was not acknowledged by the Library of Congress until 1972, when that acknowledgment was made unofficially by the Chief of the LC Subject Cataloging Division.[3] However, during the early development of the *LCSH*, J. C. M. Hanson at the Library of Congress adopted a more pragmatic approach than what Cutter had intended, resulting in some inconsistencies in the forms of subject headings and the choice of cross-references.[4] Inverted headings, meant to bring some subjects together in logical groupings, were established in the early *LCSH* lists to a much greater extent than had been recommended by Charles Cutter.

It has also been noted that, whereas Cutter's *Rules* eventually led to much greater elaboration of rules–and examples–in the area of descriptive cataloging, in *subject* cataloging the efforts resulted in lists rather than codes.[5] Paul Dunkin believed that our excessive focus on the lists and their growth actually hindered the further development of the basic philosophy of the rules for subject headings.[6] Perhaps this explains why throughout the century the library community made numerous requests for explanations of the fundamental rules or theory behind LC's subject heading lists. Let's continue to sketch the history of *LCSH*, and see how this theme arises again and again.

The Library of Congress developed the *LCSH* for use in its own catalogs. The list was also considered appropriate for the very largest public libraries, some colleges and many university libraries. Smaller libraries continued to use the ALA *List*, last published in a 3rd edition (1911), and later, the *Sears List of Subject Headings*, which first appeared in 1923. *LCSH* was criticized for its aforementioned inverted headings, as well as its subdivided headings, which seemed to be a carryover from the days of the alphabetico-classed catalog. Also, in the 1920's and 1930's the LC list lacked some of the syndetic structure found in *ALA* or in *Sears*. (It was not until 4th *LCSH* (1943) that "refer from" references were included, in addition to the "see" and "see also" cross-references, but printed in a separate volume; the 5th *LCSH* (1948) incorporated the "refer from" references in the main list.[7]) Nevertheless, by the 1930's more and more libraries found themselves doing a retrospective conversion of subject headings. They abandoned their homegrown lists, the outdated (1911) ALA *List*, or *Sears*, and converted to the *LCSH* for several compelling reasons: as their library collections grew, the desire for more precise subject headings increased; it was no longer economically feasible to continually revise subject headings appearing on LC catalog cards; and, the *LCSH* was the only general list that made a consistent practice of keeping up to date by creating new subject headings for new topics.[8] LC had been publishing **supplements** from time to time, but many outside catalogers reported using the card distribution service as an informal notification about the newest subject headings. (In the 1940's a regular column in *Library Journal* also listed the newest LC subject headings, until finally, beginning in 1948, LC started issuing its printed supplements on a quarterly basis.)

Simultaneous to the increased adoption of *LCSH* in the 1930's, the library community began to demand a textbook on understanding and applying the *LCSH*. As a compromise, in the early 1940's "notes on L.C. methods and authorities used to establish certain types of headings, geographic headings, names of Indian and African tribes and languages, were obtained" and published in the aforementioned column of *Library Journal*, largely through the efforts of the ALA Committee on Subject Headings and the "friendly cooperation of the Library of Congress."[9] Finally in 1946 a treatise on subject headings by Julia Pettee, librarian of the Union Theological Seminary in New York, was published; later that same year the Library of Congress indicated that it was also working on a manual.[10] The latter was not published until 1951. Written by the Chief of the LC Subject Cataloging Division, David J. Haykin, it was a 140-page book that basically reiterated most of Cutter's principles and tried to explain or rationalize some of the seeming inconsistencies in *LCSH*. (Haykin's work is discussed in more detail by a couple of the authors in this collection.) Neither of these books, however, provided a true manual of practice for using and applying the *LCSH*.[11] Another controversy that flared up in the literature of the 1940's was a debate over whether or not published subject bibliographies were superior to catalog subject headings as a means of access to subject information.[12]

At mid-century there was a growing dissatisfaction with *LCSH*. Libraries were feeling the pressures of the increased publication and acquisition activities of this postwar period.[13] There was a need to improve subject access but also to make subject cataloging less costly, goals which are often in conflict with each other. Critics complained that "the basic rules and techniques for the construction of subject catalogs and the development of subject heading lists have undergone virtually no change in the last 75 years," and that such practices did not reflect any clear understanding of function or purpose.[14] One trend that gained popularity in the 1950's and 1960's was a move to the **divided catalog**. Considering the complexity of catalog filing rules, along with the ever-lengthening, more precise subject headings, the rise of the "subject catalog" (separated from the author/title catalog) undoubtedly did benefit the library staff, but some librarians worried that it often diminished access–especially access of the serendipitous sort–for the catalog user. Pettee observed the irony that libraries had gone "full circle"–from author and classed catalogs to dictionary catalogs and then back to divided catalogs.[15] (Interesting comment, but, an alphabetical, specific-entry subject catalog is *not* the same as a classed catalog.) As another result of the Cold War period's rapid expansion of knowledge and information, many catalogers felt that the Library of Congress was too slow in adopting new subjects or revising antiquated terminology. Nevertheless, LC did demonstrate a greater sense of responsibility in educating the library community during this time, principally by including in its *Cataloging Service Bulletin* explanations and guidelines on the use of certain types of subject headings or subdivisions, as well as notices of major revisions. The reporting concerning *LCSH* printed in *Cataloging Service Bulletin* has continued and increased from the 1950's to the present day. In 1957 the 6th edition of *LCSH* was published; its innovation was the increase from two to three columns of subject headings per page, a format which would remain constant through to 1999.

Another development of the latter half of the 20th century was the experimentation with **automation** as a means for resolving the problems of subject access; this resulted in several efforts to create or discover a viable alternative to the *LCSH*. In the 1950's there was much discussion of "uniterms" (later called "descriptors") designed for coordinate indexing via machine manipulation. A proliferation of keyword indexes (KWIC, KWOC, etc.) was witnessed in the 1960's-1970's, succeeded in later years by the keyword/Boolean search techniques utilized in most online public catalogs (OPACs). Thesauri became popular, particularly in special libraries, during the same period. And, in the 1970's-1980's a powerful string index language, PRECIS, was used by the British Library (and even studied briefly by the Library of Congress as an augmentation to *LCSH*). These new techniques, experiments or functionalities proved to be useful, to a point. But ultimately it was generally concluded that none of these means for subject access could fully match the effectiveness of a **precoordinated, controlled vocabulary** such as the *LCSH* system.[16] In the 1980's and 1990's the emphasis shifted to enhancing, rather than eliminating, the *LCSH* access, e.g., through mapping to other vocabularies or linking to classification numbers.

Social changes also had an impact, resulting in complaints in the 1960's-1970's about **bias** in the *LCSH*. Gradually, and often after much study and input from the ALA Subject Analysis Committee or other special-focus groups, the Library of Congress did revise many of the offensive terms or subtly-discriminatory wordings of headings related to racial, ethnic, religious, or gender groups. More technical changes occurred in the 1970's: the LC practice of using free-floating subdivisions was named in 1974 and later was expanded to new types or categories of headings; the 8th *LCSH* (1975) grew to two volumes and adopted its modern title, *Library of Congress Subject Headings*; in 1976 LC discontinued its practice of dual methods for geographic subdividing ("direct" and "indirect" instructions); and the *LCSH* began to print some headings that had previously been omitted (legendary and fictitious characters, works of art, chemicals, ancient cities, structures, buildings, parks and reserves, and others). Also in 1976, the Library of Congress offered the list in a *microfiche* version for the first time. This made it affordable for libraries desiring to have multiple copies; the microfiche was portable, and very convenient for libraries that had converted to or were planning for COM (computer-output microform) catalogs.

Practitioners and professors writing in the literature began to propose the creation of a subject cataloging "code" to do for subject analysis and practice what the *Anglo-American Cataloguing Rules* 2nd ed. (AACR2) did for descriptive cataloging. Although technically *not* a general code, the expressed need was partially fulfilled by the Library of Congress in 1984 through the publication of its *Subject Cataloging Manual: Subject Headings* (SCM:SH). It was necessary, it may be argued, to publish such a manual in order to promulgate the rules for assigning the numerous and complicated free-floating subdivisions to be used under various categories or pattern headings. But the manual provided much more information, including LC policies and procedures, scope notes, and detailed guidance on applying subject headings for particular disciplines or forms of material. For the first time, "outside" catalogers were able to read the same memoranda, or instruction sheets, available to LC catalogers, and thus acquire the opportunity to become more consistent and improve the quality of the *LCSH* strings that they assigned to original-cataloging records for the bibliographic utilities. From this point forward, the *LCSH* ceased being simply a list, and became the *LCSH* **system**; a cataloger could no longer select or verify a subject heading using the *LCSH* alone, but instead must use the list in conjunction with the *Subject Cataloging Manual: Subject Headings*. The SCM:SH has been issued in a looseleaf format, to allow for the ease of updating (generally there have been two releases of added or revised pages each year). Updating of the *LCSH* also became more timely during this period. Subscriptions to the "Weekly Lists" of new and changed subject headings and references were first offered in 1984.

In 1985 the Library of Congress began to regularize its practices regarding the provision of cross-references for new subject headings, and hoped to conduct a review and revision of the syndetic structure under older headings, as time allowed, to bring them into conformity with the new criteria. The criteria called for making links between subject headings only under certain circumstances, e.g., when the concepts or objects represented by the terms had a whole/part or genus/species relationship, among other rigorous conditions. At this time, the *LCSH* converted its notation devices to those most often used in thesaurus construction, i.e., BT for "broader term," NT for "narrower term," and so forth. The late 1980's also saw the introduction of two new formats for *LCSH*: one was the *CDMARC Subjects* for use on personal computers with CD ROM drives; the other was the *Subject Authorities* in MARC format issued on magnetic tape (later also available via FTP transfer). The latter product enabled bibliographic utilities such as OCLC and RLIN to load the *LCSH* authorities in their databases and make searching of them available to their member libraries. While these improvements in the sharing of guidelines and dissemination of additions and changes were occurring, the *LCSH* continued to grow, expanding to three volumes beginning with the 11th ed. (1988). It was also in that year that new editions of the printed *LCSH* began to be published on an annual basis.

The 1990's ushered in a new era of **cooperation**, seeming to suggest that the Library of Congress no longer took a proprietary view of the *LCSH*, but rather, was finally acknowledging its responsibility to *all* users of the *LCSH* system. In May 1991, LC hosted an invitational Subject Subdivisions Conference, which resulted in many changes to *LCSH*, still ongoing and regularly summarized in *Cataloging Service Bulletin*. Perhaps even more significant has been the development, under the auspices of the Program for Cooperative Cataloging, of the **Subject Authority Cooperative Program** (SACO). The SACO process allows specially-trained "outside" catalogers to propose new subject headings based on their libraries' new acquisitions or their users' needs, rather than those exclusively of the Library of Congress. Clearly, the Library of Congress has accepted its leadership role, while encouraging the wider cataloging community to contribute to the list. That list, by the way, grew to four volumes by 1992, and reached five volumes beginning with the 21st ed. (1998).

There are many other issues and important moments in **The *LCSH* Century** which have not been addressed in this brief overview. Some are described or critiqued in the papers of this collection. The collection begins with three essays that focus on the history or theoretical aspects of *LCSH* practice. Elaine Svenonius presents an analysis of the *LCSH* system as a **language**, describing some of its semantics and syntax as well as the pragmatics of specificity, and the effect of these on precision and recall. In the paper by Hoerman and Furniss, many of these same principles are investigated in light of recent guidelines developed and approved by the International Federation of Library Associations and Institutions (IFLA). The authors discover a good deal of similarity between the *IFLA Principles* and those of the *LCSH*, but also indicate two major defects: the principles are often in conflict with each other; and, the principles are derived from tradition and practice rather than being based on users' searching behaviors and needs. The essay contributed by Hope Olson is a successor to earlier books and articles which blew the whistle on the apparent or subtle **biases** inherent in the terminology found in *LCSH*; she uses the theories of a postcolonial critic as a framework to argue that LC could choose to eschew the exclusion or marginalization of certain peoples or cultures (even though such biases may in fact be upheld by American literary warrant), and instead become a change agent aspiring to the enrichment of the lives of *all* library users.

Since these papers were all written in 1999, it is only natural that some focus be given to the prevailing form of current library catalogs. The next three authors examine various aspects of the *LCSH* as it has functioned in the **online environment**. Pauline Cochrane first covered this topic in two works published in 1981 and 1986, and now offers an "update" on the progress made and the issues that still remain in improving the *LCSH* for use in OPACs. A topic which has seldom been addressed in the literature is examined by Gregory Wool. Because librarians have relinquished their control over the traditional catalog's **filing rules** by meekly accepting the limitations imposed by programmers and designers of OPACs, the result has been an accidental (or, unintended) deregulation of standard arrangements of subject headings in the indexes. Wool illustrates in particular how the *Library of Congress Filing Rules*, which arranges entries differently according to the punctuation that is present (e.g., commas for inverted headings, parentheses for qualified headings, etc.), takes advantage of the highly developed syntax and semantic features of the *LCSH* and result in logical groups that can benefit the searcher. These structured but perceivably helpful collocations are lost, however, in most online catalogs that simply arrange *LCSH* strings in a word-by-word fashion, causing Wool to wonder if LC and the library community as a whole have virtually abandoned their faith in a precoordinated controlled vocabulary. On a more positive note, Stephen Hearn reports on the potential for **online validation and updating of *LCSH* strings**; he examines three approaches being studied, and discusses improvements to the *LCSH* authorities, including the establishment of authority records for all types of free-floating subject subdivisions.

Next, we hear from practitioners about how they use the *LCSH* in specific environments or for particular forms of material. Most significant of all, of course, is the perspective of the **reference librarian** who interacts with the user and interprets the *LCSH* for patrons every day. Thomas Mann explains how he uses and teaches others to use the *LCSH*, for the most effective and thorough results in subject searching. His techniques–illustrated by cogent examples–combine explorations of adjacencies, cross-references and precoordination in the *LCSH* "red books" with redirections and browsing within the subject catalog itself. He also addresses the differences between keyword and *LCSH* searches, pointing out several advantages to the controlled vocabulary approach.

For the **public library** perspective, we could hardly choose a better representative than the Cleveland Public Library, whose catalog was among the five library catalogs examined in order to compile the first edition (1895) of the ALA *List* later used as the foundation for developing the *Library of Congress Subject Headings.*[17] Louisa Kreider looks at a sample of subject searches executed at the urban library, and finds that *LCSH* terms and phrases match fairly well on the vocabulary used by the users. She also discusses the library's participation in SACO (through which they have proposed new subject headings that have indeed been established in *LCSH*), the application of subject headings to works of fiction, and certain accommodations made locally for differences between the *LCSH* and the standard LC Annotated Card program headings (i.e., subject headings for juvenile literature). Our entry in the **special libraries** category comes from the field of music. Co-authors Hemmasi and Young present a comprehensive history of the development of music-related headings in *LCSH*. They include discussions on the LC Music Division's long-held preference for a classed catalog, problems such as a bias in favor of Western "art" (or, classical) music, and the potential for the ongoing Music Thesaurus Project to assist in future improvements to *LCSH*. Perhaps most instructive to other "special interest" groups is the authors' account of the proactive role taken by the Music Library Association in furthering the additions and revisions to LC subject headings for music.

Although designed for library catalogs, the *LCSH* have also been used over the years in published or online bibliographies, abstracts, and periodical indexes too. Miller and Kuhr describe the vocabularies used in **periodical indexing** at the H. W. Wilson Company, with examples of various adaptations to *LCSH* that have been necessary. Their analysis highlights the fact that, whereas the *LCSH* is an excellent tool as a general system, for highly specialized indexes (such as those geared to children, or lawyers!) the LC terminologies are often either too specific or not detailed enough. David Miller treats the issue of *LCSH*'s handling of access for different **formats of materials**, an area of concern for libraries with extensive audiovisual collections, or even, for those desiring better access to the genres/forms found in collections of literature. Recent developments such as the implementation of a new MARC code for subject "form" subdivisions have made this a hot topic of the 1990's. His paper contends that, despite the *LCSH* inclusion of such terms, the form of a work is distinct from its subject; it is therefore questionable whether or not a subject heading list is really the proper venue for documenting practice.

Stepping aside from *LCSH* use in special environments or with particular forms of materials, the next three essays focus on the use of *LCSH* by

libraries outside of the United States. Heiner-Freiling reports the results of an IFLA-sponsored survey of national libraries, revealing that the *LCSH* has become the leading subject heading language for national bibliographies worldwide, most particularly in English-speaking countries, while it is also widely used in translation or adaptation into other languages. Andrew Mac-Ewan, of the British Library, describes some challenges discovered in the preliminary study that led to the MACS project (**Multilingual Access** to Subjects), in which four European national libraries will use authority records to link equivalent subject headings of the three predominant subject heading languages in English (*LCSH*), French (RAMEAU), and German (RSWK). Although the context of European unity drives this particular desire to surmount linguistic barriers, there are wider implications for other regions or countries whose citizens use different languages. A bilingual project on this side of the Atlantic is discussed by co-authors Quijano-Solís, Moreno-Jiménez and Figueroa-Servín. First, they provide a survey of Spanish-language subject authorities that either translate from or link to *LCSH* terms, particularly those in Spain, Colombia, Chile, and Mexico. Next, the authors describe the planning and initial efforts of a project overseen by the library of El Colegio de México which will **translate *LCSH* into Spanish**, for the purpose of supporting subject access to a projected online union catalog of ten (mainly university) libraries in Mexico City, and to offer such a tool to U.S. libraries serving bilingual communities. An interesting sideline here is the fact that the catalogers at El Colegio de México have received NACO/SACO training from the Library of Congress, and intend to propose new *LCSH* terms or phrases reflecting concepts that are unique to the Latin American culture.

In the concluding piece of this collection, Lois Mai Chan and Theodora Hodges present a summary of the early development and later improvements of the *LCSH* and the reasons for its success. Then the authors speculate about the possible **directions the *LCSH* might take in the future**, with a particular view towards adapting the *LCSH* for optimum effectiveness in the "web" environment (information resources accessible via the Internet).

The 100th birthday of the *LCSH* is the *raison d'être* of this collection of papers, similar to those books of essays written in honor of a scholarly and esteemed colleague. As in any good Festschrift, one would expect to see included a comprehensive bibliography of the honoree's own published works. Here this takes the form of a chronology of *LCSH*-related publications issued by the Library of Congress over the years. However, this is where our collection's resemblance to a Festschrift ends. Typically the Festschrift is planned to celebrate the honoree upon her retirement, or near the end of her career. It is our hope and expectation that this best of all generalized subject heading systems, the *Library of Congress Subject Headings*, will expand, evolve and endure for many years to come.

NOTES

1. Gail Fineberg, "Happy Birthday, 'Big Red Book': ALA Reception Honors *LCSH* Centennial," *Library of Congress Information Bulletin*, 57 (1998), p. 202.

2. Thelma Eaton, *Cataloging and Classification: An Introductory Manual*, 3rd ed. (Champaign, Ill.: Illini Union Bookstore, 1963), p. 125.

3. Richard S. Angell, "Library of Congress Subject Headings–Review and Forecast," in *Subject Retrieval in the Seventies* (Westport, Conn.: Greenwood Press, 1972), p. 143.

4. A. C. Foskett, *The Subject Approach to Information*. 5th ed. (London: Library Association Publishing, 1996), p. 336-7. For a more complete history of the early development of the *LCSH* list, see: Francis Miksa, *The Subject in the Dictionary Catalog from Cutter to the Present*. (Chicago: American Library Association, 1983).

5. Doralyn J. Hickey, "Subject Analysis: An Interpretive Survey," *Library Trends* 25 (1976): 273.

6. Paul S. Dunkin, *Cataloging U.S.A.* (Chicago: American Library Association, 1969), p. 83-84.

7. Eaton, *Cataloging and Classification*, p. 116.

8. Harriet Dorothea MacPherson, *Some Practical Problems in Cataloging* (Chicago: American Library Association, 1936), p. 18.

9. American Library Association. Division of Cataloging and Classification, *In Retrospect: A History of the Division of Cataloging and Classification of the American Library Association, 1900-1950* (Chicago: A.L.A., 1950), p. 11.

10. The two manuals were: Julia Pettee, *Subject Headings: The History and Theory of the Alphabetical Subject Approach to Books* (New York: H.W. Wilson, 1946); and, David Judson Haykin, *Subject Headings: A Practical Guide* (Washington, D.C.: U.S. Govt. Print. Office, 1951). Selections from both works are reprinted in: Lois Mai Chan, Phyllis A. Richmond and Elaine Svenonius, eds., *Theory of Subject Analysis: A Sourcebook* (Littleton, Colo.: Libraries Unlimited, 1985), p. 94-111.

11. Jessica Lee Harris, *Subject Analysis: Computer Implications of Rigorous Definition* (Metuchen, N.J.: Scarecrow Press, 1970), at p. 18: " . . . Miss Pettee was too occupied, as was Haykin later, with the need to arrange inherited practice into a system with some meaning."

12. See, for example: R.C. Swank, "Subject Catalogs, Classifications, or Bibliographies? A Review of Critical Discussions, 1876-1942," *The Library Quarterly* 14 (1944): 316-322.

13. Hickey, "Subject Analysis," p. 273-74.

14. Carlyle J. Frarey, "Subject Headings," v. 1, pt. 2 of *The State of the Library Art*, ed. Ralph R. Shaw (New Brunswick, N.J.: Graduate School of Library Service, Rutgers–The State University, 1960), p. 57, 63.

15. Pettee, *Subject Headings*, p. 42.

16. Indeed, as recently as 1998, in Martha M. Yee and Sara Shatford Layne, *Improving Online Public Access Catalogs* (Chicago: American Library Association, 1998), the authors provide much evidence that, for the best subject-searching retrievals, "the default subject search should be a search of the controlled vocabulary and that free text searching should be used only as a backup if controlled vocabulary searching fails, and even then it should be used as a gateway to the controlled vocabulary" (p. 155).

17. Eaton, *Cataloging and Classification*, p. 113.

APPENDIX

Chronology of Official *LCSH*-Related Publications

1906	**Preliminary List of Subject Subdivisions Under Names of Countries or States, and of Subject Headings with Country Subdivisions.**
1909-14	**Subject Headings Used in the Dictionary Catalogues of the Library of Congress.**
1910	Preliminary List of Subject Subdivisions: (a) Under Names of Countries or States; (b) Under Cities; (c) Under General Subjects.
1913	**Preliminary List of Literature Subject Headings.**
1915	Preliminary List of Literature Subject Headings. 2nd issue.
1916	Preliminary List of Subject Subdivisions. (2nd ed.]
	Preliminary Lists of Subject Headings with Local Subdivision: (A) Headings with Indirect Subdivision; (B) Headings with Direct Subdivision; and (C) Preliminary List of Local Divisions (States, Provinces, etc.) to Which Subdivision Is Always Direct.
1917	Preliminary List of Literature Subject Headings, with a Tentative List for Shakespeare Collections. 3rd issue.
	Preliminary Lists of Subject Headings with Local Subdivision. 2nd ed.
1919	Subject Headings Used in the Dictionary Catalogues of the Library of Congress. 2nd ed.
	European War: Preliminary List of Subject Headings.
1920	Literature Subject Headings with List for Shakespeare Collections and Language Subject Headings. 4th ed.
	Subject Subdivisions: (A) Under Names of Countries, States, Etc.; (B) Under Names of Cities; (C) Under General Subjects. 5th ed.
	Subject Headings with Local Subdivision. 3rd ed.
1924	Subject Subdivisions. 6th ed. *(reprinted 1928, 1936)*
1925	Subject Headings with Local Subdivision. 4th ed.
1926	Literature Subject Headings with List for Shakespeare Collections and Language Subject Headings. 5th ed.
1928	Subject Headings Used in the Dictionary Catalogues of the Library of Congress. 3rd ed.
1935	Subject Headings with Local Subdivision. 5th ed.

1943	Subject Headings Used in the Dictionary Catalogs of the Library of Congress. 4th ed.
1945–	**Cataloging Service Bulletin.** *(Ongoing publication; issued quarterly; includes, among other topics on LC cataloging and classification, information on new subject headings, revised subject headings, and changes in practice or procedures.)*
1948	Subject Headings Used in the Dictionary Catalogs of the Library of Congress. 5th ed.
1950	**Period Subdivisions Under Names of Places Used in the Dictionary Catalogs of the Library of Congress.**
1951	**Subject Headings: A Practical Guide/by David Judson Haykin.**
1952	**Music Subject Headings Used on Printed Catalog Cards of the Library of Congress.**
1957	Subject Headings Used in the Dictionary Catalogs of the Library of Congress. 6th ed.
1966	Subject Headings Used in the Dictionary Catalogs of the Library of Congress. 7th ed.
1969	**Subject Headings for Children's Literature.**
1975	Library of Congress Subject Headings. 8th ed. (2 v.)
	An Introduction to *Library of Congress Subject Headings*. *(Reprinted from the 8th LCSH, principally for users of the microfiche ed.)*
	LC Period Subdivisions Under Names of Places. 2nd ed.
	Subject Headings for Children's Literature. 2nd ed.
1975–	***Library of Congress Subject Headings* [microform].** 8th ed. (22 microfiches). *Publication in microfiche has continued from Jan. /Mar. 1976- , with slight title variations, issued quarterly.*
1978	Working List of Subject Headings for Children's Literature.
1980	Library of Congress Subject Headings. 9th ed. (2v.)
1981	***Library of Congress Subject Headings*: A Guide to Subdivision Practice.**
1982	Working List of Subject Headings for Children's Literature.
1984	**Subject Cataloging Manual: Subject Headings. Prelim. ed.**
1984–	**L.C. Subject Headings Weekly Lists.** *(published 1984-1994 in monthly cumulations; continued 1995- by an online file accessible via the LC website, updated weekly)*
1985	Subject Cataloging Manual: Subject Headings. Rev. ed. (loose-leaf)

APPENDIX (continued)

1986–	**Subject Authorities [database]** *(Ongoing publication of LCSH authority records in MARC format; issued weekly; available as 9-track magnetic tape, on IBM tape cartridge, or via Internet FTP; 1996- also include Subject Headings for Children's Literature)*
1987	LC Period Subdivisions Under Names of Places. 3rd ed.
1988	*Library of Congress Subject Headings.* 11th ed. (3 v.)
	Subject Cataloging Manual: Subject Headings. 3rd ed. (2 v., loose-leaf)
1988-96	**CDMARC Subjects [computer laser optical disk]** *(Replaced quarterly; consisted of machine-readable LCSH on compact disk; ceased with final issue of 1996)*
1989	*Library of Congress Subject Headings.* 12th ed. (3 v.)
	Free-floating Subdivisions: An Alphabetical Index.
1990	*Library of Congress Subject Headings.* 13th ed. (3v.)
	LC Period Subdivisions Under Names of Places. 4th ed.
	Free-floating Subdivisions: An Alphabetical Index. 2nd ed.
	***Library of Congress Subject Headings*: Principles of Structure and Policies for Application**/by Lois Mai Chan.
1991	*Library of Congress Subject Headings.* 14th ed. (3v.)
	Subject Cataloging Manual: Subject Headings. 4th ed. (2v., loose-leaf)
	Free-Floating Subdivisions: An Alphabetical Index. 3rd ed.
	Revised *Library of Congress Subject Headings*: Cross-References from Former to Current Subject Headings. 1st ed.
1992	*Library of Congress Subject Headings.* 15th ed. (4 v.)
	Free-Floating Subdivisions: An Alphabetical Index. 4th ed.
	The Future of Subdivisions in the *Library of Congress Subject Headings* System: Report from the Subject Subdivisions Conference/ed. by Martha O'Hara Conway.
1993	*Library of Congress Subject Headings.* 16th ed. (4v.)
	Free-Floating Subdivisions: An Alphabetical Index. 5th ed.
	Subject Headings for Children's Literature [Microform]. *(Ongoing publication, issued quarterly as part of the LCSH-microfiche described above.)*
1994	*Library of Congress Subject Headings.* 17th ed. (4 v.)

	LC Period Subdivisions Under Names of Places. 5th ed.
	Free-floating Subdivisions: An Alphabetical Index. 6th ed.
1994-	**Catalogers Desktop [Computer Laser Optical Disk]** *(Ongoing publication, replaced quarterly; includes the full* Subject Cataloging Manual: Subject Headings*)*
1995	*Library of Congress Subject Headings.* 18th ed. (4 v.)
	Free-Floating Subdivisions: An Alphabetical Index. 7th ed.
1996	*Library of Congress Subject Headings.* 19th ed. (4 v.)
	Subject Cataloging Manual: Subject Headings. 5th ed. (4 v., loose-leaf)
	Free-Floating Subdivisions: An Alphabetical Index. 8th ed.
1996-	**Classification Plus [Computer Laser Optical Disk]** *(Ongoing publication, replaced quarterly; includes the full* Library of Congress Subject Headings*)*
1997	*Library of Congress Subject Headings.* 20th ed. (4 v.)
	Free-Floating Subdivisions: An Alphabetical Index. 9th ed.
1998	*Library of Congress Subject Headings.* 21st ed. (5 v.)
	Free-Floating Subdivisions: An Alphabetical Index. 10th ed.
1999	*Library of Congress Subject Headings.* 22nd ed. (5 v.)
	Free-Floating Subdivisions: An Alphabetical Index. 11th ed.

THEORY AND PRINCIPLES

LCSH:
Semantics, Syntax and Specificity

Elaine Svenonius

SUMMARY. This paper looks at changes affecting *LCSH* over its 100-year history. Adopting a linguistic conceptualization, it frames these changes as relating to the semantics, syntax and pragmatics of the *LCSH* language. While its category semantics has remained stable over time, the *LCSH* relational semantics underwent a significant upheaval when a thesaural structure was imposed upon its traditional *See* and *See also* structure. Over time the *LCSH* syntax has become increasingly complex as it has moved from being largely enumerative to in large part synthetic. Until fairly recently the *LCSH* pragmatics consisted of only one rule, *viz,* the injunction to assign specific headings. This rule, always controversial, has become even more debated and interpreted with the move to the online environment. *[Article copies available for a fee from The Haworth Document Delivery Service: 1-800-342-9678. E-mail address: <getinfo@haworthpressinc.com> Website: <http://www.haworthpressinc.com>]*

Elaine Svenonius is Professor Emeritus, Department of Information Studies, UCLA.

[Haworth co-indexing entry note]: "*LCSH*: Semantics, Syntax and Specificity." Svenonius, Elaine. Co-published simultaneously in *Cataloging & Classification Quarterly* (The Haworth Information Press, an imprint of The Haworth Press, Inc.) Vol. 29, No. 1/2, 2000, pp. 17-30; and: *The LCSH Century: One Hundred Years with the Library of Congress Subject Headings System* (ed: Alva T. Stone) The Haworth Information Press, an imprint of The Haworth Press, Inc., 2000, pp. 17-30. Single or multiple copies of this article are available for a fee from The Haworth Document Delivery Service [1-800-342-9678, 9:00 a.m. - 5:00 p.m. (EST). E-mail address: getinfo@haworthpressinc.com].

KEYWORDS. Subject heading languages, *Library of Congress Subject Headings*, semantics, syntactics, specificity

INTRODUCTION

Over a hundred years ago, *LCSH* was conceived in a spirit of optimism and democratic zeal. A grand old lady, she has been ever earnest in her aim to adapt to users' habitual ways of looking at things, helping them to find what they want using a language they know. But this has not made her universally loved. She has suffered the scorn of theorists, the belittling of rivals and the general indifference of users. She has tried to remake herself in response to the criticisms leveled at her, and the demands put upon her by the new technologies. In her later years, she has become increasingly self-aware, apologetic about her inconsistencies and worried about keeping up. Her life, though not exemplary, has been one whose story is worth telling, both for its own sake and as it holds a mirror up to the history of subject languages generally in the 20th century. The purpose of this paper is to relate certain of the incidents in this life.

It is useful to regard a tool for providing subject access to information as a language, since this provides a ready-to-hand conceptual framework that can be used in its analysis and description. This framework characterizes a language in terms of its vocabulary, semantics, syntax and pragmatics. To regard any language, whether it be a natural or a subject language, within such a framework conceptualizes it at a level of generality that allows it to be evaluated and compared with other languages. In the particular case of this paper, the framework provides a convenient way to categorize incidents in the life of *LCSH*, challenges it has faced and changes it has undergone during the last century.

The conceptualization of a tool that provides subject access to information as a language is not new. Its provenance is almost as old as *LCSH* itself, reaching back to 1911, when Julius Otto Kaiser employed it in the description of the indexing system (called Systematic Indexing) he designed for the Tariff Commission in London.[1] In this system simple terms are classed into semantic categories (of the kind later to be referred to as *facets*) and then subject headings are constructed using syntax rules defined with respect to these categories. A number of other theorists since Kaiser have embraced linguistic conceptualizations, among them Ranganathan, the members of the Classification Research Group, the information retrieval researchers at Cranfield (England), and, more recently, the IFLA Working Group on Principles Underlying Subject Heading Languages.[2]

Some definitions are in order. The *vocabulary* of a subject language consists of the terms admitted into it. (Much has been written about the *LCSH* vocabulary and it will not be dealt with in this paper.) The *semantics* of a subject language is of three kinds: category, referential, and relational.[3] *Category* semantics consists of the classes of terms recognized by the language, e.g., topical terms, geographical terms, and so on. A major reason for classifying terms in a subject language is that the resulting categories can be used to formulate the syntax rules of the language.

The *referential* semantics of a subject language consists of the techniques used to fix the denotational meaning of terms. An example is the use of parenthetical qualifiers to pinpoint one of several dictionary meanings a term might have, e.g., **Banks (Oceanography)**. The purpose of referential semantics is to address the generalized homonym problem that causes false drops or poor precision in retrieval. The need to control for homonyms in information retrieval is recognized in the *Principles Underlying Subject Heading Languages* as the homonymy principle.

The *relational* semantics of a subject language consist of the totality of meaning relationships that exist between terms in the language. The most important of these is the relationship of synonymy, e.g., that which exists between **Bobber fishing** and **Bait fishing**. The need to control for equivalence-of-meaning in information retrieval is enshrined in the *Principles Underlying Subject Heading Languages (SHL)* as the synonymy principle. Its purpose is to improve recall in retrieval. The relational semantics of most subject languages include in addition to synonymy relationships, those of hierarchy and general conceptual relatedness.

The *syntax* of a subject language consists of the rules for ordering component elements of constructed expressions in the language. An example of a constructed expression in *LCSH* is a subject heading that consists of a main heading and one or more subheadings. Syntax rules may be defined with respect to classes of terms (syntactic or semantic) or with respect to individual terms.

The *pragmatics* of a subject language consist of the policies, specifications, or conditions for the application of the language. Examples are specifications indicating how many headings should be given, and the conditions under which a given heading may be applied to a work. The oldest and most debated of such specifications (and the one to be discussed in this paper) is Cutter's injunction to assign to a work the most specific heading possible.[4] This injunction appears in the *Principles Underlying Subject Heading Languages (SHL)* as the only application principle common to a number of different subject heading languages. As yet the pragmatics of subject heading languages are not well-developed, but this may be expected to change as advances are made in automatic subject heading assignment.

LCSH SEMANTICS

Category Semantics

LCSH recognizes five major classes of terms:

1. a class of terms used as main or focal headings. Functioning as lead terms in subject headings, these terms are used to denote the essential aboutness of documents being described.
2. a class of terms used as topical subheadings. The purpose of these terms is to qualify main headings and subheadings.
3. a class of terms indicative of form or document types, used for the purpose of qualification.
4. a class of terms indicative of chronological periods, used for qualification.
5. a class of terms indicative of geographical areas, used for qualification.

The second class, topical terms used as subheadings, needs special mention. A condition put on terms in this class is that they should not introduce hierarchy into a subject heading; a heading like Domestic animals-Cats is not an allowable expression in the *LCSH* language. A defining characteristic of *LCSH* since its inception has been that it should be classification-free. Its approach should be alphabetic and direct (Cats), rather than classified and indirect (Domestic animals-Cats).[5] Thus the semantic function of topical terms used as subheadings is not classification, but qualification.[6]

The first serious challenge to the *LCSH* category semantics came in 1991 at a conference convened by the Library of Congress to consider the future of the *LCSH* subdivisions. At this conference the question was raised whether all the five major classes of terms used in *LCSH* were really necessary in a post-coordinate digital environment. In the interest of simplification might not nontopical terms be disassociated from headings and located in separate fields?[7] The matter was debated and the decision was to keep the status quo. The chief argument against removing nontopical terms to separate fields was that confusion would result if qualifiers were separated from what they qualified. Also such a move would generate false drops in retrieval.

Given that the five major *LCSH* classes of terms are necessary, are they also sufficient? Significantly *LCSH* has resisted pressures to follow fashion by swelling its category semantics with additional classes of terms, like the "action" or "material," categories found in many faceted languages. In retrospect, given the difficulties in defining semantically cohesive facets[8] and the sometimes unnatural constructions that result using a syntax based upon them, resistance seems to have been a wise stance. On the other hand, *LCSH* has been introducing other categories of terms, but these are syntactic, as opposed to semantic; that is, they are defined with respect to placement in a heading, e.g., a class of terms that can be used after a geographic term. More will be said about these later in the section on syntax.

Referential Semantics

A usual way for subject-heading languages to control for homonyms is, as mentioned, to ply apart the various meanings of the term using parenthetical qualifiers, e.g., **Banks (Oceanography)**. *LCSH*'s use of qualifiers, however, has not been restricted to the disambiguation of homonyms. They have also been used to provide general contextual information, e.g., **Cookery (Onions)** and **Marriage (Canon law)**. The use of a single device for more than one function can be problematic, particularly in times of technological change. For instance, a new technique might come along which would provide a more efficient way to accomplish one but not other of the functions, yet could not be exploited because of the difficulty of a post-hoc untangling of the functions. As early as 1967 *LCSH* was criticized for its multifunctional use of parenthetical qualifiers[9] but refused to budge, defending the practice by observing that so long as parenthetical qualifiers were used consistently for groups of like headings, its multifunctionality was not a detriment.[10] Today, while the use of a parenthetical qualifier to indicate a special application of a concept is generally proscribed, there are still a few situations where the device may used other than for qualifying homonyms, e.g., to make explicit a term that is obscure, e.g., **Seal Finger (Disease)** and to qualify certain kinds of terms, e.g., those denoting computer programming languages.

There are many terms, which, while not homonymous in a narrow sense, have meanings that vary with the contexts in which they are used. An example is **Flight**. *LCSH* has methods other than the use of parenthetical qualification to fix the referential semantics of such terms: for instance, it could be embedded in a "In" type heading, e.g., "Flight in birds"; or established as part of a phrase heading, e.g. "Bird flight"; or qualified by a subheading, e.g., **Birds–Flight**. Disambiguation techniques are used by subject languages to increase their precision power; this is an important function and the degree to which a subject language incorporates such techniques is one of the criteria by which it is evaluated.[11] *LCSH* is superior to many subject languages in its disambiguation capabilities. Somewhat of a problem, however, is that little guidance is given when to prefer one technique over another–except to say that subdivision is generally favored.

Relational Semantics

Except for its vocabulary (which is not discussed in this paper), nowhere has *LCSH* suffered more the slings and arrows of criticism than with respect to its relational semantics. For most of the last century it used two devices to indicate relatedness in meaning: *See* references linking unused terms to their nearest equivalents in the language; and *see also* references linking two related terms both belonging to the language. The semantics of these relationships were defined only approximately. Theoretically, *see* references were to link terms roughly equivalent in meaning. In actual fact, however, they were used to link not only synonyms, but also near synonyms; at times, they were even used to link narrow to broad terms, e.g., **"Classical music**, *see* **Music,"** as a way of limiting the specificity level of the language. Theoretically, *see also* references were to be either one-way broad to narrow references or two way collateral references. In practice, however, they were interpreted with great–sometimes astonishing–latitude. A Library of Congress memo dating from the beginning of the century advised that two terms could be considered *see-also* related if they occurred in the same book.[12]

The twentieth century has been marked by one information explosion after another. To keep pace, the relational semantics of subject languages developed in two ways: specific relationships replaced general relationships; rigorously defined relationships replaced fuzzy ones. These developments were spearheaded by the information retrieval thesauri that began appearing in mid century. In 1982, attendees at a conference in Dublin, Ohio advised the Library of Congress to take cognizance of these developments and emend *LCSH's* relational structure accordingly.[13] This structure should be made compatible with that of information retrieval thesauri in order to facilitate cross-database searching and it should employ the more rigorous BT, NT, RT and USE terminology familiar to thesaurus users, i.e., semantic relationships were to be more rigorously defined. In response to this charge, the Library of Congress settled for a quick-fix and automatically converted all *see* and *see from* references to *use* and *use-from* references; one way *see also's* to narrower term references (NT's), and two way *see also's* to related term references (RT's).[14] The quick fix would have worked had the *see* and *see also* references been used consistently in the manner described above, but such was not the case; consequently, what resulted gave the appearance but not the reality of a new semantic structure. There were those who viewed this as a scandal ("no amount of disguise can turn *LCSH* into a thesaurus!"[15]), but the general public, which is generally indifferent, seemed to take the change in stride. Nevertheless, a few "Band-Aid" reparations were made to fix some of the more egregious structural deficiencies emanating from the automatic conversion. At the same time, *LCSH* set about defining its new BT,NT, RT and Use relationships by stipulating conditions for their use, in the manner of prevailing thesaurus guidelines.

The restructuring and redefinition of the *LCSH* semantic structure makes it at least weakly compatible with other index languages. It also ensures for the future a greater degree of semantic consistency than was achievable in the past. Still, it would have been theoretically satisfying if at the time of the restructuring certain foundational questions had been addressed. Why, for instance should *LCSH* be more like a thesaurus? (A classification has quite a different semantic structure from a thesaurus.) Are all relationships that are useful in retrieval really capable of precise definition? (As is known, rigor and consistency often go against the public's habitual way of looking at things.) And, perhaps the most important question: in a subject heading language, which meaning relationships belong in the semantics of the language and which should be expressed by its syntax? Several thesauri guidelines suggest the former should be limited to those relationships that are always true (all parrots are birds), as opposed to those that are contingently true (some parrots are pets) But is this useful? Realistic?

SYNTAX

An enumerative syntax is distinguished from a synthetic one in that all allowable expressions in the subject language in question are established editorially and listed in an authority file. With a synthetic syntax, only the basic terms of a subject language are enumerated; complex terms are created by the cataloger following syntax rules that specify which combinations of basic terms constitute allowable expressions in the language. For most of the century the *LCSH* syntax was largely enumerative. There were some few exceptions such as the use of the "May Subd Geog" device, the "etc." device, the "in" device and model headings, but generally the work of subject cataloging consisted of determining what the document in hand was about and then looking in "Big Red" to find the best-fit subject heading(s). In 1974 a greater degree of synthesis was introduced in the form of floating subdivisions–terms, which, conditions for their use being met, could be appended to any heading. The move towards incorporating increasing synthesis into subject languages is probably the most significant trend in subject language design in the 20th century. Given the flexibility, expressiveness, and economies a synthetic syntax offers, it was inevitable that *LCSH* should become part of it.

It was inevitable as well, given increasing costs of cataloging, that the work of subject headings should begin to be distributed outside the Library of Congress. This made it imperative that the Library of Congress consolidate, formalize and make generally available its rules for the construction and application of the *LCSH*.[16] The Library of Congress's *Subject Cataloging Manual: Subject Headings* is now in its fifth edition. A large, four-volume work, much of its bulk consists of syntax rules.[17] These rules are complex, in part because they just 'growed like Topsy' and in part because a certain amount of complexity, even inconsistency, is unavoidable if headings are to be user-friendly and capable of expressing shades of meaning.

It is not possible in a short paper to do justice to the *LCSH* syntax, but briefly, and at the risk of some oversimplification: An expression in the *LCSH* language begins with a main heading whose purpose is to bring out the major concepts in a document, to capture its essential aboutness. This may or may not be followed by qualifying terms called *subdivisions*. Syntax rules specify when subdivisions can be used and in what order. Like the prototypical synthetic languages designed by Kaiser, Ranganathan, and Austin, *LCSH* defines its syntax with respect to large semantically homogeneous classes of terms. These are the above-mentioned: Topic, Place, Time, and Form. The three most common syntactic constructions in *LCSH* are:[18]

- Topical main heading–Place–Topic–Time–Form, e.g.,
  Art criticism–France–Paris–History–18th century–Bibliography
- Topical main heading–Topic–Place–Time–Form, e.g.,
  Art–Censorship–Europe–20th century–Exhibitions
- Geographic main heading–Topic–Time–Form, e.g.,
  France–Intellectual life–16th century–Periodicals

Contributing to the complexity of the *LCSH* syntax is that in addition to a syntax defined with respect to semantic categories of terms, two other syntactic constructions are used as well: a syntax defined with respect functional categories of terms and an enumerative syntax defined with respect to individual terms.

Functional categories of terms referenced by the *LCSH* syntax consist mostly of main headings. Syntax rules defined with respect to main-heading types are basically of two sorts:[19]

- those that list subdivisions permissible for a main heading type, e.g., names of ethnic groups, corporate bodies, persons, groups of persons, places, bodies of water, etc.
- those that specify a pattern to be followed for a main-heading type, such as languages and diseases. The pattern may be shown in the form of a subdivided model heading, which is taken to be emblematic of other like headings; e.g., the subdivisions enumerated under **English language** may also be used under **Swedish language**. Else it may be shown in the form of a schema, as is done in free-floating phrase headings, e.g., **[Name of city] Metropolitan Area [geographic qualifier]**.

Also referencing main-heading types are syntax rules that impose restrictions on individual free-floating subdivisions. For instance the subdivision *Directories* can be used "under names of countries, cities, etc., individual corporate bodies and families, and under classes of persons, ethnic groups, Christian denominations, types of organizations, and topical headings for individual directories containing names, addresses and other identifying data."[20] The *LCSH* syntax rules defined with respect to main-heading types appear in the form of notes and references in the authority list of *LCSH* terms and also in the form of lists of subdivisions and information sheets for individual subdivisions in the *Subject Cataloging Manual: Subject Headings.*

Although the *LCSH* syntax is becoming increasingly synthetic, it still retains enumerative features such as rules defined with respect to individual terms. An example is the editorially established string **Food–Labeling**; the subdivision–**Labeling** is authorized for use with the main heading **Food**. Generalized syntax rules using the "May Subd Geog," the "In" and the "Etc." devices are also defined with respect to individual terms. Term-specific syntax is often used with main headings designating countries, e.g., **Sudan-History-Coup d'etat, 1985**. Most but not all term-specific syntax is enumerative.[21] The advantage an enumerated syntax has over the boiler-plate syntax of more synthetic subject languages is that it permits customized breakdowns, as in the Sudan example where the subdivisions are tailored to the major events in the country's history.

Given the complexity of the *LCSH* syntax, it is perhaps not surprising that in 1991 a conference should be convened to discuss the possibility of simplifying it.[22] PRECIS (PREserved Context Indexing System), developed by Derek Austin and used by the British Library from 1971 to 1990, pointed a possible direction for simplification in that its syntax was marvelously simple, consisting of three basic rules, which allowed for three different patterns of arrangement of terms in a heading. This syntax was so algorithmic, it could be automated: all the indexer had to do was to select the terms needed to indicate the various aspects of a document's aboutness; the computer would take over from there and (in most instances) construct a single-entry specific heading containing them. Recognizing the benefits of a regular syntax, the attendees at the 1991 conference recommended that under topical main headings, the order of subheadings should be standardized to Topic-Place-Time-Form. But this was not to be. After some reflection on the part of practicing subject catalogers, full compliance with the recommendation was deemed not practicable because it would detract from the expressiveness of certain headings, particularly those used in the disciplines of art, literature, history and law. For instance, Music-Brazil-History and criticism has a meaning somewhat different from that of Music-History and criticism-Brazil. The question was raised whether such shades of meaning were perceptible to users. Although a study was undertaken to find this out, its results were inconclusive[23] and the decision was made to retain *LCSH*'s custom-tailored specificity and expressiveness, even at the cost of complexity.

SPECIFICITY

The *LCSH* pragmatics includes general and specific rules for assigning subject headings. The latter pertain to headings authorized for use in special situations, e.g., when a work presents a principle and illustrates it with a particular case. General rules pertain to such things as the number of headings to be assigned to a document, the percentage of a document on a topic needed to warrant a heading for it, and the specificity level at which to apply headings.[24] As mentioned the oldest and most widely recognized of these is the specificity rule. Important as the rule is, it has never been altogether clear what was meant by *specificity*. In his paper, which asked "How Specific is specific?" Oliver Lilley speculated "well, it all depends,"[25] and Paul Dunkin observed that "'Specificity' is a magic word which we all accept, but seldom really define."[26]

Basically there are two interpretations of what Cutter meant when he wrote that a work should be entered under its subject heading, not under the class which includes that subject.[27] The first, and most traditional of these is that a heading should be direct, rather than indirect. Cutter was opposed to classified catalogs, which at the end of the last century were the prevailing means for accessing books by subject. Although logical, systematic, and exceptionally good at collocating, such catalogs were designed for scholars and could not meet the needs of the ordinary public, which included children and desultory users. How, for instance could a nonscholar find something on the badger if it was necessary first to look under **Science**, then under **Natural history**, then under **Zoology**, then under **Vertebrates**, then under **Mammals**, then under **Monodelphi**, then under **Carnivora**.[28] Cutter designed the alphabetic subject catalog to be what the classified catalog was not: it was to have headings that were directly accessible and alphabetically arranged. Lady Cust's book was to be entered under **Cats**, not under "*Domestic animals–Cats.*"

The alphabetic subject catalog in providing specific and direct access furthers the finding function of the catalog. However, even with its syndetic structure of *see* and *see also* references it does less well than the classified catalog in meeting the collocating function.[29] It is therefore not surprising that as the *LCSH* language developed it began to take on some of the aspects of an alphabetico-classed catalog. Nor is it surprising that the rule of specificity should at times be blatantly abrogated, as when a biography is given a class of persons heading, with the subdivision–**Biography**, as well as a personal name heading for the biographee. Although theoreticians pointed the accusing finger,[20] once again *LCSH* was not about to budge–a confirmation perhaps of Dunkin's observation that "'Specificity' means all things to all men and little to most, particularly when we are prepared to abandon our definition at any point when the 'convenience of the public' can be argued."[21]

A second, less traditional interpretation of Cutter's specificity rule is that a heading should be coextensive with the subject of the work being cataloged. A *coextensive* heading is one that summarizes a book's topic, fits it like a cap that is neither too loose, nor too tight. This interpretation was introduced by Eric Coates[22] and underlies the conception of string index languages, such as Chain indexing and PRECIS. One advantage of using co-extensive or single-entry specific headings is that this prevents the over application of a broad term, like *Phrenology*, which can then be reserved for books on general topics. An even greater advantage is that coextensive entries set each of the terms describing some aspect of the aboutness of a document in an understandable context, thus pinpointing the meaning of the term and establishing its semantic-syntactic relationships.[23]

How much does coextensivity matter? In a postcoordinate environment the possibility exists of dispensing with the complicated precoordinate subject heading syntax altogether and substituting for it a simpler post-coordinate Boolean syntax. (This possibility was touched upon earlier in the section on syntax.) The need for precoordinated headings was first questioned 50 years ago by Mortimer Taube, who as the father of coordinate indexing introduced Boolean operators into computerized information retrieval. Taube argued that given the capabilities of the computer, subject headings would eventually give way to descriptors as the preferred method of subject access.[24] To buttress his argument he conducted a comparative evaluation of subject heading vs. descriptor languages.[25] The upshot was that while descriptor languages (in particular his own uniterm language) were better in some respects, subject-heading languages (in particular the ASTIA subject headings) were superior in providing a context for descriptive terms. While Taube grudgingly admitted the value of context as a means of disambiguation, others esteemed it so highly as to make it a key element in the design of their index languages. Hans Peter Luhn, the modern reincarnator of keyword indexing, provided for contextual disambiguation in his KWIC (Keyword in Context) indexing system[26] as did Derek Austin in his PRECIS system. As to *LCSH*, as mentioned earlier, when the proposal was made to remove nontopical terms from *LCSH* headings, rendering them less specific (less precoordinated, less coextensive) and more like descriptors, the need for contextual resolution of meaning prevailed and the proposal was rejected–and wisely so, given the need for precision devices to stem the mounting deluge of information in retrieval.[27]

CONCLUSION

On the whole, it would seem that over the century *LCSH*, despite the baggage she has accumulated, has generally acted wisely, being neither not being the first by whom the new is tried, nor yet the last to set it aside. In some instances she has changed and given into pressures to be more user friendly, more consistent, simpler and cheaper to apply, and in some instances she has resisted them. As the new century begins, the question of her future arises. Change being inevitable, it seems likely she will develop in the direction of a more sophisticated semantics, syntax and pragmatics. It also seems likely that in the future, as in the past, bibliographic conservatism will prohibit radical change. Her advances will be halting, in disjointed increments. One thing seems sure: she will continue to be vulnerable and (sadly) misunderstood, particularly in the United States, even while she is being emulated and adopted by countries outside this country. If the precision and recall objectives of the catalog are to be honored–and they surely will–there will always be a need for controlled precoordinate subject languages. As the pre-eminent of such languages, *LCSH* is not only a national treasure, providing access to many millions of documents, she is on her way to becoming a significant force for bibliographical control at an international level.

NOTES

1. Julius O. Kaiser, *Systematic Indexing*, The Card System Series, Vol. II (London: J. Gibson, 1911).

2. International Federation of Library Associations and Institutions, *Principles Underlying Subject Heading Languages (SHL)*, edited by Maria Inês Lopes and Julianne Beall for the Working Group on Principles Underlying Subject Heading Languages, Section on Classification and Indexing. UBCIM Publication, New Series, Vol. 2. (Munich: K.G. Saur, 1999).

3. Elaine Svenonius, "Design of Controlled Vocabularies," in The Encyclopedia of Library and Information Science, v. 45, Supplement. (New York: Marcel Dekker, Inc., 1990), 82-109.

4. Charles A. Cutter, *Rules for a Printed Dictionary Catalog, U.S. Bureau of Education, Special Report on Public Libraries, Part II* (Washington, DC.: Government Printing Office, 1876), 37.

5. Cutter wrote that the "rule of 'specific entry' is the main distinction between the dictionary catalogue and the alphabetico-classed." Cutter, *ibid.*

6. Cutter approved of divisions, but not subdivisions in alphabetic-subject catalogs. It is not certain what this means. In his Boston Athenaeum catalog he made limited use of form subheadings, e.g., **Law-Bibliography, Law-History, and Law-General Works**; yet he also used **Cattle-Diseases**. David Judson Haykin, writing in 1951, distinguished subdivision from qualification; qualifying was to be done using form, time and place subdivisions, but not topical subdivisions as their use contravened the

principle of specific entry. See David Judson Haykin, *Subject Headings-A Practical Guide* (Washington, D. C.: U.S. Government Printing Office, 1951). John Metcalfe, writing a few years later using a strict interpretation of the hierarchical relationship, distinguished specification, which is subdivision by a species or subclass of a subject, from qualification, which is subdivision by an aspect of a subject. See John Metcalfe, *Subject Classifying and Indexing of Libraries and Literature* (New York: Scarecrow Press, 1959).

7. Library of Congress, *The Future of Subdivisions in the Library of Congress Subject Headings System, Report from the Subject Subdivisions Conference Sponsored by the Library of Congress, May 9-12, 1991*, edited by Martha O'Hara Conway (Washington, D.C.: Library of Congress, Cataloging Distribution Service, 1992) 46-56.

8. Elaine Svenonius, "Facets as Semantic Categories," in *Klassifikation und Erkenntnis_II*, Studien zur Klassifikation, Bd.5 (Frankfurt: Gesellschaft fur Klassifikation, 1979): 57-79.

9. Jay E. Daily, "Many Changes, No Alleviation," *Library Journal* 92 (1967): 3962.

10. Dick Angell, "Library of Congress Subject Headings–Review and Forecast," in Subject Retrieval in the Seventies: New Directions: Proceedings of an International Symposium Held at the Center of Adult Education, University of Maryland, College Park, May 14 to 15, 1971, edited by Hans H. Wellisch and Thomas D. Wilson (Westport, Conn.: Greenwood Publishing, 1972), 150.

11. Elaine Svenonius, *"Precoordination or Not,"* in *Subject Indexing: Principles and Practices in the 90's: Proceedings of the IFLA Satellite Meeting held in Lisbon, Portugal, 17-18 August 1993*, edited by Robert P. Holley, Dorothy McGarry, Donna Duncan and Elaine Svenonius. (Munich: K.G. Saur, 1995), 231-255.

12. Personal communication from Mary K.D. Pietris, Chief, Subject Cataloging Division, Library of Congress, November 1985.

13. Keith. W. Russell, ed. Subject Access: Report of a Meeting Sponsored by the Council on Library Resources, Dublin, Ohio, June 7-9, 1982. (Washington, D.C.: Council on Library Resources, 1982).

14. The idea for this conversion seems to have originated with Dick Angell. See Angell, Dick, *op. cit.* The change was implemented with the 11th *LCSH* (1988).

15. Mary Dykstra, "LC Subject Headings Disguised as a Thesaurus," *Library Journal* 113 (March 1, 1988)): 43.

16. Keith. W. Russell, *op. cit.*

17. Library of Congress, Cataloging Policy and Support Office, *Subject Cataloging Manual: Subject Headings*. 5th ed. Washington, D.C.: The Library, 1996).

18. Lois Chan, *Library of Congress Subject Headings: Principles of Structure and Policies for Application*. Advances in Library Information Technology, No. 3 (Washington, D.C.: Library of Congress, 1990), 22-23. Frequently facets in these constructions may be left out; the order of the remaining facets is observed.

19. The two kinds of rules differ only at a surface level, in their genesis having been developed at different times to achieve similar constructions.

20. Library of Congress. Cataloging Policy and Support Office, *op. cit.*, H1095 (p. 18, August 1997).

21. An example of a nonenumerative term syntax is the templated phrase (May Subd Geog) after a term to indicate the next term in a well-formed string can be the name of a geographic locality.

22. Library of Congress, Cataloging Policy and Support Office, *op. cit.*

23. L. Franz, J. Powell, S. Jude and K. M. Drabenstott, "End User Understanding of Subdivided Subject Headings," *Library Resources & Technical Services* 38,3 (1994):213-26.

24. See H180 in Library of Congress. Cataloging Policy and Support Office (1996), *op. cit.*

25. Oliver L. Lilley, "How Specific is Specific?," *Journal of Cataloging and Classification* 2 (January 1955): 8.

26. Paul S. Dunkin, "Cataloging and CCS: 1956-1966, "*Library Resources & Technical Services* 2 (Summer 1967): 284.

27. There are as well other possible interpretations. See Elaine Svenonius, "Metcalfe and the Principle of Specific Entry," in *The Variety of Librarianship: Essays in Honour of John Wallace Metcalfe,* edited by W.B. Rayward. (Sydney, Australia: Library Association of Australia, 1976) 171-189.

28. Charles A. Cutter, "Library Catalogues", in *Public Libraries in the United States of America: Their History, Condition, and Management. Special Report. Part 1,* 526-622. (Washington, D. C.: United States Bureau of Education, 1876.), 531.

29. Cutter worried about this. See his "Library Catalogues"*, op. cit., 541, 548.*

30. Patrick Wilson, "The End of Specificity," *Library Resources & Technical Services 23(Spring 1979): 116-122.*

31. Paul S. Dunkin, *op. cit.*

32. Eric J. Coates, *Subject Catalogues: Headings and Structure* (London: the Library Association, 1960), pp. 33 ff.

33. In 1972 Dick Angell grudgingly admitted that the specificity in the sense of coextensivity obtainable by *LCSH* was inferior to that of PRECIS. Angell, *op. cit.*

34. Mortimer Taube and Associates, *Studies in Coordinate Indexing* (Washington, D.C.: Documentation Incorporated, 1953-1957).

35. Among these was a retrieval experiment that predated the Cranfield (England) experiments, but did not use the measures of precision and recall. *Ibid.*, v. 2, p. 44.

36. Hans Peter Luhn, Keyword-In-Context Index for Technical Literature (KWIC INDEX), Technical Report RC-127. (Yorktown Heights, N.Y.: IBM: 1959).

37. This need was recognized in the middle of the 19th century by Samson Low (see Cutter, "Library Catalogues," *op. cit.*, 535). Indeed the history of subject languages since then might be framed in terms of advances made in harnessing precision power.

Turning Practice into Principles: A Comparison of the IFLA *Principles Underlying Subject Heading Languages (SHLs)* and the Principles Underlying the *Library of Congress Subject Headings* System

Heidi Lee Hoerman
Kevin A. Furniss

SUMMARY. The IFLA Section on Classification and Indexing's Working Group on Principles Underlying Subject Headings Languages has identified a set of eleven principles for subject heading languages and excerpted the texts that match each principle from the instructions for each of eleven national subject indexing systems, including excerpts from the LC's *Subject Cataloging Manual: Subject Headings*. This study compares the IFLA principles with other texts that express the principles underlying *LCSH*, especially *Library of Congress Subject Headings: Principles of Structure and Policies for Application*, prepared by Lois Mai Chan for the Library of Congress in 1990, Chan's later book on *LCSH*, and earlier documents by Haykin and Cutter. The

Heidi Lee Hoerman, BA, MLS, CPh, is Instructor, College of Library and Information Science, University of South Carolina, Columbia, SC 29208. Kevin A. Furniss, BEd, MLIS, is Authority Control Librarian, Dacus Library, Winthrop University, Rock Hill, SC 29733.

[Haworth co-indexing entry note]: "Turning Practice into Principles: A Comparison of the IFLA *Principles Underlying Subject Heading Languages (SHLs)* and the Principles Underlying the *Library of Congress Subject Headings* System." Hoerman, Heidi Lee, and Kevin A. Furniss. Co-published simultaneously in *Cataloging & Classification Quarterly* (The Haworth Information Press, an imprint of The Haworth Press, Inc.) Vol. 29, No. 1/2, 2000, pp. 31-52; and: *The LCSH Century: One Hundred Years with the Library of Congress Subject Headings System* (ed: Alva T. Stone) The Haworth Information Press, an imprint of The Haworth Press, Inc., 2000, pp. 31-52. Single or multiple copies of this article are available for a fee from The Haworth Document Delivery Service [1-800-342-9678, 9:00 a.m. - 5:00 p.m. (EST). E-mail address: getinfo@haworthpressinc.com].

31

principles are further elaborated for clarity and discussed. *[Article copies available for a fee from The Haworth Document Delivery Service: 1-800-342-9678. E-mail address: <getinfo@haworthpressinc.com Website: <http://www.haworthpressinc.com>]*

KEYWORDS. IFLA, subject headings, principles, *LCSH*

INTRODUCTION

The subject approach to information in library catalogs and bibliographic databases is highly valued by information seekers, yet there is widespread dissatisfaction with the capabilities of present subject access systems to satisfy information needs effectively. As long as there have been bibliographic catalogs and indexes, their designers have struggled with enabling subject-based approaches to them. Debate has raged over the "best" way to provide that subject approach. One of the difficulties in the debate is a lack of agreement on the principles that underlie an effective subject access system.

Much of the complaint about present subject approaches in online catalogs and bibliographic databases centers on perceived inadequacies in the Library of Congress Subject Headings (*LCSH*). Although originally designed for use as the subject access system for the Library of Congress' catalogs only, this system is used in both paper- and computer-based catalogs for libraries of all types and sizes and is used, or serves as the basis for, subject access systems in a wide variety of bibliographic systems, both in the United States and internationally. *LCSH* is the most widely used alphabetical subject access system in the world. Over the last century, *LCSH* has evolved into what has been called "a monumental encyclopedia of knowledge in the form of a controlled vocabulary"[1] and "an overall entity of genius."[2] Millions of both paper- and computer-based bibliographic records residing in thousands of catalogs and retrieval systems include *LCSH* as the basis for a subject approach to retrieval.

LCSH was developed without an underlying code of rules. Intner[3] and Studwell[4] are among those who have suggested that a subject cataloging code similar to the *Anglo-American Cataloguing Rules*, 2nd edition (AACR2–which gives instructions for descriptive cataloging) should be created for subject analysis and classification. AACR2 has been the ongoing effort of many cataloging experts and the present code grew out of previous sets of rules established and periodically updated throughout this century. No effort similar in magnitude to the effort that was necessary to create AACR2 is yet underway for subject cataloging, nor is one expected. The development of the IFLA (International Federation of Library Associations and Institutions) principles is welcome in that it is, perhaps, the first step toward an international standard for subject headings.

> Over fifty years ago, Prevost made a statement that is equally true today.
>
> No existing general list of subject headings, in its entirety, is a logically thought-out product. All are full of the inconsistencies and conflicting ideas concurrent on just growing. This does not mean that no rules have been made and followed; rather, it means that the rules are inconclusive and, particularly, that they themselves were not disciplined and co-ordinated prior to application, nor was there any intention to make them inflexible. Concession (mostly tacit) has been made to habit and to the difficulties of change. An attempt to arrive fully at the principles underlying any list from an examination of the list itself is foredoomed to failure. All existing lists are inadequate, not easy to lean upon mentally, unscientific. Nowhere are we directly instructed or sufficiently assisted by analogy in the assignment of headings to new subjects or to new aspects of old subjects. And up to the present we have spent our thought on detail in the effort to improve things as they are–an approach that has got us nowhere.
>
> The only way to produce a clear theory is to cast loose all ties with the past for the time being; to analyze our objectives and practices; and then to reconstitute.[5]

It may not be possible to fully discard all ties with the past in developing a set of principles for a widely established activity like subject heading creation in library catalogs. Whether, during the development of the IFLA *Principles Underlying Subject Heading Languages (SHLs)*,[6] such independence from the past was even a goal is not stated in the document. What the document does do is provide a list of principles and identifies confirming evidence for each principle's verity in existing subject heading systems, including texts from LC's *Subject Cataloging Manual: Subject Headings*.[7]

This study compares the IFLA principles with other texts that express the principles underlying *LCSH*, especially *Library of Congress Subject Headings: Principles of Structure and Policies for Application*, prepared by Lois Mai Chan for the Library of Congress in 1990,[8] Chan's later book on *LCSH*,[9] and earlier documents by Haykin[10] and Cutter.[11] The principles are further elaborated for clarity and discussed.

THE IFLA PRINCIPLES UNDERLYING SUBJECT HEADING LANGUAGES

In 1990, the IFLA Section on Classification and Indexing established a Working Group on Principles Underlying Subject Headings Languages (hereinafter referred to as the Working Group) which took the first step toward producing clear theories for subject heading lists. During its first three years, the Working Group, under the direction of Elaine Svenonius, identified a set of eleven principles for subject heading languages. In the years following, the Working Group related the principles back to existing subject headings systems. It clarified and simplified presentation of the principles and compiled the texts that matched each principle found in the instructions for each of eleven national subject indexing systems, from the United States, Germany, Portugal, Iran, Canada (English and French), Norway, Spain, Poland, France, and Russia. *Principles Underlying Subject Heading Languages (SHLs)* comprises a list of principles with short definitions and relevant excerpts from the eleven subject indexing systems.[12]

The Working Group divided the principles into two main categories: construction principles and application principles. Construction principles are those that refer to the choice and use of terms and the overall grammar of subject headings. These are "uniform heading principle," "synonymy principle," "homonymy principle," "semantic principle," "syntax principle," "consistency principle," "naming principle," "literary warrant principle," and "user principle." Application principles are those that refer to the assignment of subject headings in practice. These are "subject indexing policy principle" and "specific heading principle."[13]

In describing the efforts of the Working Group, Lopes provided useful subcategories of the construction principles by dividing them into those that address "control of terminology" (uniform heading, synonymy, homonymy, and naming principles), "guidance through the paradigmatic structure" (semantic principle), "predictability of representations" (syntax and consistency principles), "dynamic and documented development" (literary warrant principle), and "audience oriented vocabulary" (user principle).[14]

The purposes of the *Principles* document, as stated by the Working Group, were to set out "general directives for the construction and application of subject heading languages," to serve "as a useful guide to those countries, institutions and agencies planning to develop a new subject heading language or to adopt one that already exists," to help researchers in "the development of multi-lingual thesauri and of search engines," to postulate "and then empirically verify the existence of general principles underlying subject heading languages," and to contribute "scientific generalization within the field of library science."[15] In part one of the document, the purposes of the definition of principles are more formally stated.

1. To **facilitate subject access** to information on an international level.
2. To **assist in developing SHLs** by stating what is meant by a good SHL and what desirable construction and application principles are for such languages.

3. To **promote understanding of different SHLs** by identifying commonalities underlying them and providing a structure for their comparative study.
4. To **provide a theoretical rationale** for particular standards or guideline for SHL construction and application.

An examination of the IFLA principles finds that they very closely reflect the practices evident in *LCSH*. The Working Group states, "That library and information professionals from several different countries have agreed upon the principles . . . is *prima facie* evidence that feasibility is demonstrable."[16]

It is not surprising that many of these agreed upon principles are mirrored in *LCSH*. The worldwide influence, imitation, and use of *LCSH* is incalculable. U.S. Library of Congress cataloging practice, including use of *LCSH*, has long been the standard for English language academic and research libraries in Canada, with adjustments made for particularly Canadian political or historical topics. The *Répetoire de vedettes-matière*, created for French libraries in Canada and broadly used throughout the French speaking world, is based upon translation of *LCSH*. The English/Dutch/French thesaurus of Belgium is likewise based upon *LCSH* and the *Répetoire*.[17] As Cochrane notes, while many researchers suggest that adding the strengths of good thesaurus design to *LCSH* would improve its use in online catalogs, "no one" suggests the complete re-indexing of the millions of bibliographic records throughout the world that now carry *LCSH* headings.[18] In *LCSH* and other systems based on it and resembling it we have a subject headings system that works, although not as well as we would hope. The key to making *LCSH* work better or to developing new, improved subject heading systems may well reside in this articulation of principles.

THE SOURCES FOR PRINCIPLES UNDERLYING *LCSH*

The excerpts illustrating the principles for *LCSH* in the IFLA document were selected by Julianne Beall and Dorothy McGarry from LC's *Subject Cataloging Manual: Subject Headings*, 5th edition (1996). The manual was chosen as the source of the excerpts because it "contains the same instructions used by the subject catalogers at the Library of Congress in their daily work . . . [and] most of the instructions are essential for those who wish to understand and apply the *Library of Congress Subject Headings*."[19] Chan (1995) cites this as one of two documents the Library of Congress published since the mid-1980s that filled a void for those seeking explicit descriptions of the principles underlying *LCSH*. The other was Chan's own *Library of Congress Subject Headings: Principles of Structure and Policies for Application* prepared for the Library and published in 1990. Chan's work provides more succinct and formal statements of principles than does the manual. Chan incorporated these two sources into her descriptions of the principles in her 1995 textbook entitled *Library of Congress Subject Headings: Principles and Application*, 3rd edition. Earlier documents that form the basis for the *LCSH* principles include Charles A. Cutter's *Rules for a Dictionary Catalog* and David Judson Haykin's *Subject Headings: A Practical Guide.*[20]

THE IFLA PRINCIPLES EXPLAINED AND COMPARED TO LCSH PRINCIPLES

This paper compares the IFLA principles with principles underlying *LCSH* by first quoting each IFLA principle and matching it with text from *Library of Congress Subject Headings: Principles of Structure and Policies for Application* (hereinafter referred to as "Chan 1990"). Chan's 1990 document was chosen for the direct comparison to the IFLA principles because it gives the most formal statements of principles and was issued by the Library of Congress itself. Each principle will be described for clarity as best the present authors understand them. Some of the principles are easy to understand even by those new to the study of subject heading systems. Others are less clear without reference to the matching text from the national systems. Still others are best clarified by the use of examples. Frequent reference is made to Chan's 1995 text, *Library of Congress Subject Headings: Principles and Application* (hereinafter referred to as Chan 1995). As Chan rests upon Haykin's *Subject Headings: A Practical Guide,* and Haykin upon Cutter's *Rules for a Dictionary Catalogue*, frequent references will also be made to these texts. REFERENCES to other works on *LCSH* and subject analysis and examples from the list of subject headings itself will further illustrate the principles.

THE INDIVIDUAL PRINCIPLES

IFLA Uniform Heading Principle

To facilitate synonym control and to collocate subjects in the display of bibliographic records, each concept or named entity that is indexed by a SHL should be represented by one authorized heading.

LCSH Principles: 3.3 Uniform Heading (one heading per subject-control of synonyms) [in part]

"In order that all materials on a particular subject are collocated so that recall may be increased, each subject is represented by only one heading."

Taylor's edition of Wynar defines collocation as the "process of bringing together in a catalog records for names, titles, or subjects that are bibliographically related to one another."[21] As Chan (1995) puts it, "It has long been a tenet of subject cataloging practice that, in order to show what a library has on a given subject, each subject should be represented in the catalog under only one name and one form of that name."[22] Cutter embraced this principle because it overcame the scattering of items on the same subject caused by the use of whatever words the author used, a system espoused by Andreas Crestadoro in his 1856 pamphlet, "The Art of Making Catalogues of Libraries." Using Crestadoro's method, books were indexed under important title words and other words used by the author that reflected the main topic of the book. Since it was likely that different authors and even different books by the same author would use different terms to refer to the same subject (e.g., "capital punishment" and "death penalty"), cross-references were made to lead the user from the books listed under one term to those listed under the other. Cutter espoused the uniform heading principle of listing all items about a single topic under a single heading by saying, "Why is it not likewise a greater inconvenience to be compelled always to look in two places for the works on a given subject than half the time to be referred from one heading to the other?"[23]

The terminology used for a subject heading need not match the term used in the material being indexed but rather is a single term chosen from among a group of synonyms to match a particular concept. Thus, if it is agreed that the terms "car" and "automobile" are synonymous, only one of these terms would occur in a subject heading system. The term "authorized" for this concept by *LCSH* is **Automobiles**. "Car" would thus not be a valid subject heading unless it were not synonymous with automobile. Haykin puts it elegantly in his description of fundamental concepts.

> A subject catalog must bring together under one heading all the books which deal principally or exclusively with the subject, whatever the terms applied to it by the authors of the books and whatever the varying terms applied to it at different times. The cataloger must, therefore, choose with care the term to be used and apply it uniformly to all the books on the subject. He must choose a term which is unambiguous and does not overlap in meaning other headings in the catalog, even where that involves defining the sense in which it is used as compared with, or distinguished from, other closely related headings.[24]

Thus, the underlying purpose of this principle is truly the bringing together into a single list documents that address the same concept.

The uniform heading principle's value rests on the assumption that the user is best served by bringing related materials together. Cutter recognized the deceptiveness of the simplicity implied by this idea. Some headings are so similar in meaning that, although they may address different concepts, index documents that discuss such similar topics that both headings must be consulted, for example *LCSH*'s **Sex (Psychology)** and **Sex role**. Other subjects have different names at different periods in their history. Sometimes there is an exact equivalence in meaning between the older and newer terms, for example, phthisis and tuberculosis. At other times, the meaning really has changed with the terminology change, for example, natural philosophy and physics.

IFLA Synonymy Principle

To collocate all material on a given subject and to increase the recall power of a SHL, synonymy should be controlled in the SHL.

LCSH Principles: 3.3 Uniform heading (one heading per subject–control of synonyms) [in part]

Synonymous terms and variant forms of the same heading are included as entry vocabulary, i.e., as referred-from terms.

LCSH Principle: 5.3 Cross references

Cross references are made for the purpose of guiding the catalog users from their entry vocabulary to valid headings and linking related headings. This principle is related to the Uniform Heading Principle. If the subject heading system uses only one from among a great list of synonyms for the same topic, then some mechanism should be provided to the enable the user to get from his chosen term to that of the system. Control of synonymy requires not only that a single term is chosen to represent a concept but that other, synonymous terms are linked to the chosen term by some device. In a traditional library catalog that device is the cross-reference. As Cutter said, "Of two exactly synonymous names, chose one and make a reference from the other."[25] Bates suggests that the "Side-of-a-Barn Principle" should be evident in our construction of subject index systems. "Any reasonable English language word or phrase should get the searcher started and linked to explanatory, guiding information to assist the search."[26]

According to the synonymy principle, a user searching *LCSH* should find a pointer that leads him from his chosen term to that used in the system. In an *LCSH* catalog, the user that searches for "cars" should be led to **Automobiles**. With Bates's "Side-of-a-Barn Principle," it is also reasonable to expect that a fully developed referencing system would lead a user from a search for "car" to the authorized *LCSH* term **Automobiles**. This is not the case. A user who searches the singular term "car" may find such *LCSH* terms as: **Car**

axles, **Car-couplings**, and **Car fenders**, among others, each of which refers to railroad cars, not automobiles; and the *LCSH* terms **Car pools**, **Car wash industry**, and **Car washes**, which do relate to automobiles. To find the cross-reference to the term **Automobiles**, the searcher must scan alphabetically past hundreds of unrelated terms that start with c-a-r, for example, **Career education**, **Carols**, and **Carpentry**, before reaching c-a-r-s and finding the necessary cross-reference, "Cars (Automobiles) *see* **Automobiles**." Adding cross-references from singular forms to plural forms whenever another word intervenes alphabetically between the singular form and the plural form would resolve this problem but would be a huge undertaking.

IFLA Homonymy Principle

To prevent the retrieval of irrelevant materials and to increase the precision power of a SHL, homonymy should be controlled in the SHL.

LCSH Principle: 3.4 Unique heading (one subject per heading–control of homographs)

In order to ensure precision and to minimize false hits in subject retrieval, each heading represents only one subject. Homographs are distinguished by parenthetical qualifiers.

As Chan (1995) points out, this is a "corollary to the principle of uniform heading."[27] As Haykin states, "The same term must not be used for more than one subject. If a term is used in more than one sense, as when it is used in more than one field of knowledge, it must be qualified in such a way that the reader will know precisely which meaning to attach to the term."[28] This seems a straightforward idea with a simple solution. If a word has two meanings and is used to represent those different meanings in the subject access system, simply qualify each parenthetically to indicate which meaning is being used. Chan (1995) gives the examples **Iris (Eye)** and **Iris (Plant)** or **Rings (Algebra)** and **Rings (Gymnastics)**.[29]

Existing *LCSH* homographic subject headings are not always so clearly indicated as the homonymy principle would indicate. For example, the subject heading **Poles** refers to individuals from Poland, whereas **Poles (Engineering)** refers to structural poles. The user must examine the postings at **Poles** to understand which meaning is intended; the meaning is not clarified in the heading itself. Even more cryptically, **Turkey** is the country whereas **Turkeys** is the bird. The user must know the syntactic practice of using plural forms for common nouns to find the heading for the bird; there is no cross reference from "Turkey (Bird)" to **Turkeys**.

IFLA Semantic Principle

To express the semantic (paradigmatic) structure of a SHL, subject headings should be linked by equivalence, hierarchical and coordinate relationships.

LCSH Principle: 10.0 Term relationships

Three types of relationships are represented in the cross-reference structure of *Library of Congress Subject Headings*: equivalence, hierarchical, and associative. These relationships are expressed in terms of USE (Used for), BT (Broader term), NT (Narrower term), RT (Related term), and SA (See also) references. Each reference links a term or heading with another heading or with a group of headings.

To some extent, the semantic principle overlaps with the synonymy principle in that equivalence relationships are often links between synonyms. It is through the use of semantic references that some of the strengths of a classified order for subjects are added to a dictionary arrangement. In the dictionary arrangement, such disparate subjects as **Collared peccary, Collars, Collateral circulation**, and **Collation (Law)** are next to each other in an alphabetical list yet they share no subject relationships. As Cutter put it, the dictionary catalog's "subject entries, individual, general, limited, extensive, thrown together without any logical arrangement, in most absurd proximity . . . are a mass of utterly disconnected particles without any relation to one another, each useful in itself but only by itself. But by a well-devised network of cross-references the mob becomes an army, of which each part is capable of assisting many other parts. The effective force of the catalogue is immensely increased."[30]

LCSH provides semantic links from equivalent terms and to related headings. **Collared peccary** has equivalence relationships indicated from Latin species names "Dicotyles tajacu," "Dicotyles torquatus," "Tayassu angulatus," and "Tayassu tajacu," and a hierarchical link from the broader term for the group of animals to which it belongs, **Peccaries**. These relationships provide a structure to the alphabetical display that forms the "concealed classification" in *LCSH* described by Richmond.[31]

IFLA Syntax Principle

To express complex and compound subjects, the syntax of a SHL should link the component parts of a subject heading by syntagmatic relationships rather than semantic (paradigmatic) ones.

LCSH Principle: 4.0 Structure of Subject Headings

A subject heading may consist of one or more words. A one-word heading represents a single concept, whereas a multiple-word heading may represent a single concept or multiple concepts.

LCSH Principle: 4.1 Single concept headings

A subject heading representing a single concept may appear as a single word or a multiple-word phrase, usually an adjectival phrase but occasionally a prepositional phrase. Each such heading represents a single object or idea. *Examples*: Automobiles, Botany, Budget deficits, Electric interference, Boards of trade, Clerks of court.

LCSH Principle: 4.2 Pre-coordinated and multiple-concept headings

A pre-coordinated multiple-concept heading contains two or more otherwise individual or independent concepts coordinated or related through one or more linking devices. Pre-coordination results in phrase headings or main-heading/subdivision combinations.

Syntax refers to structure whereas semantics refers to meaning. Syntax is applied to the development of individual headings within the SHL. Meaning of headings, or their semantics, can only be understood in terms of the relationships of the headings to each other (and, to some extent, to the postings related to those headings). Chan (1995) addresses this under the rubric "Precoordination and Postcoordination." Precoordination is the bringing together of more than one idea to form a multi-topical heading to address a multi-facetted topic. Some of these are specified in *LCSH*, for instance **Television and children**, which is used to index documents on the relationships between children and television. Others are constructed as needed using the extensive and complex subject subdivision practices of *LCSH*.[32]

The wording of this principle can be distilled into "Do this; don't do that." The "Do this" is the taking into account the syntax of the language of construction into the development of the SHL. Therefore, the syntax of individual headings varies from language to language as do the rules for each national system. For example, the German *RSWK-Regeln für den Schlagwortkatalog* as excerpted in the IFLA document gives instructions for dividing the very long compound terms that are possible in German into discrete segments more suited for the SHL, e.g., breaking "Luftverschmutzungbioindikator" into the subdivided "Luftverschmutzung/Bioindikator."[33] Such a rule would not be much needed in English.

The "Don't do that" indicates that a heading cannot be expected to show its entire meaning by itself. The *LCSH* heading **Toes** is, while a one-word heading, a complex concept. **Toes** are parts of the foot. The whole-part concept is not explicitly shown in the syntax of the term (i.e., the form of the term is not "Foot–Toes), rather the meaning of Toes is augmented by the semantic link from the broader term **Foot**. Semantic relationships within a SHL are shown by relating specific subject headings to each other within the language system. A complex concept can be expressed in a single precoordinated subject heading, e.g., **Television and children** or **Toes–Diseases** but the full meaning of the heading, whether simple or compound, is not.

IFLA Consistency Principle

To achieve and maintain consistency, each new subject heading admitted to a SHL should be similar in form and structure to comparable headings already in the language.

LCSH Consistency

Wherever feasible, attempts are made to maintain consistency in form and structure among similar headings through the use of recurring patterns.

Chan (1995) states that, "Predictability is an essential factor in successful subject retrieval, and predictability is higher if, under analogous circumstances, a given heading pattern occurs throughout the system. Thus, consistency as well as stability is a factor in end-user ease of consultation."[34] A simple example of such consistency is the use of the same term for the same thing within complex subject heading phrases, for example, "motion picture" in **Motion pictures, Animals in motion pictures**, and **Motion picture cameras**. Great retrieval confusion would result if the last term was changed to "Movie cameras" even though this may be a more commonly used term in natural speech. Cutter said that "it is better that the [choice of subject headings] should be made to conform when possible to some general system as there is then more likelihood that they will be decided alike by different cataloguers, and that a usage will grow up which the public will finally learn and profit by."[35]

IFLA Naming Principle

To facilitate integrated retrieval, names of persons, places, families, corporate bodies and works when used in a SHL of a given catalogue, bibliography or index should be established according to the rules used for that catalogue, bibliography or index.

LCSH Principle: 6.21 Names borrowed from the Name Authority File

With few exceptions, names of persons, corporate bodies, places and other entities may be borrowed from the Name Authority File (the machine-readable database containing headings and cross references for personal names, corporate names, and uniform titles) for use as subject headings for works about them. Forms of such headings are based on *Anglo-American Cataloging Rules*, 2nd edition (*AACR*).

Cutter stated that "The importance of deciding aright where any given subject shall be entered is in inverse proportion to the difficulty of the decision. If there is no obvious principle to guide the cataloguer, it is plain there will be no reason why the public should expect to find the entry under one heading rather than another . . . But it is better that such decisions should be made to conform when possible to some general system."[36] Cutter puts this statement with his version of the naming principle but you could easily apply it to several of the principles. The practice from Cutter forth has been to use the rules found in creating descriptive cataloging headings to create the subject headings for persons and corporate bodies. Haykin[37] and Chan (1995)[38] specify following the descriptive cataloging codes of their times for the establishment of names, but neither explains why this is a good idea.

IFLA Literary Warrant Principle

To reflect the subject content of documents, the vocabulary of a SHL should be developed dynamically, based on literary warrant, and integrated systematically with existing vocabulary.

LCSH Principle: 3.2 Literary Warrant

The Library of Congress collections serve as the literary warrant (i.e., the literature upon which the controlled vocabulary is based) for the *Library of Congress Subject Headings System*. The number and specificity of heading included in the Subject Authority File (the machine-readable database containing the master file of Library of Congress subject headings from which the printed list, the microform list, the CDMARC Subjects, etc., are generated), are determined by the nature and scope of the Library of Congress collections. Subject headings are established as they are needed to catalog items being added to the collection or to establish links among existing headings. In recent years, headings contributed by libraries engaged in cooperative activities with the Library of Congress based on the needs of their collections have also been included.

Chan (1995) lists this as the second basic principle (after user and usage) and describes the two fundamental bases upon which a subject list or classification scheme can be built: on a conceptual framework of the universe of knowledge or on the content of the literature that needs to be indexed by the system. The literary warrant principle specifies that subject headings lists follow the latter method. Subject heading lists are not built upon a theoretical construct for the universe of knowledge. They are instead reactive and reflective creations. They are "enumerative" in that they enumerate the topics in a collection of documents. As Haykin states, "Since all existing lists are limited to such headings as have been devised to cover actual books, pamphlets, and articles in periodicals found in a particular library (or group of libraries), even relatively small libraries and, particularly, special libraries find it necessary to establish new headings for their own catalogs. This need arises from two circumstances: no list is complete enough and sufficiently up-to-the-minute to keep up with the increase of knowledge, and no list is adequate to the needs of a library when the library [catalogs materials it has not previously cataloged]."[39]

What Haykin goes on to say, and Cutter says in a more convoluted way, is that if a subject is new to the literature, a library may need to enlist the assistance of experts in that subject area. In fact, the use of literary warrant is *de facto* consultation with subject experts; if the terms used in the documents are used for the subjects and the authors of the documents are assumed to be expert over that which they write, then expert opinion is reflected in literary warrant. However quite often subject experts come up with subject heading terms that an average person would never think of because experts have specialized vocabularies others do not know. Bates demonstrated this is her dissertation. The greater the subject knowledge, the less likely people are to be able to guess the *LCSH* that are applied to documents in their own areas of expertise.[40]

To some degree, the literary warrant principle links directly to the user principle; using terms with literary warrant is using terms that are used by users of the term. But applying the literary warrant principle affects application of semantics, syntax, consistency, naming, and user principles and may at times conflict with all of them.

IFLA User Principle

To meet users' needs, the vocabulary of a SHL should be chosen to reflect the audience for the SHL, whatever that may be, for example for the general public or users of a specific type of library.

LCSH Principle: 3.12 Current Usage

User needs are best met if headings reflect current usage in regard to terminology. Thus, terms in current use are selected in establishing new subject headings. Current usage is ascertained through research in reference works, general indexes and thesauri, current literature in the appropriate field, and the work(s) being cataloged.

Chan (1995) puts user and usage first among the principles of *LCSH* and referred back to what is perhaps Cutter's most famous statement from the 4th edition of his rules which were published posthumously in 1904, "The convenience of the public is always to be set before the ease of the cataloger."[41] Cutter also stated, "General rules, always applicable, for the choice of names of subjects can no more be given than rules without exception in grammar. Usage in both cases is the supreme arbiter–the usage, in the present case, not of the cataloguer but of the public in speaking of subjects."[42] If choices must be made among synonyms, the term chosen for the subject heading should be the one that the users of a particular catalog would expect to find.

Cutter uses the term "public" rather than user and, indeed, his rules were published as part two of a document distributed by the U.S. Bureau of Education called *Public Libraries in the United States of America*. But from the start, the definition of user has been a difficult one and this problem makes application of the user principle difficult. The catalogs Cutter knew were those that were created and printed in book form for individual libraries. They were discrete unto themselves. A new catalog was expected to be created and replaced periodically and to serve a single "public." This means that Cutter's ideal catalog was a temporary and local device. As Cutter said in his essay in the first part of the Bureau's report, "A catalogue is designed to answer certain questions about a library, and that is the best which answers most of the questions with the least trouble to the asker. It [the catalog] may, however, for reasons of economy, decline to answer certain classes of inquiries with very little practical loss of utility, and different libraries may properly make different selections of questions to be answered."[43]

In reference to practices at the Library of Congress, Haykin states, "The reference to our lack of knowledge in regard to the approach of various classes and categories of readers to the subject catalog clearly points to the fundamental principle that the reader is the focus in all cataloging principles and practice. All other considerations, such as convenience and the desire to arrange entries in some logical order, are secondary to the basic rule that the heading, in wording and structure, should be that which the reader will seek in the catalog, if we know or can presume what the reader will look under."[44]

Working subject heading lists like *LCSH* grow one heading at a time and the creators of new subject headings for those lists must take into account conflicting principles and needs. The User Principle would lead one to use "movie camera" whereas applying the Consistency Principle results in the heading **Motion picture cameras**. Following both User Principle and Literary Warrant, the *LCSH* headings for species of animals in a given group are a mix of Latin and common names because some animals are written about in the popular literature and others are only written about in the scientific literature. The term **Bottlenose dolphin** is used as the heading rather than the

Latin name *Tursiops aduncus*, whereas the Latin term **Lagenorhynchus electra** is used as the heading for the broad-beaked dolphin. Haykin assumes the supremacy of the User Principle over the Consistency Principle because the user approaches the catalog "resting on psychological rather than logical grounds."[45] This runs counter to Cutter's idea that the user finding a consistency will be able to infer the underlying rules of the catalog and therefore be better able to predict where to look. Prevost would seem to value consistency when she argues that, "we must make plain the truth that no one can use a catalog who does not know how, and, for those who do know how, we must make its use quicker, easier, and more sure, disavowing openly and without shame the pretense that it can be, successfully, a free-for-all."[46]

IFLA Subject Indexing Policy Principle

To meet user needs and give consistent treatment to documents, indexing policies giving guidance for subject analysis and representation should be developed.

LCSH Part II.A: General Guidelines for Assigning Subject Headings

[Sections 20.0 through 42.7 fulfill the recommendation of this principle.]

Chan (1995) describes Haykin as "the closest thing to a set of rules for subject headings since Cutter . . . It contains an account and exposition of Library of Congress practice, with occasional apologetics, but is not cast in the form of a code."[47] Actually, the clearest statement of the principles in Haykin is found in a set of instructions to the "faculty specialists" a subject cataloger would consult when doing subject analysis outside their areas of expertise.[48] Despite repeated calls in the literature for a subject cataloging code that would meet the spirit of the IFLA principles, the closest that exists for *LCSH* is its own description of internal practices, the *Subject Cataloging Manual* section on subject headings. It is not therefore surprising that no direct equivalent to this principle can be found in Chan (1990). It seems to be a principle that states there ought to be principles.

If it is appropriate to include this among the principles, then perhaps it and the other "Application Principle," the Specific Heading Principle, should appear before the "Construction Principles." Arguably, one need not know how to construct a heading if one does not know when a heading needs to be constructed. Missing, for instance, among the principles is one that specifically addresses the problem of determining aboutness. The principles address mechanics first and only cryptically in the Subject Indexing Policy Principle make a reference to subject analysis. Without knowing how to do the analysis we cannot know what subject headings need to be constructed.

IFLA Specific Heading Principle

To increase the precision power of a SHL, a subject heading or set of subject headings should be coextensive with the subject content to which it applies. However, to prevent too little or too much from being retrieved, the level of coextensivity of assigned headings should be adjusted to take account of file size and subject trends in collection development.

LCSH Principle: 22.0 Specific (co-extensive) entry

The heading that represents precisely the subject content of the work is assigned as the primary subject heading, unless such a heading does not exist and cannot be established. In the absence of a co-extensive heading, a heading broader or more general than the content of the work may be assigned. In this case, the broader or more general heading is the most *specific* authorized heading in the hierarchy which covers the content of the work. In some cases, several related headings may be assigned.

Chan (1995) addresses specificity and coextensivity together but differentiates the two. Specificity is related to a subject term whereas coextensivity is related to the span of a document. She also quotes extensively Oliver Linton Lilley, John Balnaves, and Elaine Svenonius in her explanation of specificity.[49] It is not surprising that her discussion of specificity is longer than that for any of the other principles. Specificity in indexing comes as a surprise to users. Markey noted that most users fail to match an *LCSH* heading on their first try. Indeed many do not know that there is a controlled vocabulary specified for the subject headings but there is strong evidence that users wish to retrieve lists of subject headings related to their searches.[50] Only a controlled vocabulary provides such a list. Bates's findings indicate that when a user identifies a valid subject heading in a catalog, two-thirds of the time that heading is not at the right level of specificity for the information need. Users are misled into thinking that they have found what the library has on a topic when they have missed the best materials for the topic.[51]

As the IFLA principle indicates, be as specific as possible but not too specific. To Cutter, specificity was a moving target.

> Some subjects have no name; they are spoken of only by a phrase or by several phrases not definite enough to be used as a heading. . . . There are thousands of possible matters of investigation, some of which are from time to time discussed, but before the catalogue can profitably follow its "specific" rule in regard to them they must attain a certain individuality as objects of inquiry, and be given some sort of *name*, otherwise we must assign them class-entry [index them under a broader term].[52]

Thus, level of specificity is dependent on literary warrant and user expectations. Ideally, perception of sufficient literary warrant to create a specific heading on the part of the cataloger coincides with the expectation that a new subject may be looked up on the part of the user. Such coincidence is rare. Anyone cataloging in the field of education in the early 1980s was aware that the term "mainstreaming" was prevalent in the field long before the subject term **Mainstreaming in education** entered *LCSH*. Earliest items on mainstreaming (the practice of putting children of all ability levels in the same classroom) were indexed by the heading **Exceptional children–Education**. This heading has now been replaced by **Special education**, a heading particularly ill-suited for the topic of mainstreaming. During Cutter's day, such problems would not have been irreparable; when a new book catalog was constructed, new subject headings would be assigned. Since the widespread implementation of the card catalog and online catalogs, however, we expect the subject analysis represented in bibliographic records to be valid in perpetuity. Rarely do catalogers go back and reanalyze when more specific subject headings become available.

Specificity problems are often addressed in critiques of *LCSH*. Clack (1973) assesses how well *LCSH* met the needs of those in search of information about Blacks and African-Americans by defining a "fully adequate" heading as one that precoordinated the concept of the Black race with the specific subject being discussed. To Clack, the greater the specificity, the greater the adequacy of the heading. Following Clack's measurement, a single subject heading such as "**Afro-American women government executives**" would be more "adequate" than the two current *LCSH* headings, **Afro-American government executives** and **Women government executives**.[53] Wang examines the treatment of Chinese literature in *LCSH* and also finds it lacking sufficiently specific subject headings.[54] Mischo identifies several shortcomings in both the structure of *LCSH* and in its application. Specificity of headings and their application varies. In some cases, multi-element topics are addressed through one precoordinated heading, e.g., **Television and children**. In other cases, items on multi-element topics are treated as if they were multitopical through the application of two or more single element headings. Additionally, there are concepts for which no heading exists and the heading for a broader concept is employed despite a large number of postings at that broader heading, and a narrower heading could be developed.[55]

THE PRINCIPLES AND THE "REAL WORLD"

If the IFLA principles and the *LCSH* principles coincide and if the IFLA principles "stat[e] what is meant by a good SHL and what desirable construction and application principles are for such languages,"[56] then *LCSH* must be a good SHL. It is a good SHL but it is certainly not a perfect one. Herein lie some of the problems with the IFLA *Principles* document.

First, the IFLA principles are well-grounded in statements of practice, but are existing practice and historical statements of principles appropriate bases for "a useful guide to those . . . planning to develop a new subject heading language?"[57] Intner suggests that "we should go back to what ought to be the basis for all subject heading principles: Observations about the search behavior and expectations of subject heading users."[58] Do the practices that have evolved through the years based on statements of principle by Cutter and Haykin reflect user approaches to information seeking?

Second, in reality, the principles identified as being appropriate for subject headings lists cannot be fully followed. Some of the principles are in direct conflict with others, and fully following some of the principles may be impractical or impossible. Inconsistencies in *LCSH* demonstrate this. As Holley and Killheffer noted, "the Library of Congress subject heading system has not been tried and found wanting; it has never been tried."[59]

Chan (1995) identifies an *LCSH* principle that does not appear among the IFLA principles and "receives little attention in the literature," that of "Stability."[60] Ideally, stability provides a predictability for the user. Stability run amok results in complaints like that of Gabbard: "The frequent Victorian terminology in *LCSH* is unfamiliar to the typical subject searcher."[61] Stability exacerbates the conflicts between consistency and usage, literary warrant and specificity. Anyone who has been involved with subject headings can cite instances of the Library of Congress dragging its feet before making changes but there are also instances of leaping to make changes too soon. Stability is a real world principle in *LCSH* whose impact cannot be overlooked. If the IFLA principles are to serve as the basis for future systems, then stability is an issue that should be addressed by them.

CONCLUSION

The IFLA *Principles Underlying Subject Heading Languages (SHLs)* meets its goal as expressed in the foreword by Elaine Svenonius. It "postulates and then empirically verifies the existence of general principles underlying subject heading languages."[62] Principles were enumerated and then matching text was found. Similarly, this paper has found matching text for the principles in documents that form the framework for *LCSH*. Whether the principles as identified "stat[e] what is meant by a good SHL and what desirable construction and application principles are for such languages" is open to question.[63]

The document does not test the efficacy of the principles. It only postulates and demonstrates that they exist. It is only through the testing of these principles in real world retrieval systems that we can determine whether these are principles that ought to be followed. What the IFLA *Principles* document represents for the present is codification of existing practice. If the aim is improved retrieval, then the evaluation of the principles must be based upon information retrieval research, not compilation of rules. Perhaps the true success of the document is in its having articulated principles that can now be tested.

NOTES

1. Paule Rolland-Thomas, "Preface," in *Library of Congress Subject Headings: Philosophy, Practice, and Prospects*, by William E. Studwell (New York: The Haworth Press, Inc. 1990), 1.

2. William E. Studwell, *Library of Congress Subject Headings: Philosophy, Practice and Prospects* (New York: The Haworth Press, Inc. 1990), 12.

3. Sheila Intner, "ASCR: The American Subject Cataloging Rules (Part 1)," *Technicalities* 8 (July 1988): 7.

4. William E. Studwell, "Why Not an 'AACR' for Subject Headings?" *Cataloging & Classification Quarterly* 6 (Fall 1985): 3-9.

5. Marie Louise Prevost, "An Approach to Theory and Method in the General Subject Heading,' *The Library Quarterly* 16 (April 1946): 141.

6. Working Group on Principles Underlying Subject Heading Languages, IFLA Section on Classification and Indexing, *Principles Underlying Subject Heading Languages (SHLs)*, edited by Maria Inês Lopes and Julianne Beall. (The Hague: International Federation of Library Associations and Institutions, 1999.) Recently also published in a hardcover edition: München: K.G. Saur, 1999.

7. Library of Congress. Cataloging Policy and Support Office, *Subject Cataloging Manual: Subject Headings*, 5th ed. (Washington, D.C.: Library of Congress, 1996).

8. Lois Mai Chan, *Library of Congress Subject Headings: Principles of Structure and Policies for Application*, Annotated Version (Washington, D.C.: Cataloging Distribution Service, Library of Congress, 1990).

9. Lois Mai Chan, *Library of Congress Subject Headings: Principles and Application* (Englewood, Colo: Libraries Unlimited, 1995).

10. David Judson Haykin, *Subject Headings: A Practical Guide* (Washington, D.C.: Library of Congress, 1951), 7.

11. Charles Cutter, *Rules for a Dictionary Catalogue*, 3rd ed. (Washington, D.C.: U.S. Bureau of Education, 1891).

12. Maria Inês Lopes, "Principles Underlying Subject Heading Languages: An International Approach," 61st IFLA General Conference-Conference Proceedings–August 20-15, 1995 from IFLANET [Accessed at http://www.ifla.org/IV/ifla61/61-lopm.htm].

13. Working Group, *Principles*, 10-11.

14. Lopez, "Principles."

15. Working Group, *Principles*, 5.

16. Ibid., 9.

17. Rolland-Thomas, "Preface," 2.

18. Pauline A. Cochrane, *Improving LCSH for Use In Online Catalogs: Exercises for Self-Help with a Selection of Background Readings* (Littleton, Colo.: Libraries Unlimited, 1986), 24.

19. Working Group, *Principles*, 15.

20. Chan, *Library of Congress Subject Headings*, 1995, 15.

21. Bohdan S. Wynar, *Introduction to Cataloging and Classification*, 7th ed. by Arlene Taylor (Littleton, Colo.: Libraries Unlimited, 1985), 604.

22. Chan, *Library of Congress Subject Headings, 1995*, 19.

23. Charles A. Cutter, "Library Catalogues," in *Public Libraries in the United States of America: Their History, Condition, And Management: Special Report*. Part I. (Washington, D.C.: U.S. Department of the Interior, Bureau of Education, 1876), 536.

24. Haykin, *Subject Headings*, 7.

25. Cutter, *Rules*, 1891, 49.

26. Marcia J. Bates, "Subject Access in Online Catalogs: A Design Model," *Journal of the American Society for Information Science* 37, no. 6 (1986): 357-376.

27. Chan, *Library of Congress Subject Headings*, 1995, 24.

28. Haykin, *Subject Headings*, 8.

29. Chan, *Library of Congress Subject Headings*, 1995, 50.

30. Cutter, *Rules*, 1891, 57.

31. Phyllis Allen Richmond, "Cats: An Example of Concealed Classification in Subject Headings, " *Library Resources & Technical Services* 3 (Spring 1959): 102-112.

32. Chan, *Library of Congress Subject Headings*, 1995, 32-36.

33. Working Group, *Principles*, 105.

34. Chan, *Library of Congress Subject Headings*, 1995, 30.

35. Cutter, *Rules*, 1891, 46.

36. Ibid., 46.

37. Haykin, *Subject Headings*, 37.

38. Chan, *Library of Congress Subject Headings*, 1995, 55.

39. Haykin, *Subject Headings*, 90-91.

40. Marcia Jeanne Bates, "Factors Affecting Subject Catalog Search Success." Ph.D. diss., University of California, Berkeley, 1972.

41. Charles A. Cutter, *Rules for a Dictionary Catalog*, 4th ed., rewritten (Washington, D.C.: U.S. Government Printing Office, 1904), 6.

42. Cutter, *Rules*, 1891, 49

43. Cutter, "Library Catalogues," 526-527.

44. Haykin, *Subject Headings*, 7.

45. Ibid., 7.

46. Prevost, "An Approach to Theory and Method in the General Subject Heading," 97.

47. Chan, *Library of Congress Subject Headings*, 1995, 11

48. Haykin, *Subject Headings*, 91

49. Chan, *Library of Congress Subject Headings*, 1995, 24-30.

50. Karen Markey, "Integrating the Machine-Readable *LCSH* into Online Catalogs," *Information Technology and Libraries* 7 (September 1988): 299.

51. Marcia J. Bates, "Factors Affecting Subject Catalog Search Success," *Journal of the American Society for Information Science* 28 (May 1977): 166-167.

52. Cutter, *Rules*, 1891, 46.

53. Doris Hargrett Clack, "An Investigation into the Adequacy of Library of Congress Subject Headings for Resources for Black Studies," Ph.D. diss., University of Pittsburgh, 1973.

54. Sze-Tseng Wang, "The Structure of Library of Congress Subject Headings for Belles-Lettres in Chinese Literature," *Library Resources & Technical Services* 17 (Spring 1973): 231.

55. William Mischo, "Library of Congress Subject Headings: A Review of the Problems, and Prospects for Improved Subject Access," *Cataloging & Classification Quarterly* 1, no. 2/3 (1982): 105-124.

56. Working Group, *Principles*, 9.

57. Ibid., 5.

58. Intner, "ASCR," 7.

59. Robert P. Holley and Robert E. Killheffer, "Is There an Answer to the Subject Access Crisis?" *Cataloging & Classification Quarterly* 1 no. 2/3 (1982):132.

60. Chan, *Library of Congress Subject Headings*, 1995, 31.

61. Paula Beversdorf Gabbard, "*LCSH* and PRECIS in Music: A Comparison," *The Library Quarterly* 55 (1985): 193.

62. Working Group, *Principles*, 5.

63. Ibid., 9.

Difference, Culture and Change:
The Untapped Potential of *LCSH*

Hope A. Olson

SUMMARY. The *Library of Congress Subject Headings* have traditionally attempted to reflect reality neutrally. The result is bias in representing cultural margins. While neutrality is one of the ethical stances espoused by librarianship, another is universal and equitable access to information for the betterment of humanity. This paper views *LCSH* as a potential tool for cultural change using Homi Bhabha's postcolonial concept of a Third Space as a model. *LCSH* functions as a Third Space where the meanings of documents are constructed and enunciated for library users. Therefore, it is in *LCSH* that there is potential for instigating change. *[Article copies available for a fee from The Haworth Document Delivery Service: 1-800-342-9678. E-mail address: <getinfo@haworthpress inc.com> Website: <http:www.haworthpressinc.com>]*

KEYWORDS. *Library of Congress Subject Headings*, cultural bias, postcolonial criticism

Use what is dominant in a culture to change it quickly.

Jenny Holzer[1]

Hope A. Olson, PhD, is Associate Professor, School of Library & Information Studies, 3-20 Rutherford South, University of Alberta, Edmonton, AB T6G 2J4, Canada (E-mail: hope.olson@ualberta.ca).

[Haworth co-indexing entry note]: "Difference, Culture and Change: The Untapped Potential of *LCSH*." Olson, Hope A. Co-published simultaneously in *Cataloging & Classification Quarterly* (The Haworth Information Press, an imprint of The Haworth Press, Inc.) Vol. 29, No. 1/2, 2000, pp. 53-71; and: *The LCSH Century: One Hundred Years with the Library of Congress Subject Headings System* (ed: Alva T. Stone) The Haworth Information Press, an imprint of The Haworth Press, Inc., 2000, pp. 53-71. Single or multiple copies of this article are available for a fee from The Haworth Document Delivery Service [1-800-342-9678, 9:00 a.m. - 5:00 p.m. (EST). E-mail address: getinfo@haworthpressinc.com].

This epigraph from artist Jenny Holzer is the starting point in this paper for suggesting that a mainstream tool such as a standard library controlled vocabulary is potentially an agent of cultural change. The *Library of Congress Subject Headings* (*LCSH*) seems to be such a standard. This paper will explore three questions about *LCSH*:

- Is *LCSH* dominant in our culture?
- Should we seek cultural change through *LCSH?*
- Is it possible to use *LCSH* for cultural change?

The concept of the Third Space from the work of the well-known postcolonial critic, Homi Bhabha, is useful for exploring the possibility of *LCSH* as a change agent. The Third Space is the medium of communication–"the structure of symbolization" that produces meaning.[2] It is the in between space where meaning is enunciated. In this sense, *LCSH* is a Third Space between documents being represented and users retrieving them. *LCSH* constructs the meanings of documents for users.

This paper will be organized into three parts paralleling the three questions above: (1) an explanation of how *LCSH* enunciates the authority of the dominant patriarchal, Euro-settler culture; (2) an examination of the limits of *LCSH* where the dominant culture interacts with cultural differences and how the ethic of librarianship treats these limits; and (3) an explication of how Bhabha's idea of the Third Space offers a model for employing *LCSH* for cultural change.

LCSH AS A DEVICE OF CULTURAL AUTHORITY

LCSH has the intended audience of users of the Library of Congress, with a clear recognition that it also serves library users throughout the United States. It is also used in libraries and national bibliographies in much of the English-speaking world (e.g., Australia and the United Kingdom), in heterogeneous environments that are more or less officially English-speaking (e.g., Canada and South Africa), in countries with diverse languages that use English as a common language (e.g., Singapore and Nigeria), in countries that use English for its practical external value (e.g., Iceland), alongside translations of *LCSH* (e.g., in Turkey and Malaysia), and in translation alone (e.g., the Spanish versions which are widely used in Latin America). *LCSH*-derived lists of subject headings are used in some countries (e.g., Portugal) and in other types of subject access tools (e.g., indexes published by H.W. Wilson Company). This widespread use as an official vocabulary and as a foundational vocabulary illustrates the authority of *LCSH*.

LCSH has long been criticized for not adequately representing marginalized groups. In a recent study Rose Schlegl and I found 68 critiques on the basis of gender, race, religion, ethnicity and other factors.[3] Given the frustrating experience of Lynne M. Martin and Barbara J. Via[4] in searching *Library and Information Science Abstracts* and *Library Literature* (an H. W. Wilson index) for material on recruiting minorities to the profession, we, too, undoubtedly missed some relevant works. Our investigation was stymied by the very problem we were investigating. However, failure to locate material is not the only result of poor representation of marginalized groups. It is also important to bear in mind the impact of *LCSH* on individual library users. Marielena Fina describes her experience in searching, such as finding "a card with the heading **Libraries and the socially handicapped** (having been changed from **Library service to the culturally handicapped**) to cover the topic of access to information by a Latina(o) in 1972."[5] This example (unchanged since 1972) indicates the potential impact of *LCSH* as a cultural authority. The authority of the catalogue confronts the individual with a reflection of his or her reality. The mirror may be cracked or crazed to send back a distorted image, affecting self-esteem for some and just making others angry.

Acknowledgment of the generally-accepted notion that *LCSH* usage is both widespread and influential suggests an examination of how *LCSH* operates as this device of cultural authority through three discourses. The first discourse of authority requires a return to *LCSH*'s historical link with Charles Cutter's *Rules for a Dictionary Catalog*. Cutter's *Rules* set the tone for the relationship between *LCSH* and "the public," theoretically putting "the public" in charge of the standard. The second discourse of the authority of *LCSH* is the concept of literary warrant, which puts the literature of disciplines or knowledge domains in charge of the standard. Finally, there is the authority of the Library of Congress as the institution governing *LCSH*, mediating between the knowledge domains and the public, and, at least *de facto*, governing application through documented policies and procedures and through copy cataloging.

Charles Cutter and the Historical Discourse of "the Public"

Cutter's *Rules* govern the choice of what terminology will be used to represent a given concept. His first reason for choice of an entry is overtly democratic: "choose that entry . . . that will probably be first looked under by the class of people who use the library."[6] The public is to be the arbiter of the language used in the catalogue:

> *The convenience of the public* is always to be set before the ease of the cataloger. In most cases they coincide. A plain rule without exceptions is not only easy for us to carry out, but *easy for the public* to understand and work by. But strict consistency in a rule and uniformity in its application sometimes lead to practices which clash with *the public's habitual way of looking at things*. When these habits are general and

deeply rooted, it is unwise for the cataloger to ignore them, even if they demand a sacrifice of system and simplicity.[7] (emphasis added)

The public, then, is to be the authority, even over the cataloguer who understands the workings of the system. However, the phrases "[t]he convenience of the public," "easy for the public," "the public's habitual way of looking at things" and "the class of people who use the library" give indications of a type of exclusivity. The use of the singular, especially of the definite article "the," in these phrases indicates that Cutter is envisioning one public with one convenience and one way of looking at things, at least for any particular library. Cutter is envisioning a community of library users with a singular perspective and a singular way of seeking information. The convenience of this community is the cataloguer's primary consideration. All rules are subject to this community and it is the singular public who defines usage. Nonetheless, a community in the singular is not totally inclusive. It excludes those who do not fit, those who are *different*. It results in what Alexis de Tocqueville described as the tyranny of the majority: the majority opinion is imposed on everyone, including all of the minorities. "The public" is, then, the dominant view (not even necessarily a numerical majority of more than 50% of the population). The result is that Cutter's approach tends to reinforce the status quo of a society. The authority of "the public" is the authority of an established mainstream perspective.

In consulting the public, the current practices of the Library of Congress show a significant modification of Cutter's approach. For example, in the establishment of the heading **Gays–Nazi persecutions**, the Library of Congress authority record notes a variety of sources for the content and form of the heading (established in 1995 and revised in 1998) including the Library of Congress's catalogue, a World Wide Web search, and the gay newspaper *The Washington Blade*.[8] This array of sources represents a diversity of voices and combines voices of various publics with literary warrant.

Literary Warrant and Canonicity

While the public, in the tradition of Cutter, determines the choice of form of a heading, the Library of Congress follows the principle of literary warrant in deciding whether or not a heading will be established at all. Literary warrant is a second element in the operation of *LCSH* as a device of cultural authority. The *Subject Cataloging Manual: Subject Headings* (*SCM:SH*) defines literary warrant in its instruction regarding establishment of a new topical subject heading:

> Establish a subject heading for a topic that represents a discrete, identifiable concept when it is first encountered in a work being cataloged, rather than after several works on the topic have been published and cataloged.[9]

Literary warrant contributes to the reinforcement of a mainstream canon in any particular knowledge domain. In 1972, Steve Wolf condemned the treatment of gays and lesbians in the *Dewey Decimal* and *Library of Congress* classifications.[10] He documented how both classifications lump "gayness" with crime and sexual disorders, prostitution and pornography, disorders of character, rapists, seducers, and perversions through context and references. In contrast, the nuclear family and sex within marriage are set up as the norm. Wolf quotes C. Sumner Spalding, then Assistant Director for Cataloging of the Library of Congress, as replying to Wolf's concerns that the Library of Congress does not *establish* usage, but *reflects* it. In a similar situation, in response to the criticisms of Thomas Yen-Ran Yeh regarding the use of the word "massacre" when Native Americans killed European settlers as opposed to the word "battle" when white soldiers killed Native Americans, Eugene Frosio, LC principal subject cataloguer at the time, suggested that literary warrant dictated this usage in the text of the *Library of Congress Classification*.[11] The tradition of literary warrant at the Library of Congress has been the same for both classification and subject headings. It has echoed the mainstream and rejected the margins. The topics that are represented in *LCSH* on the basis of literary warrant are more or less (as will be discussed below) the topics that are represented in published materials received and catalogued by the Library of Congress. While this includes a wide range of materials, the barriers to publication of marginal views are well known and marginal presses are not always represented in the Library of Congress's collection, especially if they are published outside of the United States without even legal deposit to assist in their collection. Further, literary warrant introduces a decidedly US bias to *LCSH* simply because of the collection developed through legal deposit–understandable, but unfortunate and with far-reaching consequences.

Another limitation, even to the opportunities offered by literary warrant, is that not all types of headings are included in *LCSH*:

> When a work being cataloged is on a topic that appears to be new but is judged to be not yet discrete and identifiable, assign the available subject headings that most accurately designate the topic of the work.[12]

So if a topic is represented in one book, *SCM:SH* instructs its immediate inclusion unless the terminology for the topic is not well-developed. New ideas on marginalized topics are among the most likely to fall outside of the category of "discrete and identifiable." Terminology in areas such as women's studies is especially problematic because the concepts are typically interdisciplinary, quickly changing and unconventional. The "problem without a name" (the anomie felt by suburban housewives who had "everything" a housewife is supposed to want) identified by Betty Friedan in *The Feminine*

Mystique in 1963, is quite concrete, but still unnamed more than thirty years later.

As a final factor, it is important to realize that literary warrant is not, for whatever reason, consistently applied. For example, there is no heading for *unpaid work*. The idea of work or labour seems a basic concept, but in our society what is valued is *paid* work. Unpaid work is essential to the function of our society and our economy; however, it generally goes unrecognized. This lack of recognition is likely a factor of who does most of the unpaid work in the world: women. Unpaid labour–including household work (cooking, cleaning, laundering, managing family finances, etc.), child care, elder care, care of family members with disabilities, volunteer work, and work in family businesses and agricultural work–is typically labour done with no expectation of remuneration or labour performed as a family investment over which women may have little control or that may disappear in the event of divorce. The Library of Congress has catalogued at least a dozen books (found in a superficial keyword search) on this topic and still does not have a heading for it. The establishment of a heading to cover persecution of Gays by the Nazis (discussed above) followed the cataloguing of at least nine titles by the Library of Congress as indicated by a note in the *LCSH* authority record. Some of these titles were held well before the heading was established. Whether or not the omission of a heading for unpaid work and the late addition of a heading for persecution of Gays by the Nazis relate to the fact that these topics are not studied within the canons of mainstream of economics and history is impossible to know for certain. However, such omissions raise concerns that the discourses of the status quo are very strong in *LCSH*.

The Library of Congress as an Authoritative Source

LCSH applied in a canonical form is the third enactment of authority, explaining how *LCSH* operates as a device of cultural reinforcement. Not only is it used in many parts of the world beyond the United States and in languages other than English, but the Library of Congress's application of *LCSH* is also used worldwide through copy cataloguing. OCLC, for example, has a database containing approximately 42 million bibliographic records of which over 7 million originated with the Library of Congress. In addition, it contains the Library of Congress authority database including *LCSH*. Over 35,000 libraries in 64 countries use OCLC.[13] They include public, school, special and academic libraries. OCLC may well be the single greatest distributor of Library of Congress catalogue records, but it is certainly not the only one. A trip to the American Library Association conference's exhibitors' halls illustrates that dozens (if not hundreds) of vendors offer online and CD-ROM products, cataloguing services and print bibliographic records, most of which originate at the Library of Congress. While the Library of

Congress may never have asked for the distinction of being the world's arbiter of subject cataloguing practice, it has acquired that role. Not only do libraries copy records from the Library of Congress, but many also endeavour to follow Library of Congress policies and procedures documented in its *SCM:SH* and *Cataloging Service Bulletin*s. The result is that Library of Congress decisions regarding issues such as levels of exhaustivity (how much of a work needs to be about a topic before it is represented) and specificity (application of broad and/or narrow headings) are replicated across libraries.

* * *

The authority of the public, the authority of the canons of various knowledge domains, and the authority of the Library of Congress as an institution all work together to largely reinforce the limits of the status quo.

PROBLEMATIZING LCSH AT THE BOUNDARIES OF CULTURAL DIFFERENCE

The above discussion has stressed the international use of *LCSH* and Library of Congress cataloguing copy. While it is easy to see how a standard designed in a US institution funded by US tax dollars is likely to cross international boundaries with some difficulty, it should also be remembered that boundaries are not just between national states. They also exist between cultures within a state. The United States, like so many other countries, is a diverse political jurisdiction within which difference may be celebrated, derogated or ignored. Such differences as gender and sexuality function as limits within our cultures. If a cultural authority reinforces the status quo then it will also reinforce the ascendancy of some and the subordination of others. Like any limited system (and a controlled vocabulary is by definition a limited system), *LCSH* has boundaries defining what it includes and what it excludes. It is at these boundaries that problems with the system are visible. Viewing *LCSH* as a text of cultural authority reveals its exclusions.

It is only by exclusion that authoritative culture is defined. Homi Bhabha states that "The concept of cultural difference focuses on the problem of the ambivalence of cultural authority: the attempt to dominate in the name of a cultural supremacy which is itself produced only in the moment of differentiation."[14] Differentiation is, then, the definition of what is *included* in a cultural authority by defining what is *excluded*. What is left out of *LCSH* defines its boundaries and illustrates the culture it endorses and enforces. This section of the paper will reveal exclusions, marginalizations, and distortions through specific examples from *LCSH* and its shortcomings in representing specific concepts in published works contained in the Library of

Congress's catalogue. It will then look at the expressed views of librarianship on the cultural role such standards should be playing.

Exclusions, Marginalizations, and Distortions

As mentioned earlier, there are numerous existing critiques of bias in *LCSH*. Certainly the Library of Congress has done much to address many of the acute problems raised in these critiques (such as the recent change of the heading "Man" to **Human beings**). The problems that remain are mainly subtle and systemic–systemic in that they result from the authority of "the public" and the authority of literary warrant that are at the foundations of the system. The following examples are intended to demonstrate these systemic problems rather than to flag specific headings or their lack.

Exclusions. Following are two examples of topics excluded from *LCSH*. In both cases a broader heading is allowed to cover a specific topic. This decision is in contradiction of the *SCM:SH* instruction regarding assigning and constructing subject headings to "[a]ssign headings that are as specific as the topics they cover."[15]

The first example is *Wicca*, a topic that is not given a heading in *LCSH* although the Library of Congress database contains many books on *Wicca*. Instead, *Wicca* is an equivalence reference (usually expressed as *see* or USE) under **Witchcraft**. Further, there is an equivalence reference from *Wiccans* to *Witches* compounding the concatenation of the very different meanings of *Witchcraft*. Other topics considered synonyms of **Witchcraft** are *Black art (Witchcraft)* and *Sorcery*; and **Witchcraft** has the broader term, **Occultism**. As a result, the religion of Wicca is categorized under *Occultism*. The Library of Congress catalogue lists nearly 500 titles under the main heading *Witchcraft* followed by numerous screens of **Witchcraft** with subdivisions, but a keyword search using the term *Wicca* produces only 33 titles about *Wicca* (plus 49 false drops). Therefore, material on *Wicca* cannot be effectively retrieved using subject headings because the materials are lost in the wider and largely unfriendly territory under the heading **Witchcraft**.

A similar instance is the lack of a heading for the concept of *Corporate welfare* (government support of corporations that have inadequate means of self-support, as though they were people, typically through tax advantages and loans). *Corporate welfare* has been used in five titles that are listed in the Library of Congress catalogue. One of these titles is the proceedings of a Congressional budget committee. However, there is no subject heading that will draw these titles together. **Corporations–Taxation** has been used in two records, the only instance of commonality amongst the five. This heading is far too broad to substitute. Other works on *Corporate welfare* that do not have the term in the title are completely lost.

Marginalizations. Marginalization of a topic is the process of placing it outside of the cultural mainstream–making it *"other."* One way of marginal-izing a topic is to focus on the qualities that make it *other* and fail to recognize the qualities that are similar to the mainstream. Since, as Bhabha notes above, "cultural supremacy . . . is itself produced only in the moment of differentiation,"[16] it is in this differentiation and concomitant omission of similarity that the authority of the mainstream is established. Examples of this practice are headings for groups of people consisting only of adjectives, such as: **Handicapped**, **Poor** and **Aged**. What is included is what differentiates these groups from the mainstream. What is excluded is the fact that they are people just as able-bodied people are people, affluent people are people, and middle-aged people are people. That the Library of Congress has recognized the lack of a noun is indicated by the equivalence references to **Handicapped** from *Disabled people* and *Handicapped people*. Sometimes the differentiation is multiplied by using two adjectives such as **Poor aged** or **Learning disabled**. This kind of differentiation essentializes groups, that is, it homogenizes their internal differences by using one defining characteristic or essence to differentiate them from the cultural mainstream.

Distortions. A more subtle systemic problem uses the structure of the subject heading list to shift the meaning of a term in a particular direction. An example is the subject heading for **Feminism**. There is nothing wrong with the heading itself, but its references to narrower terms create a peculiar picture of the concept:

> Narrower Term: Feminist therapy
> Narrower Term: Feminists
> Narrower Term: Radical therapy
> Narrower Term: Sex discrimination against women
> Narrower Term: Women–History
> Narrower Term: Women–Legal status, laws, etc.
> Narrower Term: Women–Social conditions
> Narrower Term: Psychoanalysis and feminism
> Narrower Term: Feminist theory
> Narrower Term: Ecofeminism
> Narrower Term: Lesbian feminism
> Narrower Term: Bisexual feminism
> Narrower Term: Feminist geography
> Narrower Term: Nationalism and feminism

Only three specific streams of **Feminism** are listed: **Ecofeminism**, **Lesbian feminism**, and **Bisexual feminism**. Indeed, these are the only three feminisms established in *LCSH*. The typical stance of the 1960s and 1970s, *Liberal feminism*, is not given a heading, but seems to be implied in the general term *Feminism* by the references to **Sex discrimination against**

women and **Women–Legal status, laws, etc.** *Radical feminism* is implied
only by reference to the unrelated heading **Radical therapy**. There is no
indication at all of other major streams such as *Cultural feminism, Marxist
feminism* and *Socialist feminism*, even though far more has been written
about each of these than about **Bisexual feminism**, for example. None of the
culturally-inspired feminisms are present either such as *Chicana feminism,
Womanism* or *Third World feminism* (although there is a heading for **Woman-
ist theology**). The three equivalence references under **Feminism** also suggest
a particular view: *Women's lib, Women's liberation movement* and *Women's
movement*. These are consonant with the activist stance implicit in most
feminist work, but are at odds with the significant theoretical content of
Feminism acknowledged in the narrower term, **Feminist theory**. That the
derogatory phrase *Women's lib* is still included is probably indicative of the
workload at the Library of Congress, but it could have been deleted at the last
revision of this heading in 1996.

   The picture of **Feminism** that arises from the *LCSH* heading and its references is of a dated white, middle-class, liberal movement with a few in-your-
face splinter groups. The most prominent streams of contemporary feminist
thought are not represented. This view of feminism is so homogenized that
the main heading by itself has over a thousand entries in the Library of
Congress catalogue. Further, topics of active research within the academy,
such as feminist epistemology, are unrepresented. If feminism is frozen in the
amber of history or relegated to the fringes of *other*ness, then it is safely
differentiated from topics to be treated seriously. This kind of distortion
makes it easier to ignore topics that are outside of the cultural mainstream,
just as exclusion makes topics invisible and marginalization sets them aside.

Librarianship's Views on Inclusion and Application

   At this point a second question arises: should we use *LCSH* for cultural
change? The examples described in the previous section illustrate that typical
systemic biases in *LCSH* reflect a mainstream status quo. Is it appropriate for
LCSH to fill this role? Is it what we as librarians want? According to Jesse
Shera:

> Society has determined what the library of the past has been, and it is
> society that will determine what the library of the future shall be. This
> statement does not mean that the patterns of social acceptance cannot be
> shaped and molded in response to the activities and insistence of spe-
> cialized groups, nor does it deny the values of such social "pressures";
> indeed, man [*sic*] as a responsible member of society has the obligation
> to contribute his [or her] share to the directing of social action toward
> those goals which seem to him [or her] to promise the fullest and richest

life. But one must remember that a society, consciously or unconsciously, creates its own goals, and that these establish the outer boundaries within which any agency must operate.[17]

Shera seems ambivalent here about the power of librarianship and libraries. If the discourses of "Society" create libraries, do we have any power over those discourses and their effect? "Specialized groups" seem to have some power and the rest of us have an obligation to pursue our values within the confines of "Society."

Historically librarianship has had a strong activist aspect linked to ethical goals. Missionary zeal has developed as a characteristic expected of librarians since the feminization of the profession. Melvil Dewey, in establishing the first library school, encouraged women, particularly college graduates, to take up the mission of librarianship. He said "if we are to educate and elevate the masses and make their lives better worth living, . . . we should in some way put in their hands the *best* reading."[18] He claimed that librarians were more influential than teachers or clergy because their influence went beyond the school years of their clients and was not confined to Sundays.[19] This role of missionary of culture required certain moral qualities.

> In the library profession, the best work will always be done on the moral plane, where the librarian puts his [or her] heart and life into his [or her] work with as distinct a consecration as a minister or missionary and enters the profession and does the work because it is his [or her] duty or privilege. It is his [or her] "vocation."[20]

Reinforcing this missionary zeal was the political climate of Progressivism. Suzanne Hildenbrand interprets the development of librarianship as a force in legitimating those policies of Progressivism which gave government support to individuals via social welfare programs:

> Teachers, librarians, social workers, and medical workers were largely legitimators–their work made the basic arrangements of the state seem just and acceptable. They not only actively inculcated belief in the state but also made available worthwhile services to individuals who would not otherwise have access to them.[21]

Thus, our public-spirited ethic was implicated in the support of the status quo. However, its intention was the liberal notion of educating the citizens of democracy for a better life for all. Steve Wolf, in response to the assertion of Sumner Spalding that the Library of Congress responds to rather than establishes usage, points out that because we flatter ourselves to be educators so do we, indeed, expect to have an affect on our users.[22] Indicative of the current manifestations of this ethic is the American Library Association's Council motion to adopt as policy a statement titled "Libraries: An American Value" that endorses universal access to "resources and services" and embraces the principles of "freedom of speech in a world that celebrates both our similarities and our differences, respects individuals and their beliefs, and holds all persons truly equal and free."[23] The ethic is obviously still part of the values of librarianship as a profession, but we have some problems with implementation. The clash between Wolf's and Spalding's perspectives described above reflects an ambivalence between ideals and their application in our profession.

The profession of librarianship has a long history in the area of collection development of trying to evaluate documents on the basis of sound criteria before offering them to the public. We have traditionally been dedicated to providing "the best." However, as Wayne Wiegand describes, we often abdicate responsibility for evaluation to experts.[24] Wiegand identifies designation of best books (and best sellers) as a function we have given either to experts or to assertive groups of library patrons. When it comes to vocabulary for subject retrieval we seem to have abdicated all responsibility to two external sources–the singular, mainstream public and the published literature. Our difficulty in coming to terms with the power we hold is evident in another item in the same ALA Council minutes cited above. Before endorsing the all-embracing statement of the value of libraries, ALA Council passed two motions to send to committees for study two aspects of the implementation of the previously adopted "Poor People's" policy: budget and subject headings. Budget is an obvious factor, but why would subject headings need further study? The answer is that the motion brought forward asked the Council to "urge" the Library of Congress to make specific changes (such as adding *people* to the heading **Poor**) and additions (such as *Corporate welfare*) to *LCSH*. Why would such a request cause hesitation? It was not a demand to the Library of Congress, it was an encouragement. Given ALA Council's adoption of the "Poor People's" policy it seems peculiar that this motion would cause problems.

My own speculation is that ALA Council found the *topic* rather than the *action* to be controversial. One of the illusions we try to maintain is that we can keep our own biases out of describing documents. This motivation is undoubtedly one of the reasons we seek some kind of external warrant for establishing subject headings. If we give way to the convenience of the public and to literary warrant we feel that we are enacting a neutral, if not objective, stance. In its instructions of how to assign and construct subject headings the *SCM:SH* instructs:

> Avoid assigning headings that label topics or express personal value judgments regarding topics or materials. Individual cataloger knowl-

edge and judgment inevitably play a role in assessing what is significant in a work's contents, but headings should not be assigned that reflect a cataloger's opinion about the contents. Consider the intent of the author or publisher and, if possible, assign headings for this orientation without being judgmental.[25]

We do not, however, seem to realize that these sources have significant biases and exclusions, and that by choosing to follow the convenience of a singular public and the canon of literary warrant we are introducing a bias toward the mainstream status quo that is just as much a bias as any professional judgment we are likely to employ.

LCSH AS A THIRD SPACE AND AGENT FOR CULTURAL CHANGE

How then can we go about taking action? Do we want to return to an ethic of missionary zeal in which *we* decide what is "best"? Ethically, we cannot afford to forget that a missionary stance has been recognized for some time as one that imposes the values of some onto others. Missionaries do not always have a positive reputation for helping to preserve cultures and respect others' ways of living. The postcolonial critic, Homi Bhabha offers another approach. The critical philosophy of postcolonialism looks at the current state of the world as the product of colonialism, especially its diasporization and hybridization of cultures. Unlike much poststructuralism, with which it shares a rejection of universals, it takes an overtly political stance. If our purpose, as Shera described it, is to fulfill a responsibility to take social action in directions that "promise the fullest and richest life," then a postcolonial model is an appropriate approach.

A Third Space

The model that Homi Bhabha offers is that of a Third Space. A statement and its meaning are not the same thing. Meaning is determined not only by the content of the statement, but also by its context–"its cultural positionality, its reference to a present time and a specific space."[26] The "pact of interpretation is never simply an act of communication between the I and the You . . . "[27] That is, the interpretation of a statement is not just a negotiation between the statement or the person originating it and the person perceiving it. There is a space in between, a context, that shapes the meaning of the statement. This is the Third Space. Bhabha suggests that the Third Space is a place of enunciation. It is the "structure of symbolization" or "process of

language" that gives a context to a statement. In terms of connecting information (statements) and people, our practice as librarians might be considered a Third Space. More particularly, *LCSH* and all of its policies and
practices constitute a Third Space. It is a dynamic space of passage between
documents catalogued and library users. It is a space of ambivalence in which
meaning is constructed. That is, *LCSH* shapes the meaning that is conveyed
from a document to a user. In this sense *LCSH* and its application form a
cultural practice of authority. To view *LCSH* as a simple hegemonic tool of
dominance would be simplistic. It is actually an ambivalent tool. It seeks to
be a universally applicable vocabulary treating topics with the neutrality of
equality. Yet it is under constant revision as not only the universe it represents
changes, but also as the concepts of neutrality and equality change. Because
the Third Space is one of ambivalence, it is one with potential for change:

> It is that Third Space, though unrepresentable in itself, which consti-
> tutes the discursive conditions of enunciation that ensure that the mean-
> ing and symbols of culture have no primordial unity or fixity; that even
> the same signs can be appropriated, translated, rehistoricized and read
> anew.[28]

Viewed in this manner, *LCSH* has the power to create meaning whether that
power is used consciously or not. It cannot be neutral because there is no
neutrality or universal meaning–no "primordial unity." Therefore, it should
be used with a consciousness of that power.

Cultural Change

With the location of this Third Space in *LCSH*, cultural change has a
venue. But what direction should this cultural change take? Shera suggests
seeking what will "promise the fullest and richest life"–presumably not just
for oneself, but also or even primarily for others. Cultural change has historically been viewed in western culture as a teleological progression towards a
goal. That goal is some superior form of society, some ideal culture, that we
can achieve step-by-step through a developmental process of cultural evolution. This evolutionary model of change reached a peak in modernist thought,
but has more recently been viewed as suspect for several reasons. One is that
we seem no nearer to achieving it in a global sense than we have ever been.
More fundamentally, it is not clear that we can define the goal we seek and,
moreover, such a goal is suspect in the contexts of globalization and postco-
loniality.[29] Evolutionary progress as a model simply does not work anymore
(if it ever did). In this realization it is easy to throw up one's hands altogether
or live a life of existential individualism within the status quo.
    Bhabha offers an alternative to this bleak prospect. He suggests that cultur-

al authority is questioned in the "moment of *enunciation*" of cultural difference.[30] The expression or representation of cultural difference undermines the appearance of cultural uniformity–it destabilizes the status quo. However, indicating the existence of difference is not sufficient:

> For example, if the interest in postmodernism is limited to a celebration of the fragmentation of the 'grand narratives' of postenlightenment rationalism then, for all its intellectual excitement, it remains a profoundly parochial enterprise.
>
> The wider significance of the postmodern condition lies in the awareness that the epistemological 'limits' of those ethnocentric ideas are also the enunciative boundaries of a range of other dissonant, even dissident histories and voices–women, the colonized, minority groups, the bearers of policed sexualities.[31]

It is at the margins of our cultural identities that change can take place. Our systems that reflect the mainstream status quo can be identified by critical practices such as postmodern interpretations that focus on who is *Other*. However, it is also necessary to accommodate the dynamic change not only of the content of what is represented, but also the relationships:

> The representation of difference must not be hastily read as the reflection of *pre-given* ethnic or cultural traits set in the fixed tablet of tradition. The social articulation of difference, from the minority perspective, is a complex, on-going negotiation that seeks to authorize cultural hybridities that emerge in moments of historical transformation.[32]

It is at the limits of our systems that these changes take place. "Cultural hybridities" mean that our preconceived categories shift and intermingle. As cultures meet and interact–such as the western influence on indigenous cultures worldwide–purity of culture no longer exists. Nostalgia for that purity will not retrieve the irrevocably changed realities. "Historical transformation" means that our foundations are realigned. "The time of liberation is . . . a time of cultural uncertainty, and most crucially, of significatory or representational undecidability . . . "[33] We can encourage change by recognizing and allowing the representation of cultural differences in all of their dynamic, boundary-crossing hybridization.

LCSH as an Agent of Change

How can *LCSH* play a role in this theoretical stance regarding change? *LCSH* is the Third Space in which enunciation takes place. On either side of this space sit the two sources of our ambivalence: the authoritative literatures and the singular, authoritative public. We operate at the junction of literatures and the public–documents and users. In this sense our practices and standards such as *LCSH* form the boundary. In this Third Space we can enunciate cultural difference that can set both of our sources of authoritative ambivalence just a bit off balance. According to Bhabha, "[i]t is in this sense that the boundary becomes the place from which *something begins its presencing* in a movement not dissimilar to the ambulant, ambivalent articulation of the beyond. . . . "[34] What this calls for in a concrete way in *LCSH* is the willingness to represent cultural difference and to change those representations as they shift. It is also a willingness to take risks in these representations. According to Homi Bhabha, then, enunciation in aid of cultural change will have the following characteristics:

• it will articulate cultural difference
• it will take place at the boundaries of the dominant culture
• it will change with the differences
• it will be ambivalent–representing hybrids, not just discrete concepts

These characteristics overlap, but in the following discussion I will treat them roughly in order. As in the earlier discussion on the mainstream biases of *LCSH*, cultural difference here includes racial, ethnic, gender, sexuality and many other *Other*nesses that transect our societies.

To articulate cultural difference, *LCSH* must be more explicit in representing marginalized cultures and must actively identify and eliminate exclusions. This kind of effort may require significant labour, but is not intellectually demanding. If there is no heading for a concept one must be created.

To work at the boundaries, we must take risks in representing concepts and using terminology in *LCSH* even though they will be alien to some of the singular public. By placing them in useful syndetic contexts, providing scope notes and actively and appropriately applying them, the public will come to recognize their meanings. If some members of the public find them disturbing it may help them to question unfounded presumptions. Other users will appreciate the efforts made as we work toward eliminating experiences like that of Marielena Fina described above.

Change of subject headings has always been regarded as an expensive process to be avoided whenever possible. However, considerable capacity for change is indicated by the fact that *LCSH* added 5000 subject headings between its last two annual editions and made 1000 changes to headings. When changes on this scale are made annually (and advertised in the marketing of the Cataloging Distribution Service), it is obvious that change is not totally impracticable. Further, what is the purpose of libraries if not to make information accessible? Using inadequate and ethically dubious subject headings hinders access. It can only be justified if our intent is to enforce the status quo and banish the margins.

Finally comes the most difficult aspect of this process for us to recognize– the necessity to be ambivalent. What is meant by ambivalence in this instance is the ability to accommodate hybridity. We need to overcome our compulsion to put concepts into *either/or* categories. We need to overcome the need for mutual exclusivity. The notion of mutually exclusive categories has been with us at least since classical Greece, but it is nevertheless a constructed concept. Many cultures do not feel uncomfortable with categories that overlap.[35] One of the reasons that we choose to employ mutually exclusive categories is to fulfill Charles Cutter's second object of the catalogue: to gather all works with some common attribute. This gathering is a matter of differentiation. It is through differentiation that cultural authority is established as discussed above. However, we can look at gathering in another way. Homi Bhabha quotes a metaphor from Martin Heidegger that Bhabha likens to the operation of the Third Space: "Always and ever differently the bridge escorts the lingering and hastening ways of men [and women] to and fro, so that they may get to other banks. . . . The bridge *gathers* as a passage that crosses."[36] If we think of our gathering as a bridge to facilitate the crossing of the Third Space from documents to users, rather than some ideal categorization of what is and what is not something in particular, then ambivalence should cause us fewer problems. A bridge is a practical construction. It conforms to the topography of a particular landscape. It is wider or narrower as traffic requires. Its surface will need patching and its piers will need shoring up. There are not always bridges for every possible convenience, but we can build bridges to and from all kinds of neighbourhoods and communities if we wish to make them accessible and they are likely to serve more than one community at a time. Periodically they will be redesigned or even replaced. The metaphor works reasonably well for what we require. A bridge is anchored at both ends, but provides access to a wide range of places and it can carry a variety of pedestrians and vehicles. Yet it funnels all of them through a controlled space.

CONCLUSION

Since librarianship is committed to an ethic of universal access to information the lack of neutral meaning seems an obstacle in meeting that goal. However, tools such as *LCSH* can be used to open up the exclusionary cultural supremacy of the mainstream patriarchal, Euro-settler culture. The responsibility for this change is typically focussed on the Library of Congress as the arbiters of *LCSH*. However, for librarians and libraries in general to abdicate responsibility for subject access to a "universal" standard is unethical. Every member of the profession of librarianship shares the responsibility for Jesse Shera's quest for "the fullest and richest life" for all library users. Therefore, each individual librarian is responsible for *LCSH* in its standard form and, to an even greater degree, in its application. We cannot foist off responsibility onto the Library of Congress or onto the singular public or the literature. We must take responsibility along with the Library of Congress and use it according to the long-standing ethic of our profession to promote universal access. We must take it the next step and follow Jenny Holzer's injunction to "use [*LCSH* as] what is dominant in a culture to change it quickly" and we can do so by permeating the limits of cultural authority.

NOTES

1. Jenny Holzer, *Kickstand*, [art installation for computer], ([S.l.]: antenna tool & die co., 1997).

2. Homi K. Bhabha, *The Location of Culture* (London: Routledge, 1994), p. 36.

3. Hope A. Olson and Rose Schlegl, "Bias in Subject Access: A Content Analysis," 1999, available at: *http://www.ualberta.ca/~holson/margins/bias.html*; and Hope A. Olson and Rose Schlegl, "Bias in Subject Access Standards: A Content Analysis of the Critical Literature," in James Turner (ed.), *Information Science: Where Has It Been, Where Is It Going? Proceedings of the 27th Annual Conference of the Canadian Association for Information Science=Les science de l'information: D'où viennent-elles et où s'en vont-elles? Actes du 27e Congrés annuel de l'Association canadienne pour les scienes de l'information*, pp. 236-247. (Montréal: CAIS/ACSI, 1999).

4. Lynne M. Martin and Barbara J. Via. "Looking at the Mirror: Reflections on Researching the Recruitment of Minority Librarians to the Profession in 'LISA' and 'Library Literature' on CD-ROM" *Reference Librarian*, 45-46: 253-78 (1994).

5. Marielena Fina, "The Role of Subject Headings in Access to Information: The Experience of One Spanish-speaking Patron," *Cataloging & Classification Quarterly*, 17 (1993), p. 269.

6. C. A. Cutter, *Rules for a Dictionary Catalog*, 4th ed. (Washington: Government Printing Office, 1904; republished London: The Library Association, 1962), p. 12.

7. *Ibid.*, p. 6.

8. Library of Congress authority and bibliographic records in this article were verified on 23 September 1999 in the MUMS and Voyager catalogues on the World Wide Web at <http://lcweb.loc.gov/catalog/>.

9. Library of Congress. Cataloging Policy and Support Office. *Subject Cataloging Manual: Subject Headings*. 5th ed. (Washington, D.C.: Cataloging Distribution Service, 1996), H187, p. 1.

10. Steve Wolf, "Sex and the Single Cataloger: New Thoughts on Some Unthinkable Subjects," in *Revolting Librarians*, edited by Celeste West (San Francisco, CA: Booklegger Press, 1972), pp. 39-44.

11. Thomas Yen-Ran Yeh, "The Treatment of the American Indian in the Library of Congress E-F Schedule," *Library Resources & Technical Services*, 15 (2):122-128

(1971); and Eugene T. Frosio, "Comments on the Thomas Yen-Ran Yeh Proposal," *Library Resources & Technical Services*, 15 (2):128-131 (1971).

12. *SCM:SH*, H187, p. 1.

13. Statistics on OCLC are from various pages on the OCLC web site at: <http://www.oclc.org/>

14. Bhabha, p. 34.

15. *SCM:SH*, H180, p. 2.

16. Bhabha, p. 34.

17. Jesse H. Shera, *The Foundations of Education for Librarianship* (New York: Becker and Hayes, 1972), pp. 135-136.

18. Melvil Dewey, "Librarianship as a Profession for College-Bred Women," an address delivered before the Association of Collegiate Alumnae on March 13, 1986, in *Melvil Dewey: His Enduring Presence in Librarianship*, ed. Sarah K. Vann (Littleton, Colo.: Libraries Unlimited, 1978), p. 99.

19. *Ibid.*, p. 111-112.

20. *Ibid.*, p. 108.

21. Suzanne Hildenbrand, "Ambiguous Authority and Aborted Ambition: Gender, Professionalism, and the Rise and Fall of the Welfare State," *Library Trends* 28: 186-187 (fall 1979).

22. Wolf, p. 44.

23. American Library Association Council, ALA Council Actions, 1999 ALA Midwinter Meeting, available at: <*http://www.ala.org/alaorg/council/mw99acti.html*>

24. Wayne A. Wiegand, "The Politics of Cultural Authority," *American Libraries* 29: 80-82 (January 1998).

25. *SCM:SH*, H180, p. 7.

26. Bhabha, p. 36.

27. *Ibid.*

28. *Ibid.*, p. 37

29. A summary of sociological thought on change and its critiques can be found in Barry Smart, *Modern Conditions, Postmodern Controversies* (London: Routledge, 1992), pp. 1-27; and a thorough discussion of the same is available in Anthony Giddens, *Politics, Sociology and Social Theory: Encounters with Classical and Contemporary Social Thought* (Stanford, CA: Stanford University Press, 1995).

30. Bhabha, p. 35.

31. *Ibid.*, p. 4.

32. *Ibid.*, p. 2.

33. *Ibid.*, p. 35.

34. *Ibid.*, p. 5.

35. Hope A. Olson, "Cultural Discourses of Classification: Indigenous Alternatives to the Tradition of Aristotle, Durkheim and Foucault," *Proceedings of the American Society for Information Science, Special Interest Group on Classification Research Workshop, 1999* (in press).

36. Martin Heidegger, "Building, Dwelling, Thinking," in *Poetry, Language, Thought* (New York: Harper & Row, 1971): pp. 152-153; quoted in Bhabha, p. 5.

Improving *LCSH* for Use in Online Catalogs Revisited– What Progress Has Been Made? What Issues Still Remain?

Pauline Atherton Cochrane

SUMMARY. In 1986 Libraries Unlimited published Cochrane's book, *Improving LCSH for Use in Online Catalogs; Exercises for Self-Help with a Selection of Background Readings*. This was preceded in 1981 by an ERIC publication (ED 208 900) by Cochrane, with Monika Kirtland–a Bibliographic and Bibliometric Essay which documented critical views of *LCSH* and an analysis of vocabulary control in *LCSH* (parts of which were published in *Cataloging & Classification Quarterly*, 1(2/3) (1982), 71-94). Three features of *LCSH* will be re-examined to check on progress since the time of these earlier publications: notes,

---

Pauline Atherton Cochrane, PhD, is Professor Emeritus, Graduate School of Library and Information Science, University of Illinois at Urbana-Champaign, 501 East Daniel Street, Champaign, IL 61820-6211 (E-mail: pcochran@uiuc.edu).

[Haworth co-indexing entry note]: "Improving *LCSH* for Use in Online Catalogs Revisited–What Progress Has Been Made? What Issues Still Remain?" Cochrane, Pauline Atherton. Co-published simultaneously in *Cataloging & Classification Quarterly* (The Haworth Information Press, an imprint of The Haworth Press, Inc.) Vol. 29, No. 1/2, 2000, pp. 73-89; and: *The LCSH Century: One Hundred Years with the Library of Congress Subject Headings System* (ed: Alva T. Stone) The Haworth Information Press, an imprint of The Haworth Press, Inc., 2000, pp. 73-89. Single or multiple copies of this article are available for a fee from The Haworth Document Delivery Service [1-800-342-9678, 9:00 a.m. - 5:00 p.m. (EST). E-mail address: getinfo@haworthpressinc.com].

structure of relationships between headings in the list, and links between Library of Congress classification numbers and *LCSH* or other
vocabularies. *[Article copies available for a fee from The Haworth Document
Delivery Service: 1-800-342-9678. E-mail address: <getinfo@haworthpressinc.
com Website: <http://www.haworthpressinc.com>]*

KEYWORDS. *LCSH*, syndetic structure, hierarchic relationships,
LCC-*LCSH* relationships, MARC Subject Authority format, crossfile
searching, subject searching in OPACs

BACKGROUND

In 1986 the book, *Improving LCSH for Use in Online Catalogs; Exercises
for Self-Help with a Selection of Background Readings*[1] (hereinafter referred
to as *Improving LCSH*) was published. In the early 1980s library automation
developments were changing the basic design of our traditional card catalogs
and there was a need to reconsider the subject access information as it was
put into MARC format for bibliographic and authority records. The results of
catalog use studies and research into subject access problems were not being
heeded. This was the period before vendors' turnkey systems and OPAC
(Online Public Access Catalog) design was being done on college campuses
(UC-Berkeley, Mankato State, Syracuse, Ohio State, Toronto, VTI-Black-
sburg, Northwestern, to mention only a few). OPAC design efforts were not
concentrating on subject access even though we learned from the 1982 Council on Library Resources national study of OPAC use[2] that the majority of
users were searching by subject and that they needed help.

At that time, almost twenty years ago, many of us "knew the new facts
early" (to quote Phil Ochs, the late folksinger), but no matter what we did to
alert librarians and designers, OPAC system design evolved with few enhancements for the subject searcher. One reason for their reticence to embark
on such improvements may have been the slowness with which *LCSH* was
prepared to serve as a thesaurus in electronic format. The Subject Authority
File at the Library of Congress was not really ready until 1986, almost a
decade after the first OPAC design efforts. As these systems have been
revamped over the years because of developments such as graphical user
interfaces, the Internet, and computer games, we are beginning to see the
design of OPACs improve. Subject searching still needs improving.

A recent publication[3] has taken up the call for further improvements and
this effort is to be lauded because its recommendations are based on a thorough knowledge of the catalog records that make up the database being
searched and the findings of the most relevant use studies in the past twenty
years. The book by Yee and Layne and developments at IFLA should go a
long way to correct the "stagnation" which Greenberg described in 1997.[4]

Keyword searching is often touted as the best feature of OPACs, but any subject searcher knows that this mode of searching puts the burden on the user with little or no help provided to track down synonyms, homonyms, or related terms. Surely we can do better than that after twenty years of automated catalogs and indexes? This paper will investigate some developments in this area since 1986.

Another publication from almost twenty years ago and the Shubert update in 1992 provide a critical bibliography concerning the world's leading vocabulary control mechanism, namely *LCSH* (*Library of Congress Subject Headings*, hereinafter referred to as *LCSH*/SAF because this list, in the MARC Authority record format, presents the most complete version of *LCSH* records).[5] Through the years almost 300 separate articles and research reports have addressed the general structure and features of *LCSH*/SAF, with critical comments and suggestions for improvements. In *Improving LCSH* some of those suggestions were developed into a coordinated series of steps which could be taken to make improvements in subject access mechanisms in an OPAC. If the staff of the Library of Congress did not have the time or inclination to make those improvements, others could (Sanford Berman's efforts at the Hennepin County Public Library and later in NoveList have served as independent models of *LCSH*/SAF). The chapters in *Improving LCSH* covered such improvements as more notes, more entry vocabulary, more complete tracking of logical and associative relationships between terms, a better way to handle period, place, form and topical subdivisions, and links between subject headings and class numbers.

Recent changes at the Library of Congress will have an impact on the presentation of subject headings from bibliographic records. This very month (September, 1999) the new Integrated Library System has been launched at the Library of Congress. Separate products such as *Classification Plus* will probably be incorporated into that system and other OPAC systems will do likewise. Relationships between classification schedules and subject heading lists, between bibliographic records and authority files, between parts of the MARC bibliographic record and other files will all be important aspects of OPAC design and related processes such as cataloging, searching, and retrieval.[6] We are truly on the brink of a new century of developments in cataloging and classification history with new information technologies being used to good advantage.

The present review of recent progress toward improvement of *LCSH*/SAF will highlight the potential for this subject access mechanism in three feature areas: notes in *LCSH*/SAF, cross-reference structure of *LCSH*/SAF, and the linkage between *LCSH* headings and Library of Congress Classification numbers.

Notes in LCSH/SAF

In *Improving LCSH*, on pages 36-44 and several reprinted selections this aspect of a subject authority list was covered. The index refers the reader to: cataloger's note, general reference note, history note, refer from note, scope note, and see also reference note. These are the notes that appear in subject authority records, some of which are displayed for OPAC searchers. Alan M. Greenberg's[7] review prompted Lois Chan[8] to include information about the construction of such notes in later editions of her book on *LCSH* because of their importance, and the *Subject Cataloging Manual: Subject Headings* (SCM:SH) has a section (H400) to document policies followed at the Library of Congress.

What I wanted to document by reviewing developments in this area was whether or not there had been an increase in notes in *LCSH*/SAF and to compare newer editions of *LCSH* (in print) to see if some of the exercises in *Improving LCSH* had had an impact. The 22nd *LCSH* (1999) indicates that about of 2% of the headings now have scope notes.

Scope notes for the subdivision records (18X in MARC format for subject authority records) can now be found in the Subject Authority File. These notes were previously only available in a separate publication. They can now be accessed by anyone using *LCSH*/SAF.

Scope notes are now in two MARC/SAF fields, 680 and 667, the former a "public" general note and the latter a "nonpublic general note." Until February 1999 there were no 667 notes in *LCSH*/SAF, but now they appear in geographic subject heading records, for example, to record "Heading not valid for use as geographic subdivision."

Exercise One in *Improving LCSH* included eight subject headings with scope notes with revisions suggested to improve the note for catalog searchers who were not catalogers. Four had been revised, two deleted, and two remained identical. That is progress! In Exercise 2, where three headings (**New thought, Sandwich construction,** and **Open and closed shelves**) needed dictionary definitions as scope notes, there were no scope notes in the 22nd *LCSH* (1999). Apparently a third suggestion caused no overall review of the need for scope notes at such places as headings beginning with the word "State . . . , Municipal . . . , or Local . . . ". Notes still appear only erratically at such places in *LCSH*/SAF. For example, why should **Local finance** have a scope note but not **Local budgets, Local laws** but not **Local option**, etc.?

Since so few headings have scope notes (in the 680 field of the MARC/ Subject authority record), the review was not continued any further. Instead "note-type" information in *LCSH*/SAF, in fields 670, 675, and 952 was checked. As a subject cataloger at the Library of Congress (or elsewhere) prepares a subject authority record for a new term, justification for that term and any cross references (especially entry vocabulary) appears in field 670. It shows sources checked and if the *LCSH* heading is not identical to that used in each source, the variation is noted. If a source is checked and there is no entry found, that is recorded in the 675 field. Local information is given in field 952.

Let's examine the *LCSH*/SAF records given as examples in Lois Chan's book on *LCSH* to see how valuable these fields might be for OPAC users who are doing multifile or crossfile searching. Figures 1-7 illustrate seven of these records from Chan.[9] There is a wealth of information for multifile or crossfile searching if and when OPACs are redesigned to accommodate such a feature. For example:

Look at the *LCSH*/SAF record for the **Tailhook Scandal, 1991-1993** (Figure 1). Out of the four sources checked three did not agree with the approved *LCSH* heading, and the variations are shown. Three of the sources are online bibliographic databases.

FIGURE 1. *LCSH*/SAF Record for **Tailhook Scandal**

```
010   sh 93007668
040   DLC DLC
150   Tailhook Scandal, 1991-1993
550   Sexual harassment of women--United States broader term
670   Work cat.: 93-138159: Women in the military : the Tailhook
affair and the problem of sexual harassment, 1992.
670   Wash. Post index, 1992 (Tailhook Association ... sexual
harassment scandal)
670   NYT index, Jan.-Mar. 1993.
670   MAGS (Tailhook scandal scars Naval aviation)
670   LC data base, 10/5/93 (Tailhook Association)
```

FIGURE 2. *LCSH*/SAF Record for **Golden Parachutes**

```
010   sh 94002701
040   DLC DLC
150   Golden parachutes (Executive compensation)
680   Here are entered works on severance benefits paid to
executives in the event of a corporate takeover.
450   Golden umbrellas (Executive compensation) used for
550   Executives-Salaries, etc. broader term
550   Severance pay broader term
550   Consolidation and merger of corporations related term
670   UMI business vocab.
670   LIV.
670   Scott, D.L. Wall Street words, 1988: (Golden parachutes, also known as Golden
umbrellas)
```

FIGURE 3. *LCSH*/SAF Record for **Lost Architecture**

```
010    sh 93000146
040    DLC DLC DLC NjR
053    NA209 (General)
150    Lost architecture
680     Here are entered works on buildings, structures, etc., that
were accidentally or purposefully destroyed or demolished.
450    Architectural heritage, Lost used for
450    Buildings, Lost used for
450    Lost architectural heritage used for
450    Lost buildings used for
550    Architecture broader term
670    Work cat.: 92-43452: Jones, C. Lost Baltimore, c1993.
670    92-73620: DeAngelo, D. The law offices of Shook ... Kansas City
as seen through its lost architecture, c1992.
670    LC database, Dec. 15, 1992 (lost architecture; lost
architectural heritage)
670    Art. human. cit. index (lost architecture)
675    Bibl. guide art arch.; Hennepin; LIV; IAC; Readers'
guide; NYT index; Random House; Art index
```

FIGURE 4. *LCSH*/SAF Record for **Crop Circles**

```
010    sh 93000098
040    DLC DLC
150    Crop circles
450    Circle formations in crops used for
450    Circles, Corn used for
450    Circles, Crop used for
450    Corn circles used for
450    Crop circle formations used for
450    Crop field circles used for
450    Cropfield circles used for
450    Formations, Crop circle used for
550    Curiosities and wonders broader term
670    Hennepin (Crop circles x Crop field circles; Cropfield
circles)
670    LC data base, 1/8/93 (crop circles)
670    Ox. dict. new words (crop circle: a (usually circular) area
of standing crops which has been inexplicably flattened, apparently by a
swirling, vortex-like movement (sometimes also called corn circles))
670    Crop circle enigma, 1990: pp. 10, 12 (Circle formations in
crops, corn circles)
675    IAC
```

Look at Figure 2, where the heading was glossed (qualified in parentheses) in such a way that the related and broader terms are sensible relationships and the 670 fields contribute to our understanding.

Look at Figure 4, the record for **Crop circles**. Eight *"used for"* references are included in *LCSH*/SAF and justified by what was found in the Hennepin County Public Library catalog and elsewhere.

FIGURE 5. *LCSH*/SAF Record for **Health Care Reform**

```
010   sh 93007525
040   DLC DLC
150   Health care reform
450   Health reform used for
450   Health system reform used for
450   Medical care reform used for
450   Reform of health care delivery used for
450   Reform of medical care delivery used for
550   Medical policy broader term
550   Insurance, Health related term
670   Work cat.: 93-35883: Domestic Policy Council (U.S.). Health
security, c1993 (health care reform)
670   MESH 1994 (Health care reform)
670   Washington Post (health care reform, health reform)
670   IAC (health care reform)
```

FIGURE 6. *LCSH*/SAF Record for **Time Pressure**

```
010   sh 93005764
040   DLC DLC
150   Time pressure
450   Pressure, Time used for
450   Temporal stress used for
450   Time stress used for
550   Stress (Psychology) broader term
670   Work cat.: 93-11985: Time pressure and stress in human judgment
and decision making, c1993 (Time stress, time constraints, time urgency)
670   LC data base, 7/26/93 (Time pressure)
670   Keyes, R. Timelock, 1991 (Time pressure)
670   Faulkner, H.W. (Spatio-temporal stress)
675   Hennepin; Thes. psych. index terms
```

FIGURE 7. *LCSH*/SAF Record for **World Music**

```
010   sh 93002569
040   MnMHCL DLC
150   World music
680   Here are entered popular musical works combining traditional
rhythms from around the world with elements of jazz and rock.
450   World beat music used for
550   Popular music broader term
670   Work cat.: Spencer, P. World beat, 1992 : a listener's guide to contemporary world
music on CD, 1992 (World music)
670   BDNE (World Beat)
670   Hennepin (World beat music)
670   Ox. dict. new world (World music)
670   M. Ziomek visited Tower Records, 5/18/93 (World music)
```

Look at Figure 5, the record for **Health care reform**. If this information were used in multifile searching, catalog users would have direct links, with correct headings for searching, in three popular databases, Medline (where MeSH is used), the Washington Post, and IAC.

Look at Figure 6 where the field 675 tells you that the heading, **Time pressure**, is not found in the *Thesaurus of Psychological Index terms*. Such information could prompt the searcher to do a keyword search in the abstract and title fields of *PsychInfo*. The same is true in Figure 3 where the 675 field of the record for **Lost architecture**, shows that eight databases do not use this term as a descriptor.

In Figure 7, the authorized heading chosen, **World music**, must have been a toss-up in the mind of the subject cataloger. The sources checked show that various terms (World music, World beat music, and World Beat) are used. The helpful scope note in 680 provides the searcher with more useful information.

As more and more books will be in electronic form and accessible from OPACs through hyperlinks in the 856 field of the MARC bibliographic record, the information about book citations in the 670 and 675 fields of *LCSH*/SAF will become more important. (See the "work cat." notes in the 670 field of records in Figures 1, 3, 5, 6, and 7. See also the notes about reference works in Figures 2, 4, and 7.)

These fields truly contain notes for the 21st century library catalog. Thompson Yee, at the Library of Congress, reported that as of September 30, 1998 there were 87,424 of the 244,747 *LCSH*/SAF records that have a 670 field, with a mean of 2.07 occurrences, and this is only for headings established or revised after 1986.[10] There was no breakdown given by heading tag, but figures 1-7 show how full the records are for such topics as public affairs issues, technology, news events, and even humanities headings.

A follow-up study of this feature of *LCSH*/SAF is recommended so that we can judge how truly valuable this information will be as OPACs are transformed into gateways to electronic library collections and help us locate other resources on the Internet. No doubt the availability of electronic thesauri will transform the way we use metadata to access full text in the OPACs of the future.

A subfield in the 6XX fields of the MARC bibliographic records now shows the source of the subject heading if it is not from *LCSH*/SAF. This prompts me to suggest a related study of the OCLC/OLUC file to determine how many different thesauri are used and to find out how many of these thesauri are in electronic form. As we begin to experiment with relationships between *LCSH* and other thesauri, between MARC bibliographic records in OPACs and all relevant thesauri, we may find some other features which can enhance OPAC use. The early attempt of Sally Knapp[11] to provide us with tools for multifile searching can now become more sophisticated than even Mandel[12] or Milstead[13] have imagined.

Cross-Reference Structure in LCSH/SAF

Phyllis Allen Richmond's seminal 1959 paper[14] started most of us thinking about the hierarchic structure within *LCSH*. Before then all we knew was that there were relationships between headings in the printed *LCSH* such as an unapproved heading cross-reference to an approved heading (the old A *see* B reference with an *x* notation at the B heading); cross-references between two approved headings (the old B *see also* C reference, sometimes combined with C *see also* B (shown as a *sa* or *xx* tracing, or both at B and C, depending on the nature of the relationship). At the time there were no principles or theory for establishing these relationships except for some discussion by David Haykin[15]-these references were more or less made by subject catalogers at the Library of Congress "as needed." There were no computers around to manipulate and trace the entire hierarchical structure of any subject heading list if such a structure could be discerned. This is why Richmond's "manual analysis" was so very revealing.[16] Other research followed and in only a year or so some lexicographers (editors of subject heading lists) started using categorization and classification schemes to help determine hierarchic relationships in their lists. The term "thesaurus" came into vogue about 1960 in the information science field and constructing such a list of controlled vocabulary terms was defined as the practice of relating approved headings (or descriptors) in a list to each other in either a BT-NT (Broader-Narrower Term) hierarchic relationship or a RT-RT (Related term) relationship by association. (The *x* and *see* relationship were coded *used for* and *use* and talked about as entry vocabulary or synonym equivalents.) Retrieval tests at Cranfield, England and elsewhere tested the value of these relationships during the search process. By the time of the Elsinore Conference[17] in September 1964 the value of a classification scheme for the formation of a thesaurus was recognized and the relationship of subject headings and class numbers was considered as integral parts of an information retrieval system.

As thesauri were constructed for abstracting and indexing services and for special libraries in scientific and technical fields, national and international standards were developed for the construction of such vocabulary control mechanisms. The ERIC Thesaurus and MeSH (Medical Subject Headings from the National Library of Medicine) are two notable examples which have been used in library science education classes for more than thirty years. We could never use *LCSH* as an example because study after study showed how incomplete the structure was. The Library of Congress has repeatedly explained that only headings needed for cataloging were in the list and there was no attempt at an underlying structure of relationships.[18] But by 1948, in the Introduction to the 5th edition of *LCSH*, there was a telling statement:

A growing awareness of the need of a statement of principles and rules of practice in subject cataloging has tended to correct deviations from logic and consistency, and has led to the gradual improvement of the headings in the Library's catalogs.[19] (*Subject Cataloging Manual: Subject Headings* (SCM:SH) policies H373, 370, 375 document those principles and practices today.)

The Library of Congress, for many editions of the printed *LCSH*, reported that the logical arrangement of concepts in their classification scheme was a complementary structure to what seemed missing in *LCSH*. Unfortunately they have been lax in relating these two vocabulary control mechanisms for almost one hundred years. Only thirty-six percent of the headings in the 22nd *LCSH* (1999) show a corresponding LCC class number. (This will be treated in more detail in the next section.)

With a syndetic structure that did not show proper hierarchic relationships there is no wonder that there was a flurry in the professional literature when the Library of Congress decided to adopt the standard thesaurus encoding for term relationships in *LCSH*/SAF during the 1980s and 1990s.[20] There was no overall review of the structure of *LCSH*/SAF until the mid-1990s. Such a review is a monumental task, given that the number of topical headings is well over 180,000 and the linkage of all these headings to a classified outline has never been done. Now that both *LCSH*/SAF and LCC exist in electronic form, we may see more effort to get this done. For comparison purposes, consider that the total review and updating of the ERIC Thesaurus, in the late 1970s, took more than twenty man-years. It was called the Vocabulary Improvement Project.[21] A similar plan for *LCSH*/SAF will involve much more time and resources but the information technology developments such as thesaurus editing software and hypertextual thesaurus browsers that now exist should make the review more efficient.

The review of *LCSH*/SAF cannot be done fast enough if we are to provide OPAC designers with the wherewithal to show the logical structure and other relationships between headings in hypertextual thesaurus browsers and in improved intermediate displays of search results in OPACs.[22] Figure 8 shows Eric Johnson's IODyne system operating within Cancerlit using MeSH as the controlled vocabulary.[23]

Several features in this system serve as a useful model for what should be a part of every OPAC someday, because these features will prove quite useful to catalog searchers. Many of these features go beyond those recommended in Yee and Layne. For example, IODyne:

1. dynamically unifies keyword searching with controlled vocabulary searching. The searcher can open a search window and see a keyword-in-context display as the search term is entered. The searcher can decide whether this KWIC list will be for thesaurus terms and/or the concept space (made up of text co-occurrences).
2. displays in the thesaurus window all levels of the hierarchy related to the search term. In Figure 8 this looks much like the outline of a classification schedule or the MeSH tree structure–which indeed it is without the numbers. For compactness in the first thesaurus display IODyne opens only those parts of the hierarchy needed to place the search term in context (the opened parts of the hierarchy are shown by downward pointing radio buttons). The searcher is free to "punch" other buttons and open up more of the display (or close it), or switch to another hierarchy if the search term has more than one BT. (This latter feature is not shown in Figure 8 because the term only appears in one part of the MeSH tree structure.)
3. the free text searching option opens the Concept Space window where the co-occurrence analysis of the search term is shown with other terms or phrases in the title or abstract. Included in this anaylysis, but not shown in Figure 8 are authors' names and descriptors (subject index terms such as MeSH headings) that frequently co-occur with the search term in the file where the search is being made (in this case, CancerLit). The concept space information is shown in rank order. The most frequently occurring thesaurus terms could be shown in the concept space window if the scroll bar were used.
4. When any terms in these vocabulary displays are found useful by the searcher they can be moved into the search window or thesaurus window and from the search window back into the thesaurus or concept space windows by a drag and drop procedure.[24]
5. IODyne provides the user with an efficient and effective search environment to search in several repositories (or OPACs) at the same time, displaying all the available electronic thesauri associated with those files, and shows "concept spaces" if the bibliographic files have been processed for a concept space analysis.

Coupled with the useful information to be found in the 670/675 field of records in *LCSH*/SAF we could begin to see how future developments of an OPAC or a system like IODyne could provide aids to the searcher which would result in a very functional multifile and crossfile searching capability.

There is an enormous potential for *LCSH*/SAF in this new world of graphical user interface, hyperlinks and object-oriented programming. What is needed is preparation to move structure and logical relationships away from the rigidity and incompleteness of the MARC Authority Format and to free

FIGURE 8. A Search for Expert systems in CancerLit using IODyne

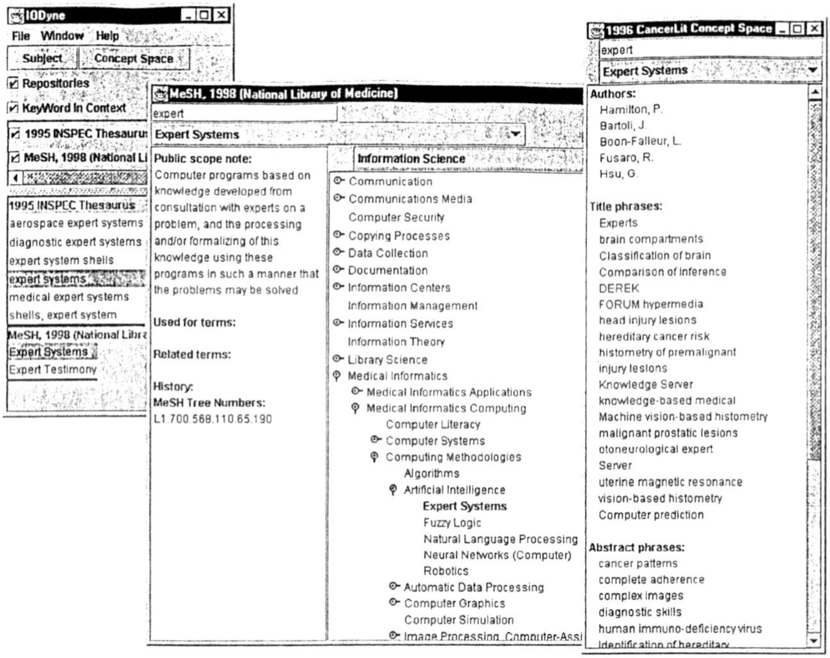

up the fixed field string of topical headings with subdivisions which are found in bibliographic records. To this day a continuing source of aggravation is the way *LCSH*/SAF records are displayed in some other bibliographic utilities or OPACs. All *LCSH*/SAF displays, in all OPACs and bibliographic utilities, must be improved. Too often the following minimum processing is not done when *LCSH*/SAF is included in various bibliographic systems:

> With well-designed thesaurus editing software, the lexicographer provides one kind of tracing (typically whichever is convenient given the particular editing circumstances), and the software automatically provides the other, automatically checking for violations in the structure of the hierarchies affected by the change. Each term in a thesaurus can have multiple NTs as well as multiple BTs.[25]

Referral back to Figure 8 shows what would be possible if retrieval system designers understood more about the value and content of thesaurus records, including all levels of the BT-NT relationships in the thesaurus. (Downward pointing "radio buttons" in the middle of the display show how MEDICAL INFORMATICS in the INFORMATION SCIENCE hierarchy has been

"opened" to show where EXPERT SYSTEMS fits under MEDICAL INFOR-
MATICS COMPUTING/COMPUTING METHODS/ARTIFICIAL INTELLI-
GENCE.)

When hierarchies in *LCSH*/SAF are more complete and when we have a
standard for complete display of subject authority records, we will have made
substantial improvements in our subject access mechanisms. Maybe this will
be done as a millenarian project. The ERIC Vocabulary Improvement Project
pointed the way but it was not followed.

The recent review and policy formation regarding Related Terms and the
cooperative work to improve entry vocabulary in *LCSH*/SAF will be covered
in other papers in this volume, so let's move on to a related and potentially
useful development.

LCSH and LCC Relationships

The 5th edition of the *National Library of Medicine Classification* is
linked to MeSH: "an effort was made to make schedule headings, subheadings and class number captions compatible with MeSH terminology. . . The
Index to the Classification provides access to classification numbers through
the terminology of MeSH."[26] Something like this for the Library of Congress
Classification and *LCSH*/SAF may finally appear. That is what has been
planned at the Library of Congress as far back as the 1920s–a comprehensive
index to the schedules of the Library of Congress Classification used as a link
to *LCSH* and LCC class numbers in *LCSH* for all headings to show those
relationships.[27]

Generations of librarians have debated the values of a dictionary catalog
over a classed catalog. Charles Ammi Cutter (upon whom rests the honor of
the first rules book for dictionary catalog creation) preferred a *combined*
catalog as the *ideal* catalog,[28] a catalog with both systematic and dictionary
portions because the combination helps to overcome the weaknesses of each
and allows specific and general questions to be answered "quickly, easily and
fully." In OPACs we may be able to plan for such a combined catalog when
the two vocabulary and organizing mechanisms are seen to be useful in
tandem.

The potential for a combined catalog in our present day OPACs will rest
on how accurately the authority files link with the bibliographic files, and
how carefully the authority files link with each other. There is more literature
on how poorly related all these files are than there are reports on their
improvement.[29] Practices in subject cataloging and classification over a century have not worked on such relationships in a reliable way, but some
attempts are worthy of note.

1. The electronic versions of the Dewey Decimal Classification (DDC) have links to at least one *LCSH* heading for each class number and sometimes show the MARC bibliographic record for some items.
2. The *LCSH*/SAF shows LCC class numbers for slightly more than one third of the headings. The CD-ROM version of the LCC, called *Classification Plus*, attempts a relationship with *LCSH*/SAF. Neither of these link to any bibliographic files in an exemplary way.

Improving *LCSH* suggested checking actual practice in various libraries to see how reliable the class numbers given in *LCSH*/SAF might be for finding books and other materials classified in a given library. If this were an accurate link, then OPACs could rely on *LCSH*/SAF information for another display of retrieval results and suggestions for alternative search strategies. If other libraries besides the Library of Congress would find these links valuable, then the updating of *LCSH*/SAF information so that every subject heading would have a LCC class number takes on more importance. The new LCC electronic version might also have more value to individual libraries and they could load it into their OPACs for another type of search vocabulary besides alphabetic keyword searching.[30]

As a start to checking the usefulness of the *LCSH*/SAF information about LCC class numbers, a preliminary study was conducted with the help of Sandra Roe at Mankato State University. Starting on page 69 of the printed *LCSH* and continuing in increments of 100 pages for a few volumes, we collected the headings with class numbers. These headings were checked in the Mankato State University Library catalog to see if those headings had been used. If yes, a check was made to see under which LCC class number the item had been classified. For 207 of the 313 *LCSH* headings checked there were no entries in the catalog. For the remaining 106 *LCSH*/SAF headings which matched the sample there was a total of 1002 records. If the first subject heading on these records matched a heading in our sample (we know of the policy to match the first subject heading with the class number), we kept that record in our study. The number of records (531/1002) had the heading we were checking listed first. Of those 531, 136 had to be excluded from our study because the class number used on these items was not LCC (these items included government documents, sound recordings, sheet music, and juvenile fiction). The remaining 395 bibliographic records were analyzed and we found the following:

- 52% (205) matched the LCC class number in *LCSH*/SAF
- 29% (115) matched the basic class of the LCC number but not the specific class number (Note: no check was made to determine if Mankato would have had to reclassify because of a new LCC number or a revision of a number from a previous edition of *LCSH*.)

- 19% (75) did not match either the basic or specific class number

The other 471 records were not examined to see if the second, third, or fourth heading matched those in our study. Time did not permit such an analysis. We hope no one will generalize from our findings as this study was, by no means, statistically valid and many variables may contribute to the lack of a match. It was merely a probe. Our study should be extended and repeated in other libraries including the Library of Congress. It is just possible that the LCC-*LCSH* links are valuable tools for creating arrays of bibliographic records during the search process. These different "neighborhood sweeps" will most likely add new items to the retrieval results. Almost every information retrieval research project has reported the retrieval of unique relevant items when a search is repeated, first searching by keyword and then by controlled vocabulary, or first by subject heading and then by classification number, or first by title word and then by words in the abstract or contents note, etc. The recommendation of these researchers has been that we should use all the means at our disposal if we want to attempt to retrieve all the relevant items in the collection. Since my work on the Subject Access Project in the late 1970s I have been calling such a system a "hybrid" search system, but now that I have read Cutter's contribution in the 1876 report I think we should call such systems "combined subject access systems" in his honor.

Even if the OPAC environment would not be the place to show LCC-*LCSH* relationships, the effort to relate these two might still be beneficial to *LCSH*'s development, adding structure from LCC when warranted. Other classification and thesaurus developers besides those at the National Library of Medicine have seen the potential recently.[31] Phyllis Allen Richmond "knew the facts early" and her pioneering research deserves a second read.[32]

CONCLUSIONS

Before the celebration for the second hundred years of *LCSH*/SAF I think we will see vast improvements in its structure and in its usefulness in OPACs and other information gateways. Links to LCC and to other vocabularies will probably be more visible and useful. Fortunately there are information technology tools on the horizon such as IODyne which will first show the weaknesses of our authority files and then help us make changes easily. No longer will we have to waste human time and effort making all the needed changes in reciprocal records or revising thousands of bibliographic records. We will be able to concentrate on the intellectual challenges of creating hierarchical relationships in alphabetic and classed information systems, links for crossfile searching, and alphabetic-classed links for alternate displays in OPACs.

NOTES

1. Pauline A. Cochrane, *Improving LCSH for Use in Online Catalogs.* (Littleton, CO: Libraries Unlimited, 1986).

2. Joseph R. Mathews, Gary S. Lawrence, and Douglas K. Ferguson, eds. *Using Online Catalogs: A Nationwide Survey; A Report of a Study Sponsored by the Council on Library Resources.* (New York: Neal-Schuman, 1983).

3. Martha M. Yee and Sara Shatford Layne, *Improving Online Public Access Catalogs* (Chicago: American Library Association, 1998). (Reviewed by Mary Beth Weber in *Library Resources & Technical Resources* 43 (1999), 60-61).

4. Jane Greenberg, "Reference Structures: Stagnation, Progress, and Future Challenges," *Information Technology and Libraries* 16 (1997), 108-119.

5. Pauline A. Cochrane with Monika Kirtland. *An ERIC Information Analysis Product in Two Parts: I. Critical Views of LCSH; a Bibliographic and Bibliometric Essay; II. An Analysis of Vocabulary Control in LCSH.* ED 208 900. (Syracuse, NY: ERIC Clearinghouse on Information Resources, 1981). (Part I was published, with authors reversed, in *Cataloging & Classification Quarterly* 1 (1982), 71-94 and updated by Steven Blake Shubert, "Critical Views of *LCSH*–Ten Years Later: A Bibliographic Essay," *Cataloging & Classification Quarterly*, 15 (1992), 37-97.

6. A forthcoming book on relationships in bibliographic information retrieval, edited by Rebecca Green and Carol Bean, in press. (Private communication from Lynn M. El Hoshy, August 9, 1999.)

7. Alan M. Greenberg, "Scope Notes in Library of Congress Subject Headings," *Cataloging & Classification Quarterly*, 1 (1982), 95-104.

8. Lois Mai Chan, *Library of Congress Subject Headings: Principles and Application.* 3rd ed. (Englewood, Colo.: Libraries Unlimited., 1995).

9. *Ibid.* pp. 149-152.

10. Private communication, August 9, 1999.

11. Sara D. Knapp, "Creating BRS/Term, a Vocabulary Database for Searchers," *Database* (December 1984), 70-75.

12. Carol A. Mandel, *Multiple Thesauri in Online Library Bibliographic Systems; A Report Prepared for Library of Congress Processing Services.* (Washington, D.C.: Library of Congress, 1987).

13. Jessica L. Milstead, "Cross-file Searching: How Vendors Help and Don't Help Improve Compatibility," *Searcher* 7 (May 1999), 44-55.

14. Phyllis Allen Richmond, "Cats: An Example of Concealed Classification in Subject Headings," *Library Resources & Technical Resources*, 3 (Spring 1959), 102-112.

15. David Judson Haykin, *Subject Headings: A Practical Guide.* (Washington, D.C.: U.S. Government Printing Office, 1951).

16. Ranganathan's writings were not well known by many American librarians, but Haykin (op. cit.) mentions his suggestion of a classed catalog on page 14. Ranganathan did not make a lecture tour in the United States until 1950. See, for example, S. R. Ranganathan, *Elements of Library Classification.* 2nd ed. (London: Library Association, 1959).

17. Pauline Atherton, ed., *Classification Research; Proceedings of the Second International Study Conference* (Copenhagen: Munksgaard, 1964).

18. See the reprinted introductions from seven different editions of *LCSH* in Cochrane-Kirtland, *An ERIC Information Analysis Product.*

19. *Ibid.* p. 76.

20. Shubert, "Critical Views of *LCSH.*"

21. Barbara Booth, "A 'New' ERIC Thesaurus, Fine-tuned for Searching," *Online,* (July 1979), 20-29.

22. Greenberg, "Reference Structures." See also Figure 3 in Pauline Atherton Cochrane and Eric H. Johnson, "Visual Dewey: DDC in a Hypertextual Browser for the Library User," *Advances in Knowledge Organization,* 5 (1996), 99.

23. Eric H. Johnson, "IODyne Java Version." August 1, 1999. Unpublished, but available from the author of this paper.

24. *Ibid.*

25. Eric H. Johnson, "The Usefulness of Hierarchical Subject Displays in Bibliographic Retrieval." Unpublished manuscript dated May 12, 1998. Available from this author.

26. National Library of Medicine. *National Library of Medicine Classification.* 5th ed. (Bethesda, Md.: U.S. Dept. of Health and Human Services, Public Health Service, National Institutes of Health, National Library of Medicine, 1994), p. x of Introduction.

27. See the reprinted introductions from seven editions of *LCSH* in the Cochrane-Kirtland publication, *op. cit.*

28. Charles A. Cutter, "Library Catalogues" in *Public Libraries in the United States.* Part I, 1876 Report. (Champaign, University of Illinois, Graduate School of Library Science), Monograph Series, No. 4 (reprint), pp. 549, 564-567.

29. Cochrane and Kirtland, *An ERIC Information Analysis Product*; and, Shubert, *Critical Views of LCSH.*

30. Cochrane and Johnson, "Visual Dewey."

31. Nancy C. Williamson, "Deriving a Thesaurus from a Restructured UDC," *Advances in Knowledge Organization,* 5 (1996), 370-377; Victoria Francu, "Building a Multilingual Thesaurus Based on UDC," *Advances in Knowledge Organization,* 5 (1996), 144-154; Karen M. Drabenstott, "Classification to the Rescue—handling the Problems of Too Many and Too Few Retrievals," *Advances in Knowledge Organization,* 5 (1996), 107-118.

32. Phyllis A. Richmond, "Hierarchical Definition," *American Documentation* 11 (1960), 91-96.

Filing and Precoordination:
How Subject Headings Are Displayed
in Online Catalogs and Why It Matters

Gregory Wool

SUMMARY. *Library of Congress Subject Headings* retrieved as the results of a search in an online catalog are likely to be filed in straight alphabetical, word-by-word order, ignoring the semantic structures of these headings and scattering headings of a similar type. This practice makes LC headings unnecessarily difficult to use and negates much of their indexing power. Enthusiasm for filing simplicity and postcoordinate indexing are likely contributing factors to this phenomenon. Since the report *Headings for Tomorrow* (1992) first raised this issue, filing practices favoring postcoordination over precoordination appear to have become more widespread and more entrenched. *[Article copies available for a fee from The Haworth Document Delivery Service: 1-800-342-9678. E-mail address: <getinfo@haworthpressinc.com> Website: <http://www.haworthpressinc.com>]*

KEYWORDS. Filing, indexing, precoordination, postcoordination, *Library of Congress Subject Headings*, online catalogs

In the online as in the card catalog, filing is a means of providing access. This is true even though in the online catalog, the "file" is read by a machine

Gregory Wool, BA, MA, MLS, is Associate Professor and Monographs Cataloger, Iowa State University Library, 204 Parks Library, Ames, IA 50011-2140.

[Haworth co-indexing entry note]: "Filing and Precoordination: How Subject Headings Are Displayed in Online Catalogs and Why It Matters." Wool, Gregory. Co-published simultaneously in *Cataloging & Classification Quarterly* (The Haworth Information Press, an imprint of The Haworth Press, Inc.) Vol. 29, No. 1/2, 2000, pp. 91-106; and: *The LCSH Century: One Hundred Years with the Library of Congress Subject Headings System* (ed: Alva T. Stone) The Haworth Information Press, an imprint of The Haworth Press, Inc., 2000, pp. 91-106. Single or multiple copies of this article are available for a fee from The Haworth Document Delivery Service [1-800-342-9678, 9:00 a.m. - 5:00 p.m. (EST). E-mail address: getinfo@haworthpress inc.com].

in response to a search request, instead of by a user selecting a drawer and thumbing through a batch of cards. It is in the outcome of a search–either as a group of keyword matches gathered from thoughout the file, or as a targeted segment of the overall file-that filing sequence becomes important to an online catalog user.

Controlled, precoordinated subject terms, such as *Library of Congress Subject Headings* (*LCSH*), are especially dependent upon filing sequence for access. Mann (1993) characterizes the advantages of controlled headings as their providing *predictability* (efficiently taking the searcher from her query to the materials she needs) and *serendipity* (calling attention to terms of interest the searcher would not have thought to look for) to subject access. Because a user's query is unlikely to match a subject string exactly, and because information needs are seldom focused enough that only a single, narrow subject category will be of interest, the ability to find a particular term quickly in a list, and to scan easily all terms sharing a particular relationship, can well make the difference between searching success and failure. It is therefore necessary that the filing create patterns that are either familiar or logical, preferably both. Moreover, the filing should serve to highlight, rather than obscure, the semantic relationships among similar terms, so that the benefits of precoordination–predictability and serendipity–can be fully realized.

The purpose of this essay is to examine the filing of LC subject headings in online catalog displays to users, in relation both to existing standards and to the structure and properties of the headings themselves. Its premise is that filing can either support or undercut the power of *LCSH* to provide effective subject access. Implicit in this statement is that such filing cannot be properly judged apart from consideration of the relative merits of precoordinate and postcoordinate indexing, and that perceptions of how subject headings are to be used ultimately determine how they are filed.

LITERATURE REVIEW

Several of the documents cited in this brief survey are discussed further below. The most comprehensive discussion of online filing issues for subject headings is in ALCTS 1992. Massicotte (1986), McGarry and Svenonius (1991), Allen (1993), O'Brien (1994), and Yee and Layne (1998, 172-176) have examined the use of compression as a practical implementation of structured filing for subjects. Daily (1972) and Hoffman (1976) provide theoretical discussions of filing that retain considerable relevance.

Many books and articles over the years have examined problems with subject retrieval in online catalogs. Of these, Yee (1991) and Borgman (1996) are among the few to discuss filing issues, while Yee and Layne (1998,

169-171) offers a particularly cogent summation of the advantages of structured subject arrangement. In a wide-ranging search for ways to enhance use of LC subject headings through machine manipulation, Drabenstott and Vizine-Goetz (1994) show how postcoordinate techniques might make good use of precoordinate structures. The precoordinate and postcoordinate approaches to subject access are debated in Chitty 1987, Duke 1989, Gregor and Mandel 1991, Svenonius 1992, Mann 1993 and 1997, and Weinberg 1995, among others.

FILING BASICS

Daily (1972) offers an essential theoretical framework for the consideration of filing issues. He depicts filing as fundamentally mathematical in nature and posits five "iron laws" of acceptability, clarity, redundancy, ambiguity, and equality as characteristic of efficient and sustainable filing sequences (410-14). Especially concerned with containing the cost of filing, he also maintains that the easier a file is to maintain (i.e., the fewer distinctions it makes), the easier it will be to use. While allowing that semantically-based filing can create a "useful sequence" based on meaning (409), he insists that exceptions to a single, widely-recognized sequence (such as the alphabet) inevitably create needless difficulties for the file user (415).

A helpful, if not completely watertight, model of the filing process can be found in Hoffman 1976. This monograph, written to clarify the principles behind the ALA filing rules, second edition (Seely 1968) dealt with the filing of complete bibiliographic records (as they appeared on cards) in a dictionary catalog. In this analysis, the record is divided into *blocks,* which are characterized by *position, content, function,* and *role.* Only certain types of block (as defined by position and content) play any role in filing. Filing blocks are divided into *sections,* which are further divided into *items,* for purposes of subarrangement.

Items correspond to individual words or their equivalents. Since these had not been rigorously defined for filing purposes, Hoffman defines them as "any typographic symbol or sequence of such symbols enclosed by spaces" and goes on to identify *latentspaces* and *pseudospaces* as functional equivalents of spacing and no spacing, respectively, where the rules effectively divide (e.g., "USA") or combine (e.g., "Los Angeles") apparent word units for filing purposes. Items meant to be ignored in filing (e.g., initial articles) are designated *pseudo-items.* Filing is fundamentally numerical rather than alphabetical, with letters implicitly assigned numeric values, and is a matter of realizing rank order, from lowest to highest. Rank order is determined by the first non-identical pair of blocks, sections, items, and units found.

Hoffman follows his analysis with an exploration of the question whether card filing can be automated (99-110). He concludes that it can, but that the more distinctions are to be supported, the more difficult and inefficient such automation would be. It would work very well, however, under conditions such as the following (105): "If we could live with catalogs filed strictly by the Basic Principle of the *ALA Rules*, allowing no exceptions, and if we could change entries at their birth to supress [sic] all leading pseudo-items, for example, we could have computer filing tomorrow. It is that simple. . . . Instead of filing a word that is a name before the same word that is not a name, a decision the machine cannot make without help, a computer filing according to the Basic Principle would file 'straightforward, item by item through the entry, not disregarding or transposing any of the elements, nor mentally inserting designations.'" While Hoffman's analysis was based on the filing of bibliographic records in card catalogs, the implications for online listing of subject headings are clear: (1) any class of objects needing to be filed can be analyzed to enable any kind of filing sequence; (2) the more complicated the criteria for determining rank order, the more work imposed on the filer, human or machine.

FILING IN THE ONLINE CATALOG

Filing in the online catalog is both simpler and more complex than in the card catalog. As automated systems developed, the mechanized filing of cards (or their equivalents) speculated about by Hoffman proved to be unnecessary. Rather, a menu of indexes offers access to records in response to a user's query. Typically the user chooses an index and types in a search term. The system then returns all the records that, within the parameters of the index, "match" the search term. If there is only one record, it will appear either in full or abbreviated form, depending on the configuration of the system and/or the expressed preference of the user. A handful of records might also appear in abbreviated form. A larger set of results, however, will typically appear as a list of titles, perhaps with additional identifying information such as author and date, but usually with each entry taking up one line apiece. One or more items from the list can then be chosen to display in full record form. Kilgour (1995) refers to such a set as a "minicat."

Most online systems respond to a subject index search by displaying an alphabetical list of all the subject strings that begin with the user's search term. Some systems will also produce minicat displays of subject headings in response to a subject-keyword index search, listing all the subject headings containing the entered word. Some offer a subject browse function, whereby a query takes the user to an alphabetical list of all the subject headings used in the catalog, displaying initially the segment where the user's search term would be "filed." A few systems also offer searching or browsing in "dictionary mode," displaying a list of all types of main entry and added entry headings; such a feature presents the nearest online equivalent to comprehensive card catalog filing. Usually, however, subject headings display online as a separate file, rather than interfiled with other entries.

PRECOORDINATION VS. POSTCOORDINATION

"Precoordination" and "postcoordination" are terms used to describe indexing, rather than filing, processes. The distinction they represent is that between the pre-combining of simple concepts by an indexer in assigning a term, and their juxtaposition by an index user in formulating a search strategy. According to Chan (1995, 32-36), *LCSH* is basically a precoordinate indexing system, though not consistently so. Single-word headings are assigned to many documents, and the practice of assigning multiple headings is a means of postcoordination. The vast majority of *LCSH* strings, however, are precoordinate in nature.

Terms in *LCSH* are precoordinated in one of four ways: subdivision, inversion, qualification, and phrase building. Each of the first three methods is indicated in the heading by a distinctive typographic means (dash for subdivision, comma for inversion, parentheses for qualification) and initial capitalization of the secondary concept. Phrase building is indicated by no punctuation and no following capitalization. Each method is meant to indicate a certain semantic relationship between the coordinated terms.

Filing that makes distinctions among these semantic relationships provides crucial support to a precoordinated, controlled vocabulary system such as *LCSH*. By collocating, rather than scattering, all manifestations of a certain semantic relationship involving the primary term (which is usually identical or nearly identical to the user's search term), it makes possible a quick overview of how the term is used in indexing, enabling a user to focus her search, and clarifying rather than muddying the distinctions among subject categories. These precoordinated categories are the hallmark of *LCSH* as a tool for subject access, but they are not self-evident to the catalog user; as is well known, search terms seldom match *LCSH* strings exactly. Without mechnisms that facilitate productive browsing of LC subject headings, the expense and trouble of using these headings to provide access will become increasingly difficult to justify.

In online catalogs, postcoordinate subject access remains represented largely by the subject keyword/Boolean search function. The apparent simplicity, flexibility, and power of keyword searching (mining terms largely, but not always exclusively, from LC subject headings assigned to records) holds wide appeal, even when the results are difficult to sift through, encumbered with wildly irrelevant items, and lacking many of the items sought. By putting category creation in the hands of the catalog user, keyword indexing and other forms of postcoordination offer users a sense of control and libraries apparent cost savings by forgoing the expense of "canned" subject identification by catalogers.

If one considers the essence of precoordination as the catalog bringing a group of similar items together in advance for access by anyone at any time, and the essence of postcoordination as letting that task be performed over and over again by catalog users, then it makes sense to speak of precoordinate and postcoordinate filing as well. Like precoordinate indexing, precoordinate filing assembles useful categories of objects in advance (through the making of distinctions that add complexity to filing) to save countless file users that trouble. Postcoordinate filing, meanwhile, by keeping things simple offers users the exhilaration or frustration of building from scratch.

CURRENT FILING STANDARDS

The term "current filing standards" must be used advisedly. First, while the ALA rules are the only ones with the imprimatur of a national professional organization, and have probably been the most widely used by libraries, several other sets of rules have been developed by individual libraries and even published, presumably to be adopted by other libraries in preference to the ALA code. One of these codes, that of the Library of Congress (Rather and Biebel 1980), wields particular influence through the arrangement of entries in the printed and machine-readable *Library of Congress Subject Headings*. Second, the ALA, Library of Congress, and other published filing rules documents all predate the era of catalog automation. The continuous updating in response to new developments in bibliography that is so evident in other types of catalog standards has not been happening here, although brief guidelines for filing have been included in recent standards for index and thesaurus construction (e.g., ISO 1996; NISO 1998).[1] With this caveat in mind, then, we will use the ALA and the LC rules as separate benchmarks for comparison with display practice in online catalogs.

The ALA rules are built upon the Basic Principle (partially quoted above) which calls for filing strings of characters just as they appear, on an item-by-item (word-by-word) basis, but also allows for exceptions, of which there are enough to result in a volume of over 200 pages (Seely 1968). Only four exceptions, however, affect significantly the filing of subject headings, and all are alluded to in the code's other foundational statement, the Basic Order. One is that subject heading strings with chronological subdivisions are filed immediately following the main heading, and before all other strings beginning with the same word or words. Another is that the chronological subdivisions of a heading are filed in chronological order, including those beginning with words rather than dates. The third, a relatively minor exception with regard to subject headings but of major impact in general, calls for personal surnames to be filed preceding other headings beginning with the same set of letters. The fourth allows certain headings containing numbers to be filed with the numbers (no matter where situated within the heading) considered last (Rule 9D; example, pp. 184-5). With these exceptions, however, the ALA rules do not support precoordinate indexing by taking semantic structure into account in organizing subject strings.

By contrast, *Library of Congress Filing Rules* (1980) explicitly provides for structured access to LC's famously structured subject headings. The second of the rules' three governing principles states: "Related entries should be kept together if they would be difficult to find when a user did not know their precise form." This principle is amplified as follows (Rather and Biebel 1980, 4): "The second principle acknowledges the fact that the more formally constructed a heading is, the less likely a user is to know its elements precisely. Therefore, headings that begin with the same elements are grouped in categories to reduce the time needed to browse in a large file for a heading that is known incompletely." Consequently, headings beginning with a particular word are organized in the following order:

- the single word heading (e.g., **Drawing)**
- the single word heading with subdivisions (set off by dashes, e.g., **Drawing-Technique)**
- inverted phrase headings beginning with the word (set off by commas, e.g., **Drawing, Rococo)**
- the single word with qualifier (in parentheses, e.g., **Drawing (Metalwork**
- phrase headings beginning with the word (e.g., Drawing ability)

Headings with subdivisions are further subarranged, with chronological subdivisions filing ahead of topical and form subdivisions, which in turn are followed by geographical subdivisions. In terms of Hoffman's model, all headings, as blocks, are sectioned at a mark of punctuation (dashes, commas or parentheses), with all identical sections kept together and subfiled by their following sections.

An early, proposed set of filing rules for online catalogs (Hines and Harris 1966) takes a middle-ground approach. Anticipating MARC, it defines headings as fields and those portions of headings suitable for subarrangement as subfields. *LCSH* subdivisions are defined as subfields and the rules call for all instances of a heading with its various combinations of subdivisions to be filed together following the heading without subdivisions.

"HEADINGS FOR TOMORROW"

From 1987 to 1991 a subcommittee of the American Library Association's Subject Analysis Committee studied the sequencing of LC subject headings in online catalog displays in the context of card catalog filing standards. The subcommittee's report, *Headings for Tomorrow* (ALCTS 1992) was offered to librarians, programmers, and vendors making design decisions for online catalogs as a guide to subject display issues, and it remains the definitive work in this area.

The report covers in turn each type of subject heading feature requiring a filing decision, presenting two or three alternative approaches with examples. Usually the more structured approach corresponds with Library of Congress filing practice, and the "straight alphabetical" with the ALA rules, but in some cases an approach is presented which is more purely alphabetical than the ALA rules allow, and which had been seen in one or more online catalogs. For each feature, current practice based on the subcommittee's investigations is noted, as are the advantages and disadvantages of each approach. Also, the introduction presents the structured and the strict alphabetical approaches in general, with the arguments in favor of each.

With regard to practice, the overall picture emerging from this report is of all systems examined following the strict alphabetical approach in most situations, and many "going strict alphabetical" throughout. Yet while the subcommittee avoided making recommendations and took care to present the issues thoroughly and evenhandedly, the concluding statement of the introduction (ALCTS 1992, p. xviii) suggests a concern that semantically structured filing receive serious consideration: "The important thing to remember in designing displays is that one should never assume users of the catalog know the subject heading they need prior to the search; systems should be designed to encourage exploration and to teach structure by example." Also, it is noteworthy that the arguments in favor of the structured approach take up four pages in this report, while those in favor of the strict alphabetical approach run just over half a page.

CURRENT FILING PRACTICE

In order to update the information on filing practices reported in *Headings for Tomorrow*, the present author examined 15 Web-accessible catalogs in September 1999. Twelve were chosen from among larger American academic and public libraries and union catalogs to represent the six leading vendors of automated library systems in the United States market (Ameritech, DRA, Endeavor, Innovative Interfaces/III, Library Corporation/TLC, SIRSI). In addition, an experimental Ameritech interface was examined at two libraries, and the new Library of Congress system, an Endeavor product, was also considered. The subject indexes of these catalogs were queried using the search terms **Children** and **France**.

If this admittedly unscientific sample is any indication, strict word-by-word alphabetical filing has put the structured approach thoroughly to rout. With a few partial exceptions, all the catalogs examined file word by word, making no distinctions among inverted headings, qualified headings, phrase headings, and headings with subdivisions; nor among chronological, geographic, and topical/form subdivisions. As a consequence, to find a heading like **Children–Wounds and injuries or France, Western** one must scroll and click through dozens, perhaps hundreds, of screens. Chronological subdivisions are filed the same way, with numerals filed at the head of the alphabet and character by character, and subdivisions beginning with a word (e.g., **–Bourbons, –Louis, –To**) interfiled with other alphabetical strings. The SIRSI catalogs' filing of ordinals in numeric rather than digit-by-digit order and MaineCat's (TLC) shifting of dates to the head of period subdivisions beginning with words or names (bringing all period subdivisions of a heading together) are the partial exceptions–two lonely nods to precoordination.

The other exceptions, by contrast, push the postcoordination envelope farther. The III and SIRSI catalogs use string permutation to expand the range of responses to a search term, bringing up headings with the search term in a subdivision along with the headings beginning with the search term, and interfiling them as if the subdivision was the lead term. (All but one of these libraries also display these strings with the subdivision as the lead term.) Examples include **Alcott, Louisa May, 1832-1888–Characters–Children** as "Children Alcott Louisa May 1832 1888 Characters" and **Abolitionists– France–Biography** as "France Abolitionists Biography." Only one catalog (the Ameritech installation at Hennepin County Public Library) displays a list of subject headings in response to a subject keyword search–and that, unfortunately, in no visible order. The Ameritech experimental interface at Columbia and Cornell universities dispenses with subject heading displays altogether, listing instead the brief records in order of their relevant subject headings (which themselves appear only in the full record display).

Most of the catalogs examined display subject heading strings without their internal punctuation, a practice that information scientists have called "normalization." This not only serves to justify straight word-by-word filing, but also presents the carefully structured headings as formless clusters of keywords. One of these catalogs, it must be noted, is the new Endeavor installation at the Library of Congress (LC). Both the abandonment of punctuation and the adoption of straight word-by-word filing in LC's new system are based on the constraints of off-the-shelf catalog software, constraints that may be altered or lifted in future versions once appropriate standards for filing in an online catalog have been established (Dulabahn 1999). But as these seemingly cosmetic changes strike at the heart of *LCSH*'s usefulness as a precoordinate system, their implementation at the home of *LCSH* sends a powerful, even if unintended, message to the library world about the future of precoordinate subject access.

DEVELOPMENTS FAVORING POSTCOORDINATION

If the compilers of *Headings for Tomorrow* hoped to raise awareness of both the benefits and the scarcity of structured filing approaches in online catalogs through a nonjudgmental guide to filing issues, the seven years since publication show little apparent impact. Indeed, it would appear that undifferentiated word-by-word filing is now a given, with enhancements tending to obscure semantic relationships further and to mine individual words within headings for additional access points.

Why has online catalog design favored postcoordination so heavily over precoordination? The lures of simplicity and cost-efficiency, given theoretical underpinning in Daily's "iron laws of filing," no doubt provide powerful motivation, as does the example of commercial index publishing. The psychological appeal of greater freedom to craft one's own access strategy combined with an expanded toolbox for data analysis makes postcoordinate features easier to "sell" to the user. In addition, though, developments within librarianship during the 1990's have displayed a weakening of support for precoordinated subject access.

"Cataloging Must Change!"

The April 1, 1991 issue of *Library Journal* offered as its cover feature an article by Dorothy Gregor and Carol Mandel with the provocative title "Cataloging Must Change!" (Gregor and Mandel 1991). In its heralding of developments in information access technology, which promised relief from cataloging costs, "deregulation" of bibliographic recordkeeping, and expansion of access, this essay struck a responsive chord throughout the profession and received numerous approving citations in the professional literature. One of its major themes was the need for catalogers to spend less time and effort seeking intellectual consistency among records, on the premise that online technology makes access possible without it. While some advantages of controlled subject headings–mainly the use of references to focus searches and offer alternate possiblilities–were duly noted, the authors devoted much more space to ridiculing catalogers' efforts to pre-package distinct and useful subject categories instead of just letting users work with the catalog software to create their own. The impact of "Cataloging Must Change!" in this regard was cited by Mann (1997) as the impetus for his own efforts to investigate the authors' claims and challenge their interpretation of the studies they cited as evidence.

Airlie House Reforms

Also in the spring of 1991, the Library of Congress convened its historic Subject Subdivisions Conference at Airlie House in Virginia (Library of Congress 1992). This gathering of subject cataloging experts from throughout the United States was asked to make recommendations for reforming *LCSH* subdivision practice in order to make heading assignment easier, improve user access, and support cooperative cataloging (Zimmerman 1992, 1). Four broad proposals and responses to them were prepared in advance, serving to stimulate discussion. While these papers in general express strong support for the principles and practice of structured subject access, highlighted by Svenonius' summary of the advantages of precoordination (1992, 36-37), at least two of the recommendations could be seen as promoting the erosion of LC's precoordinate system. The standardization of order by type of subdivision in subject strings (topical, geographic, chronological, form) was expected to limit possibilities for string construction and make many strings more ambiguous, and eventually met resistance among specialists in art and history cataloging. The merging of many pattern lists and of similar subdivisions such as–**Description** and –**Description and travel**, while perhaps making cataloging easier, risked also reducing the scope of precoordination by eliminating distinctions of meaning and in some cases bringing unrelated items together under a single rubric (Lisbon 1992, 80-81).

MeSH Deconstruction

For the 1999 edition of *Medical Subject Headings* and its new Web-based online catalog, the National Library of Medicine (NLM) altered the form and content of its subject strings, removing geographic and form subdivisions and making them separate index terms. This change was intended to bring MeSH in line with NLM's indexing practice and facilitate searching across files. At the request of several medical libraries, the strings are automatically reassembled for use in other library catalogs (Hoffmann 1999). While precoordination is thus supported alongside postcoordination, in the MeSH environment the latter is now the default.

DEVELOPMENTS FAVORING PRECOORDINATION

While developments in online catalog interfaces, national library policies, and conventional wisdom within librarianship may appear to have strength-

ened the market position of postcoordination almost to the point of dominance, precoordination is far from dead. Researchers continue to look for
ways to make it more effective in an automated environment, and investments continue to be made in its future.

British Library Adopts LCSH

Around 1995 the British Library (BL) committed itself to using *LCSH* for
subject access to its records (MacEwan 1996). This move, surprising to many
in the profession, was impelled by the widespread usage *LCSH* had achieved
in Britain's academic libraries, as well as the BL's desire to participate in a
worldwide Anglo-American authority file. However, it also entailed the dis-
continuance of COMPASS, the BL's own system of subject descriptors characterized by shorter strings than in *LCSH*, separation of geographic from
topical descriptors, and term permutation (British Library 1999).

Research Initiatives

Explicit, interface-provided guidance to navigating a precoordinate subject index has been a recurring research topic for more than a decade. Massicotte (1988) was among the first to suggest the use of compression as a way
to make long lists of headings more easily browsable. Subject strings could
be sorted by the presence of geographic, chronological, or form subdivisions
into groups offered on a menu. Building in part on this work, Karen M.
Drabenstott (with various collaborators) has conducted a number of studies
of LC subject strings and machine-assisted searching. Convinced that the
massive and ongoing investment of libraries in *LCSH* will not soon be abandoned, she has explored the concept of diagnostic system responses to subject searches ("search trees"), automatically launching a particular precoordinate or postcoordinate approach depending on the relationship of the search
term to the controlled vocabulary (Drabenstott and Vizine-Goetz 1994,
300-329).

Mention should also be made of the growing body of experimental systems using graphical, map-like interfaces to provide an overview of available
information categories. Many of them can be reached through Gerry McKier-
nan's website *The Big Picture* (http://www.iastate.edu/~CYBERSTACKS/
BigPic.htm). Though these sites for the most part use sophisticated postcoordinate techniques rather than precoordination, they offer a promising
approach to making precoordinate relationships vivid to the searcher.

MARC Form Coding for Subject Strings (6XX $v)

An especially significant investment in precoordinate subject access is the
MARC Advisory Committee's 1995 approval of a subfield $v within the

various MARC subject fields (MARC Advisory Committee 1995) and its implementation by LC in 1999. It is significant because of the role it will play in furthering precoordinate subject access online; because of the enormous effort and expense involved in implementation by libraries, bibliographic utilities, and software vendors; and because it was approved despite the presence of a separate form/genre field which could enable postcoordinate access. As the ramifications of a new wrinkle in subject coding trickle down to practitioners in the field, considerable skepticism and even hostility have emerged (as can be seen in a discussion on the AUTOCAT electronic list during 1999. Much of the debate over the benefits of the new subfield is really over the relative merits of precoordination and postcoordination in subject access.

CONCLUSION

It is a truism that advances in technology render many long-established practices obsolete, and call many others into question. Often, though, old processes may be abandoned without adequate consideration. Their drawbacks may loom large, overshadowing continued advantages. This is especially true when the technological advance offers a new way of fulfilling the purposes of the old practice. That it may not be a better way–or even as good–is often overlooked when the promise of other benefits (such as improved cost-efficiency) shines brightly.

Such is the case with library catalogs. In pursuit of the second part of Cutter's Second Objective–to show the user what the library has on a given topic–the card catalog typically used precoordinated subject terms as headings on records. These terms functioned as index entries, facilitating searching and browsing in a structured linear file, and bringing together all works on a particular subject. The structure would combine basic alphabetical order with recognition of at least some semantic relationships among terms (such as a heading with and without subdivisions), enabling the user to quickly locate the aspect or aspects of a term of greatest interest.

Online catalogs brought keyword indexing, greatly expanding the range of terms available for subject searching while promising efficiencies through the elimination of subject-heading assignment. Some twenty years later, few libraries have taken so radical a step, but keyword searching–whether restricted to titles and subject headings or encompassing whole records–has proven enormously popular, often functioning as a first approach to the catalog. Reference librarians frequently advise users to begin with a keyword search, identify the most promising records, and then search on the subject headings found in those records. As drawbacks to keyword searching (notably excessively large retrieval sets) have become apparent, research into improving online subject access is centered around improving the effectiveness of the keyword approach.

Thus it should not be much of a surprise that online subject-heading list displays do not follow filing standards established for card catalogs. Besides the convenience-for-programmers factor, there is the widespread assumption that subject headings, while retaining their value as a collocation device, are in the end only strings of discrete words and best approached as such. This assumption, however, overlooks the considerable intellectual effort involved in constructing and assigning LC subject headings, as well as the powerful alternative approach to subject access they represent. The result is an unnecessary limiting of options for searching, as well as an unconscionable squandering of library resources.

If automated library systems–whether for reasons of convenience, ignorance, or pretension to superior knowledge–fail to follow established filing standards in their displays of subject headings, users can be confused or misled by unfamiliar sequencing. If the filing does not take into account the semantic relationships among headings, those relationships can easily be lost to the user, making browsing less efficient. Stripped of their semantic content by the loss of context, headings become unstructured clusters of keywords, lacking the power that provides predictability and serendipity to subject access. When it comes to subject access, filing is not a trivial issue. Filing that makes a few sensible distinctions can provide the spark that ignites the power of precoordinate indexing.

NOTE

1. The author learned about the documents cited here shortly before the deadline for this paper, and was not able to examine them. He obtained his information about them from Taylor 1994, NISO 1999, and ISO 1999.

REFERENCES

Allen, Bryce L. 1993. Improved browsable displays: An experimental test. *Information Technology and Libraries* 12:203-208.

Association for Library Collections and Technical Services (ALCTS). Cataloging and Classification Section. Subject Access Committee. Subcommittee on the Display of Subject Headings in Subject Indexes in Online Public Access Catalogs. 1992. *Headings for tomorrow: Public access display of subject headings*. Chicago: American Library Association.

Borgman, Christine L. 1996. Why are online catalogs still hard to use? *Journal of the American Society for Information Science* 47:493-503.

British Library. National Bibliographic Service (NBS). 1999. COMPASS subject descriptors. Retrieved September 29, 1999 from the World Wide Web: <http://minos.bl.uk/services/bsds/nbs/records/compass.html>.

Chan, Lois Mai. 1995. *Library of Congress Subject Headings: Principles and application.* 3rd ed. Englewood, Colo.: Libraries Unlimited.

Chitty, A. B. 1987. Indexing for the online catalog. *Information Technology and Libraries* 6:297-304.

Daily, Jay E. 1972. Filing. In *Encyclopedia of library and information science,* edited by Allen Kent and Harold Lancour, vol. 8.

Drabenstott, Karen Markey, and Diane Vizine-Goetz. 1994. *Using subject headings for online retrieval: Theory, practice, and potential.* San Diego: Academic Press.

Duke, John K. 1989. Access and automation: The catalog record in the age of automation. In *The Conceptual Foundations of Descriptive Cataloging,* edited by Elaine Svenonius. San Diego: Academic Press.

Dulabahn, Beth. 1999. Electronic message to Alva T. Stone, 22 October; forwarded with permission of the author, 22 October.

Gregor, Dorothy, and Carol Mandel. 1991. Cataloging must change! *Library journal* 116, no. 6:42-47.

Hines, Theodore C., and Jessica L. Harris. 1966. *Computer filing of index, bibliographic, and catalog entries.* Newark, N.J.: Bro-Dart Foundation.

Hoffman, Herbert H. 1976. *What happens in library filing?* Hamden, Conn.: Shoe String Press.

Hoffmann, Christa F. B. 1999 (April 12). NLM practices for subject heading content and structure. (Posted by Andrea Demsey.) AUTOCAT [Online]. Available E-mail: LISTSERV@LISTSERV.ACSU.BUFFALO.EDU/Getpost autocat 05396 [1999 April 12]. International Organization for Standardization (ISO). 1996. *Information and documentation: Guidelines for the content, organization and presentation of indexes.* ISO 999:1996. New York: American National Standards Institute.

— 1999. ISO 999: Information and documentation–guidelines for the content, organization and presentation of indexes. Retrieved November 1. 1999 from the World Wide Web: <http://www.nlc-bnc.ca/iso/tc46sc9/standard/999e.htm#1>.

Kilgour, Frederick G. Cataloging for a specific miniature catalog. *Journal of the American Society for Information Science* 46:704-6.

Library of Congress. 1992. *The future of subdivisions in the Library of Congress subject headings system: Report from the Subject Subdivisions Conference sponsored by the Library of Congress, May 9-12, 1991.* Edited by Martha O'Hara Conway. Washington, D.C.: Library of Congress Cataloging Distribution Service.

Lisbon, Peter. 1992. Proposal #4: Arguments against. In *The future of subdivisions in the Library of Congress subject headings system: Report from the Subject Subdivisions Conference sponsored by the Library of Congress, May 9-12, 1991,* edited by Martha O'Hara Conway. Washington, D.C.: Library of Congress Cataloging Distribution Service.

MacEwan, Andrew. 1996. *LCSH* and the British Library: An international subject authority database? *Catalogue and Index* 120 (summer 1996):1-6.

Mann, Thomas. 1993. *Library research* models: A guide to cataloging, classification, and computers. New York: Oxford University Press.

—— 1997. "Cataloging must change!" and indexer consistency studies: Misreading the evidence at our peril. *Cataloging & Classification Quarterly* 23, nos. 3/4:3-45.

MARC Advisory Committee. 1995. Proposal 95-2. Retrieved September 29, 1999 from the World Wide Web: <http://lcweb.loc.gov/marc/marbi/1995/95-02.html>.

Massicotte, Mia. 1986. Improved browsable displays for online subject access. *Information Technology and Libraries* 7:373-80.

McGarry, Dorothy, and Elaine Svenonius. 1991. More on improved browsable displays for online subject access. *Information Technology and Libraries* 10:185-91.

National Information Standards Organization (NISO). 1998. *Guidelines for the construction, format, and management of monolingual thesauri.* ANSI/NISO Z39.19-1993 (R1998). Bethesda, Md.: NISO Press.

—— 1999. NISO Press online. Standards, books, and software. Document number: ANSI/NISO Z39.19-1993(R1998). Retrieved November 1, 1999 from the World <Wide Web: http://www.cssinfo.com/cgi-bin/detail?product_id=52601>.

O'Brien, Ann. 1994. Online catalogs: Enhancements and developments. *Annual review of information science and technology* 29:219-242.

Rather, John C., and Susan C. Biebel. 1980. *Library of Congress filing rules.* Washington, D.C.: Library of Congress.

Seely, Pauline, ed. 1968. *ALA rules for filing catalog cards.* Chicago: American Library Association.

Svenonius, Elaine. 1992. Proposal #2: Arguments in favor. In *The future of subdivisions in the Library of Congress subject headings system: Report from the Subject Subdivisions Conference sponsored by the Library of Congress, May 9-12, 1991,* edited by Martha O'Hara Conway. Washington, D.C.: Library of Congress Cataloging Distribution Service.

Taylor, Arlene. 1994. Letter to Myron Chace, 17 February. American Library Association, Association for Library Collections and Technical Services, Subject Analysis Committee, Pittsburgh, Pa. SAC94-ANN/4b. Photocopy.

Weinberg, Bella Hass. 1995. Why postcoordination fails the searcher. *The Indexer* 19:155-9.

Yee, Martha M. 1991. System design and cataloging meet the user: User interfaces to online public access catalogs. *Journal of the American Society for Information Science* 42:78-98.

Yee, Martha M., and Sara Shatford Layne. 1998. *Improving online public access catalogs.* Chicago: American Library Association.

Zimmerman, Glen. 1992. Conference overview. In *The future of subdivisions in the Library of Congress subject headings system: Report from the Subject Subdivisions Conference sponsored by the Library of Congress, May 9-12, 1991,* edited by Martha O'Hara Conway. Washington, D.C.: Library of Congress Cataloging Distribution Service.

Machine-Assisted Validation
of *LC Subject Headings*:
Implications for Authority File Structure

Stephen Hearn

SUMMARY. Many kinds of structure can be discerned in the headings and rules governing the *Library of Congress Subject Headings*. By addressing these structures at different levels, librarians can develop different approaches to the machine-assisted validation of subject headings, from the checking of individual words to the validation of complex forms of heading/subdivision compatibility. Using computer programs to assist with maintenance of subject headings is becoming increasingly necessary as technical services librarians strive to create consistent and useful patterns of subject collocation in library catalogs. *[Article copies available for a fee from The Haworth Document Delivery Service: 1-800-342-9678. E-mail address: <getinfo@haworthpressinc.com> Website: <http://www.haworthpressinc.com>]*

KEYWORDS. *Library of Congress Subject Headings*, subdivisions, structure, machine validation, authority control

Increasingly, technical services librarians are turning to computer programs to assist them in creating and editing catalog records. Well designed

Stephen Hearn, MLS, is Authority Control Coordinator and Database Management Team Leader, University Libraries, University of Minnesota, 160 Wilson Library, 309 19th Avenue South, Minneapolis, MN 55455 (E-mail: s-hear@ tc.umn.edu).

[Haworth co-indexing entry note]: "Machine-Assisted Validation of *LC Subject Headings*: Implications for Authority File Structure." Hearn, Stephen. Co-published simultaneously in *Cataloging & Classification Quarterly* (The Haworth Information Press, an imprint of The Haworth Press, Inc.) Vol. 29, No. 1/2, 2000, pp. 107-115; and: *The LCSH Century: One Hundred Years with the Library of Congress Subject Headings System* (ed: Alva T. Stone) The Haworth Information Press, an imprint of The Haworth Press, Inc., 2000, pp. 107-115. Single or multiple copies of this article are available for a fee from The Haworth Document Delivery Service [1-800-342-9678, 9:00 a.m. - 5:00 p.m. (EST). E-mail address: getinfo@haworthpressinc.com].

programs can carry out a complex sequence of steps, compare strings of characters, copy data accurately, check for rule violations, and generally save much wear and tear on the cataloger's wrists and elbows. One useful application of this kind of machine-based help would be a program which could validate subject headings, either at the point of cataloging or later when subject headings need to be updated. But what do we mean when we say that a Library of Congress subject heading is "valid?" There are several things that we might mean:

- The words in the heading contain no errors.
- The heading matches a Library of Congress subject authority record.
- The heading string follows LC rules for the use and order of subdivisions.
- The heading reflects the content of the item at the appropriate level of specificity.

A heading might be valid by any one of these tests, and yet be invalid by the others. So what do we mean by machine-assisted validation, and what kinds of data would a computer need to do the kinds of machine-assisted validation we want?

STRUCTURE IN LCSH

Behind these levels of validity lies an analysis of the structural levels of LC subject heading strings. "Structure," taken here to refer loosely to the arrangement of elements in a larger whole, can refer to many things in relation to *LCSH*. The heading file is built from established headings and heading strings, so they constitute structural elements of the file. A heading string may be composed of a main heading and one or more subdivisions, so each of these can also be regarded as a significant structural element in the heading. The MARC formats are used to encode subject heading elements at the heading and subdivision level, in the process explicitly differentiating types of data–e.g., topical (650) vs. geographic (651) headings, topical ($x) vs. form ($v) subdivisions.

Within main headings and subdivisions, there are also patterns and punctuation which contribute to the meaning of the heading element:

- parentheses following a heading term indicate a qualifying category for the initial term, e.g., **Power (Christian theology)**
- commas following a heading term may indicate an inversion of natural word order, e.g., **Eggs, Fossil**

- commas within a subdivision can indicate a different kind of data, e.g., **United States–History–Civil War, 1861-1865**
- These ways of indicating different kinds of data are also structural elements in LC subject headings. The arrangement of letters into words is obviously also important, but perhaps that drops below the threshold of structures specific to *LCSH*.

The Library of Congress subject heading system also has a syndetic structure, in which headings relate to other headings as "broader," "narrower," or "related" terms. Subject authority records are encoded for these kinds of relationships using the USMARC authority record structure. LC's MARC subject authority records explicitly encode some of the relationships defined above, leave some uncoded or implicit (e.g., narrower term references are implicit in the *LCSH* MARC authority system), and add levels of structure and analysis which go well beyond those already discussed, e.g., associating headings with LC classification numbers and defining patterns of geographic subdivision use.

What implications does this kind of analysis of the many structural aspects of LC subject headings have for a discussion of heading validation? First, it alerts us to the structural richness and complexity of the *LCSH* system. Second, it highlights the importance of implicitly and explicitly defined relationships in *LCSH*. The elements of a Library of Congress subject heading string are not just beads, or even beads in a predetermined order–they are beads whose defined relationships within the system determine whether and how they may be used. Lastly, it gives us a broad horizon for developing validation routines, recognizing that no one routine will be optimal for all circumstances.

Three approaches to the machine-assisted validation of LC subject headings are discussed below, in order of increasing complexity. Each depends on essentially structural comparisons–looking for equivalence between two data elements, one known and one under review. They do not offer any check of the appropriateness or semantic value of the heading, which is still in the province of the human cataloger's responsibilities.

SPELL CHECKING APPROACH

A spell checker is a program that compares the words in a document to a list of words in its dictionary and highlights any word it doesn't recognize. Running new catalog records through a spell checker offers the cataloger a chance to locate and correct various kinds of errors, including errors in subject headings. The spell checker will guess wrong–the spell checker in the word processing program which was used to write this article flagged "Follis," "Fomes," and "Fon" as dubious, though each is used in an established LC subject heading. But a program which would save the cataloger from "history" and "criticism" would be quite welcome.

The usefulness of the spell checker approach could be improved significantly if the vocabulary of LC subject headings and subdivisions were used as the checker's dictionary for comparison with the subject heading terms on the record. The kinds of mistakes cited earlier could thereby be avoided. However, because simple spell checkers tend to compare only one word at a time, without regard for relationships or other kinds of encoding, there are many kinds of errors which they would be unable to detect.

VALIDATION FILE APPROACH

A more sophisticated approach to heading validation is described by Chan and Vizine-Goetz in "Toward a Computer-Generated Subject Validation File: Feasibility and Usefulness."[1] The authors propose assembling a large file of valid LC subject heading strings for comparison with the strings in new records and files. Those headings which match the validation file are thus removed from having to undergo cataloger review. Chan and Vizine-Goetz's research indicates that such a file could reasonably be compiled by using criteria such as cataloging agency and frequency of appearance in large databases as indicators of likely validity. Their research also indicates that such a file would validate a significant number of subject headings, since some headings appear many times. Headings which did not match in the validation file would then be identified for further review.

This approach has a number of advantages. It makes few demands of existing data, data structures, or personnel, relying as it does more on the weight of accumulated bibliographic data to indicate valid strings rather than on cataloger-generated authority records or cataloger review. All headings in a file need not be perfect in order for the file to be useful as a resource in developing the validation file. The method compares whole strings, so it would match on many more headings than the current *LCSH* authority file. There is no need to ask the machine to analyze relationships between headings and subdivisions. The validation process is a fairly simple comparison, and could be run very quickly. But there are also disadvantages. The validation file's main usefulness is in validating common strings–but these are the headings that make the least demands on catalogers when validation and correction are needed. In terms of staff time, the more problematic heading strings are those which do not occur frequently, which raise questions about the appropriateness of a given subdivision under a given heading, or about the position of a geographic subdivision. When heading strings with few or no postings in existing catalogs are run against the proposed validation file, its ability to validate a new or seldom-used heading string reliably declines sharply. Yet these are just the headings which are most labor intensive to check and validate by manual means.

There are also potential problems with maintaining such a file. LC subject headings are volatile entities, undergoing frequent revision as new headings are created, old ones are modified, and new subdivisions and subdivision rules come into use. Heavily posted heading strings can become obsolete in an instant if the corresponding subject authority record is modified. Until the bibliographic files used as a basis for the proposed validation file can be updated with comparable speed, the value of the resulting validation file will be compromised by an ongoing, dynamic disjunction between it and the *LCSH* authority file.

ENCODED CATEGORIES APPROACH

A more complex approach to validation was proposed Karen M. Draben-stott in her report *Determining the Content of Machine-Readable Subdivision Records*.[2] Drabenstott called for the creation of subdivision authority records encoded to permit machine validation of the compatibility of specific head-ings and subdivisions. Work done by Gary Strawn[3] at Northwestern Univer-sity developed an encoding system to represent the relationships between different heading and subdivision types explicitly in heading and subdivision authority records, and in the process revealed the categorical complexity embedded in LC's *Subject Cataloging Manual: Subject Headings (SCM:SH)*.

A simple form of this encoding is contained in the MARC Authority Format 008/06, Direct/Indirect Geographic Subdivision Code. This code in-dicates whether a given established heading may be subdivided geographical-ly. To determine whether a geographic subdivision has been correctly added to a subject heading on a bibliographic record, a system can check the author-ity record that matches the subject heading. By comparing the 008/06 code assigned to the heading with the subfield code immediately following the subject heading on a bibliographic record, a system can report whether the use of a geographic subdivision is authorized or not.

For example, if a record contains the LC subject heading **Differential equations–United States**, a check of the authority record for **Differential equations** indicates that this heading has not been authorized to be subdi-vided geographically. The use of subfield z clearly identifies–**United States** as a geographic subdivision, so the system is able to recognize that the combination is not authorized.

The coding of geographic subdivision practice becomes more complicated when additional subdivisions are introduced. For example, the Library of Congress has recently revised many editorially established headings includ-

ing the topical subdivision–**Conservation and restoration** to permit geographical subdivisions after the topical subdivision. The base headings to
which–**Conservation and restoration** has been added are themselves authorized for geographic subdivision. However, *LCSH* rules say that geographic
subdivisions should appear in the last position for which they are authorized
in a heading string. The challenge for system designers and programmers is
to develop systems which can recognize that

* **Historic buildings–Vermont.**
  and
* **Historic buildings–Conservation and restoration–Vermont.**
  are both authorized, but that
* **Historic buildings–Vermont–Conservation and restoration.**

is not. The data necessary for this kind of validation is already present in LC
subject authority records, and could be used both to identify erroneous and
obsolete headings, and in many cases to make corrections. The Library of
Congress recently began adding 781 fields to its geographic name heading
records, giving the form of the name to be used in geographic subdivisions.
This extends further the possibilities for automated validation and correction
of geographic subdivisions.

Still, the structural problems that must be overcome to validate geographic
subdivisions are relatively simple compared to the problems currently posed
by topical and other subdivisions. The *Subject Cataloging Manual: Subject
Headings* contains an elaborate system of categories, subcategories, and exceptions which governs which subdivisions may be used with which heading
types. Further, with each additional subdivision, the category of the heading
as a whole may change, so that subdivisions not authorized after a main
heading may be authorized after a given subdivision. For example, the form
subdivision **–Personal narratives** is authorized for use under the names of
events or wars. The heading **United States** is a geographic heading, for which–
Personal narratives would not be authorized. But if other subdivisions are
interposed, e.g., **United States–History–Civil War, 1861-1865**, then the resulting string represents a war, and the addition of–**Personal narratives** is
authorized.

Gary Strawn's work on a possible notation system for encoding correla-
tions between subject heading and subdivision categories highlights the complexity which any effort at this kind of encoding will face. Strawn's system
identifies nine kinds of data relevant to determining whether a subdivision is
compatible with a given heading. Each subdivision may be authorized for use
under certain categories of headings, and explicitly excluded from use under
others; each will determine the category of the heading for the addition of
further subdivisions; each may vary from category to category in whether it

can be geographically subdivided; and so on. All of this complexity is already present in the system as defined in LC's *Subject Cataloging Manual: Subject Headings*. The ongoing effort at LC to simplify its subject subdivision practices by reducing the number of categories and exceptional cases is a most welcome process, and should also simplify the task of developing a heading/ subdivision compatibility encoding scheme.

The MARC authority record already includes fields that could contain such encoding. The 072 Subject Category Code field and the 073 Subdivision Usage field could be developed to include the kinds of encoding necessary to enable a program to validate a heading string which had never before been encountered, based on the rules for appropriate subdivision use in *SCM:SH*.

There are clear disadvantages to this approach. Putting it in place would require an analytically demanding and labor intensive effort. Validating headings would require a program not simply to compare strings, but to look up multiple authority records and compare multiple coded data elements in those records. But the promise of an automated system that could validate and propose corrections to any combination of established heading and subdivisions is too great to ignore.

The three approaches to validation discussed above are by no means mutually exclusive. It may be that the most effective system will involve a combination of these different techniques–e.g., using an authority-based encoding system to generate and authorize a heading string validation file. Indeed, many of the points in the preceding discussion are not dissimilar to those made in 1994 by the "Final Report" of the Subject Authority File Task Group to the Cooperative Cataloging Council,[4] predecessor to the Program for Cooperative Cataloging. That group's recommendations included the addition of indirect geographic subdivision forms to geographic authorities, the use of a subject heading validation file, and the development of subject subdivision authorities with coding based on *SCM:SH* rules. It is encouraging to see the progress that has been made at LC in several of these areas.

A CONTRARY VIEWPOINT

There is an assumption inherent in all of these approaches to structural validation of subject headings that a correctly structured heading is a good thing. This assumption has been called into question by Karen M. Drabenstott, Schelle Simcox, and Eileen G. Fenton in "End-User Understanding of Subject Headings in Library Catalogs."[5] drabenstott and her co-authors have conducted several studies, presenting LC subject heading strings to various kinds of library users and asking them to interpret the strings' meanings. The answers are then compared to catalogers' "expert" interpretations of the strings, and if the interpretations diverge (which Drabenstott's research shows they often do), it is taken as evidence that the string does not convey its intended meaning. More broadly, the authors call into question the useful-ness of current rules for ordering subject strings, arguing that their poor performance as clear semantic statements is indicative of a fundamental failure.

Behind this argument is an assumption that subject heading strings should perform in manner comparable to a natural language statement. Validity is tested by comparing natural language interpretations of the subject strings, as though these were reasonable substitutes for the strings themselves. But this line of reasoning fails to take into account the context in which subject strings appear, and their structural as well as semantic function in ordering subject heading files. A string which may be obscure or ambiguous in isolation may be easier to interpret in the context of a well ordered catalog, where other headings with a parallel structure can establish patterns that aid the user, and where titles are visible under the heading to assist the user in interpreting the heading. Indeed, structured subject heading strings may achieve their ends largely by collocating entries for works on a shared, complex topic, regardless of whether the heading by itself is entirely clear. Drabenstott and her co-au-thors are correct in questioning the value of long and overly complex subject headings–the goal of collocation is not well served when every heading is so custom-tailored that it becomes unique. But the fundamental value of struc-tured subject headings lies in their ability to order a large, browsable file of records into a hierarchy of categories and subcategories which is optimized to meet the needs of researchers for certain preferred kinds of collocation, not in any meaning the headings may convey in isolation. If scholars working in a given field such as art or music history tend to approach their subject chrono-logically, they will not be well served by a standard order of subdivisions which places chronological subdivisions after geographic subdivisions. The value of a given order of subdivisions lies in how well it orders a file for use, not in how easily each heading can be understood on its own.

CONCLUSION

The preceding discussion is silent on the issue of subject analysis. It assumes that the cataloger has successfully identified the subject or subjects of the item being cataloged, and has identified a heading with the intended meaning. The emphasis here on validating the structure of an LC subject heading string is not an end in itself. A subject heading that is valid but not appropriate is of no use. On the other hand, it is in the area of structural validation that automated systems hold the greatest promise for improving catalogers' efficiency and accuracy in subject heading work. Systems that can comment reliably on the appropriateness of a subject heading, or reliably propose appropriate subject headings, are much further out, for the simple reason that the semantic relationships between words in catalogable texts and words in subject headings are far more complex and indeterminate than the much more formal relationships already defined in *LCSH* or *SCM:SH* between subject headings and subdivisions.

The Library of Congress and the cataloging community have invested great effort in developing and defining the structure and vocabulary of *LCSH*. Deconstructing and reconstructing the elements of subject headings, as many systems and Boolean search strategies do, is an extension rather than a violation of the relationships established in the strings themselves. However, even in such unstructured uses, much of the value of subject heading data elements depends on the added precision and predictability which they acquire when placed in a valid, structured heading. And in this day of clickable access point displays, precoordinated subject strings can be an effective tool for quickly navigating large numbers of records for works on related subjects.

The effectiveness of LC subject headings depends on consistency. The need for consistency is in constant conflict with the need to keep heading vocabulary current, to refine the granularity of authorized subjects in an expanding topical area, and to amend the errors and infelicitous judgments of the past. The various approaches discussed above to validation of the subject strings will all assist with achieving the goal of consistent subject headings. Given the volatility of *LCSH* and the ever rising expectations of our users, it is hard to see how any sizable file will be manageable in the future without more sophisticated help from our automated systems, more work on simplifying any unnecessary complexities of the headings, and more explicit encoding of the relationships which LC has worked so hard to define in *SCM:SH*.

BIBLIOGRAPHICAL REFERENCES

1. Lois Mai Chan and Diane Vizine-Goetz. "Toward a Computer-Generated Subject Validation File: Feasibility and Usefulness." *Library Resources & Technical Services* 42:1 (January 1998), 45-60.

2. Karen M. Drabenstott, *Determining the Content of Machine-Readable Subdivision Records.* Dublin, Ohio: OCLC, September 1993.

3. Gary Strawn. *"LCSH* Subdivision Classification and Notation." Unpublished paper, appended to Association for Library Collections & Technical Services, Cataloging & Classification Section, Subject Analysis Committee, Subcommittee on Subject Authority File Recommendations. "Final Report to ALCTS/CCS Subject Analysis Committee." June 1997.

4. Cooperative Cataloging Council, Subject Authority File Task Group. "Final Report." November, 1994.

5. Karen M. Drabenstott, Schelle Simcox, and Eileen G. Fenton. "End-User Understanding of Subject Headings in Library Catalogs." *Library Resources & Technical Services* 43:3 (July 1999), 140-160.

SPECIFIC PERSPECTIVES

Teaching
Library of Congress Subject Headings

Thomas Mann

SUMMARY. An understanding of the workings of *Library of Congress Subject Headings* (*LCSH*) is one of the most valuable conceptual tools a researcher can have. The subject heading system is by no means obvious or self-evident, however; it must be taught, explained, and exemplified by librarians. Several points must be covered explicitly. The cross-reference notation of UF, BT, RT, SA, and NT has to be explained; the importance of choosing the most specific heading available, rather than a general term, must also be emphasized. There are four ways to find the most specific *LCSH* terms for a particular topic; two of them come from using the red books, two from using the online catalog itself. All four ways are important; none is obvious. Each must be taught. *[Article copies available for a fee from The Haworth Document Delivery Service: 1-800-342-9678. E-mail address: <getinfo@haworthpressinc.com> Website: <http://www.haworthpressinc.com>]*

Thomas Mann is affiliated with the Humanities and Social Sciences Division, Library of Congress, Washington, DC 20540-4660 (E-mail: tman@loc.gov).

[Haworth co-indexing entry note]: "Teaching *Library of Congress Subject Headings*." Mann, Thomas. Co-published simultaneously in *Cataloging & Classification Quarterly* (The Haworth Information Press, an imprint of The Haworth Press, Inc.) Vol. 29, No. 1/2, 2000, pp. 117-126; and: *The LCSH Century: One Hundred Years with the Library of Congress Subject Headings System* (ed: Alva T. Stone) The Haworth Information Press, an imprint of The Haworth Press, Inc., 2000, pp. 117-126. Single or multiple copies of this article are available for a fee from The Haworth Document Delivery Service [1-800-342-9678, 9:00 a.m. - 5:00 p.m. (EST). E-mail address: getinfo@haworthpressinc.com].

KEYWORDS. Library research, research methodology, bibliographic instruction

I've been a reference librarian for over twenty years; I've probably helped tens of thousands of researchers in that period. The single most important and most practically useful thing I've ever learned about how to use a research library efficiently is the *Library of Congress Subject Headings* system. I dearly wish someone would have explained it to me when I was a graduate student in English, working on my Ph.D., years before I became a librarian. In retrospect, I can see that in all of those years I used libraries only haphazardly, rather than systematically, because I didn't perceive that there *is* a system. I'm sure I routinely missed more than I found in most of my searches; but since I didn't have a clue that I was missing anything, and I could usually find *something*, I never realized the extent of my ignorance. I was missing a good overview of the range of sources available; and I was often probably missing the best material, too.

In four years of undergraduate classes and three of graduate, nobody–no professor, no librarian, no graduate assistant–ever mentioned even a word to me about how to find the right subject headings for a topic in a library catalog, in spite of the fact that I took whole semester-long classes on how to do research. I didn't even know the red books set (*Library of Congress Subject Headings*) existed during my entire pre-library school academic career. The set was probably there somewhere in the libraries I used; but no one ever pointed out to me even its existence, let alone its function. When I had my first cataloging class in library school, I was simply astonished that such an amazing system for categorizing books had been there all along, and that I had gone through so many years of using libraries without anyone at all telling me about it. Frankly, I had half a mind to go back and sue a couple professors for malpractice. Teaching library research without *LCSH* is like teaching medicine without anatomy.

Of course, finding the right subject heading in a library catalog is not the *only* way of searching that students (and others) need to know about; there are many different ways of doing subject searches, and I've tried to discuss and exemplify all of them, each with its peculiar strengths and weaknesses, in detail in *The Oxford Guide to Library Research* (Mann, 1998). It is especially important, however, that we teach students the enormous differences between controlled vocabulary searching and keyword searching. I say that not just because of my personal, daily experiences in seeing how vast those differences are, but also because over the last several years some of my colleagues and I at the Library of Congress have been teaching a weekly research orientation class to anyone who wishes to attend. In each of these sessions we lay out all of the different methods of doing subject searches: through controlled vocabularies (especially *LCSH*), via keywords, through citation searching, related record searching, stacks-browsing, and so on. And we always ask attendees to fill out evaluation forms on the lectures. The one thing that we are thanked for most–most explicitly, most often, and most heartily–is our explanation of the *LCSH* system. This happens week after week, year after year.

It is apparent to those of us who teach the classes that the researchers we talk to–and they come from all over the country–have never been told by anyone else, ever, how to find the right subject headings for their topics. This is the single factor that makes the biggest difference in the quality of library research that gets done in research libraries; and yet most librarians evidently don't bother to tell anybody how to use the system that we create ourselves. My own experience of having gone through an entire Ph.D. program without being clued in to the most fundamental technique of using a library is by no means unique; it actually seems to be the norm.

It is not enough to simply put a lot of sets of the red books out near computer terminals. It is not enough to simply tell people to look in them for their headings. *LCSH* is a lot more complicated than that. The system isn't difficult to teach; but it does have to be taught. And there is much more to it than just the red books list, or its online equivalent of headings with cross-references. The list itself is only a quarter of what needs to be taught.

There are four ways to find the right subject terms for a topic. Two of them come from using the red books; two of them come from using the online catalog itself.

The first way that we need to teach is the use of the cross-reference network in the basic red books set itself. I usually point out that works on the Bay of Pigs invasion of Cuba aren't categorized under that term; rather, they're under **Cuba–History–Invasion, 1961**. But the *LCSH* list will guide researchers from the former to the latter by means of a simple "use" cross-reference. That's not hard to follow at all–the trick is to know that the red books exist in the first place, which most people *don't* know. Beyond simple "use" references, however, the other cross-reference notations have to be explained: BT for Broader Terms, RT for Related Terms, SA for See Also, and NT for Narrower Terms. These meanings are neither obvious nor self-evident.

I've noticed over the years that many students who are aware of the list's existence nevertheless mistakenly assume that the column of BT, RT, and NT terms appearing under a heading are included within the coverage of that heading. We teachers have to point out explicitly that this is not the case; this, too, is just not obvious to inexperienced users. If anyone wants a BT, RT, or NT term, he or she has to type it in directly; such terms are not subsets or subdivisions of the heading above them.

Above all, we must emphasize that the NT cross-references are the most important ones to look for. Catalogers, as a rule, will assign the subject terms to a book that are the tightest fit for its topical coverage, and will not use general terms when more specific ones are available. In other words, if researchers want information on a specific topic, they must look under a specific heading for it, and not under some general heading that they (mistakenly) assume will *include* the narrower aspects. I once helped a reporter who wanted information on game shows on TV; he was searching under **Television**. Wrong. The right heading is **Game shows**, and the books listed under the narrower term are not duplicated under the broader one. Another reader wanted information on recreation rooms, but was searching under **Homes**. The right heading is **Recreation rooms**. And please note: reference librarians are not playing "Gotcha!" by pointing out this *necessary information*; rather, we are simply trying to do our very important job of showing researchers, in Cutter's words, *what the library has*–and we are also making sure that the wonderful work done by our cataloger colleagues gets *used*, to solve the very problems that only vocabulary control can solve (Cutter, 1904).

What this means is that there's a *rule* that goes with the red books, and *in the absence of that rule the list doesn't work*. Researchers need to be taught always to *start* by looking in the direction of specificity–by following NT references in particular–rather than in the direction of generality. (This is the very opposite of what many are in fact told.) There may be many different levels of headings available in the red books that seemingly cover **Callinectes** (blue crabs)–among them, **Chesapeake Bay, Crabs, Crustacea**, or any of a dozen more. The problem is this: If researchers look among the many levels of general headings, there is no predictable or logical stopping point, because any or all of the general headings are potentially applicable. The one, sole, and only mechanism for making the choice of *which* level to search under *predictable* is the principle of specific entry: Search in the direction of specificity until you come to the heading that is the tightest fit for your topic, and stop *there*. Without this rule, students have no guidance as to which level of headings they should use; and, left to their own devices, they will usually chose–mistakenly–general rather than specific headings; and in doing so they will miss most of the best material the library has to offer them on their subjects. We have to *teach* them the rule of specificity; it is not obvious. Without that rule the whole system has no control; and any system that does not provide a mechanism for choosing among many different possible headings is not a *controlled* vocabulary to begin with.

Beyond following the trail of NT references, the second way to find the appropriate specific heading is to look for narrower terms that are alphabetically adjacent to general terms in the red books. The heading **Monasteries** is followed by a number of NT references, none of which begin with the root

"Monast-." But right nearby, alphabetically adjacent, are whole columns of other narrower terms such as **Monasteries, Coptic, Monastery gardens, Monastic and religious life in art**, and **Monastic and religious life of women**. None of these terms show up in the cross-reference structure linked to **Monasteries**. In other words, the formal cross-reference structure among headings is only one means of aggregating related terms; the second way is through alphabetical adjacency, and researchers–or librarians–who neglect the latter are likely to miss many important subject headings.

What is especially important about alphabetically adjacent narrower terms is that they are virtually invisible in most online screen displays. I once helped a reader who wanted to set up a company that would do, in his words, "spying on other companies." I couldn't think of a term for that, so I looked under **Business** and its NT references, with no luck. But on the next page over in the red books, there was the heading **Business intelligence**, which proved to be exactly right. In our online computer display–I tried this later–the heading **Business intelligence** was separated from **Business** by over 200 screens! No screen display can possibly show this relationship as readily as the print format does. The mere existence of information in a system does not guarantee that it can or will be found; the *format of its presentation* is crucial here. And the paper copy red books have a major advantage over online screen displays in *showing* researchers the existence of alphabetically adjacent narrower terms, which are just as important as those terms given formal NT cross-references, but which are themselves outside the cross-reference structure. (Take a look in the red books around **Afro-Americans, Art, Architecture, Business, Landscape, Sports, Television**, or **Women** for other good examples.)

The first and second way of finding the proper narrow terms for a search thus come from using the red books. The third and fourth ways come from using the online catalog itself. The third way is to look for subject tracings–that is, to find a good title by some other means (either a title, keyword, or author search, usually) and then to look at the subject tracings assigned by the catalogers to that one title. Once again, however, this is something that we have to teach people to do; it is not intuitively obvious. This is especially the case if our computer software's default display is a brief record that doesn't show the tracings immediately.

While using tracings is a marvelous way to find *LCSH* terms, I must emphasize–perhaps to the annoyance of some colleagues who don't want to hear this?–that this method is not an adequate substitute for using the red books directly; it's a wonderful supplement but a terrible substitute. Why? For two very important reasons. Most students don't understand the need to search under specific rather than general headings–because *we* haven't told them–and this will throw off their efficient use of tracings. If a reader wants material on questioned document examination (i.e., the study of documentary evidence for identification, forgery detection, and so on), she may mistakenly do a keyword search for the too-general words "forensic science." A book having these words in the *title* will probably have the *tracing* **Criminal investigation**. In the red books, the heading **Criminal investigation** will provide an NT reference to **Writing–Identification**; but *tracings do not provide NT cross-references to more appropriate narrower terms*. And second, *tracings do not display alphabetically-adjacent narrower terms*. Tracings are themselves the end of the line; and if they are at the wrong level of generality to begin with, then the researcher will miss the most relevant, "tightest fit" material that she should be finding. In other words, if the researcher misses the right headings in the tracings field, she will have no formal mechanisms there that will bring to her attention the better headings that she ought to be using to find "what the library has."

Tracings, however, do offer one major advantage over the red books list: Traced headings that show up on actual catalog records often create aggregations of related headings that are not formally linked by the cross-reference structure of *LCSH*. The catalog record for the book *Document Examiner Textbook*, for example (Figure 1) has the following tracings: **Writing–Identification; Legal documents–Identification; Evidence, Documentary; Forgery;** and, **Printing–Specimens**.

Within *LCSH*, **Writing–Identification** is formally linked to the second

FIGURE 1

LC Control Number: 99172607
Type of Material: Book (Print, Microform, Electronic, etc.)
Personal Name: Dines, Jess E.
Main Title: Document examiner textbook / Jess E. Dines.
Published/Created: Irvine, CA : Pantex International Ltd., c1998.
Description: x, 566 p. : ill. ; 24 cm.
ISBN: 0962766631
Notes: "ISSN 1098-6170"--T.p. verso.
Includes bibliographical references (p. 549-555) and index.
Subjects: Writing--Identification.
Legal documents--Identification.
Evidence, Documentary.
Forgery.
Printing--Specimens.
LC Classification: HV8074 .D56 1998
Dewey Class No.: 363.25/65 21
Other System No.: (OCoLC)40613051
Quality Code: lccopycat

heading **Legal documents–Identification** by a cross-reference; but it is not linked to the other three, and clearly it should be. Tracings, then, often create aggregations of related subject headings that are not brought together by the red books. Just as tracings alone are not adequate to provide full entry into the subject heading system, *the red books themselves are not fully adequate either.*

The fourth way to find the right subject category term for a topic is to make use of the browse displays of precoordinated strings of subdivisions that appear in the online catalog. The example of Thomas Jefferson (Figure 2) is relevant here.

One researcher whom I helped wanted information on Jefferson's opinions on religious liberty. In going through the browse displays of subdivisions under Jefferson as a subject, we found the subdivision–**Views on freedom of religion**, which, of course, is right on the button. But the array of *other* subdivisions brought to our attention further options for answering the same question–options that neither one of us thought of in advance. The subdivision–**Quotations** turned up several compilations of extracts from Jefferson's writings, categorized by subject. They proved to be useful in isolating, quickly, passages from his writings that were directly relevant. And the subdivision–**Bibliography** led to annotated bibliographies compiled by Jefferson scholars that listed *dozens* of citations that were right on target.

The important points to teach are these: First, most of the arrays of subdivisions that show up in the catalog itself are not recorded in the red books set. Most subdivisions are "free-floaters," which means essentially that they can be assigned when appropriate (i.e., according to governing rules), but that the attachment of such subdivisions is not recorded in the red books. Second, if researchers are *taught* to *take the time to look through the full arrays of subdivisions* under any particular heading, they will frequently notice aspects of their topics that it would never have occurred to them to specify in advance. This recognition capability is of enormous practical use when students, in particular, don't quite know what they want to write on, or how to narrow their topics. Precoordinate strings in browse displays thus offer researchers a huge advantage over systems that require them to specify in advance which terms they wish to combine in postcoordinate Boolean combinations. In the Jefferson example, the student might well think of combining "Jefferson" and "religious liberty"–but maybe not "freedom of religion"?–but even so, who would ever think of adding "Quotations" to the mix? And most students, left to their own devices, would never think of adding "Bibliography" either. But both turned out to be of great relevance. The point is that precoordinate strings enable researchers to recognize many, many options that they could never specify in advance within their topics. But *we* have to *teach* them to look through the full array of subdivisions–

FIGURE 2

464	Jefferson, Thomas, 1743-1826	LC subject headings
51	Jefferson, Thomas, 1743-1826.	LC subject headings for children
13	Jefferson, Thomas, 1743-1826 Addresses, essays, lectures.	LC subject headings
3	Jefferson, Thomas, 1743-1826 Anniversaries, etc.	LC subject headings
1	Jefferson, Thomas, 1743-1826 Anniversaries, etc., 1926.	LC subject headings
2	Jefferson, Thomas, 1743-1826 Archives.	LC subject headings
2	Jefferson, Thomas, 1743-1826 Art collections Exhibitions.	LC subject headings
1	Jefferson, Thomas, 1743-1826 Associated objects.	not applicable
11	Jefferson, Thomas, 1743-1826 Bibliography.	LC subject headings
4	Jefferson, Thomas, 1743-1826 Books and reading.	LC subject headings
1	Jefferson, Thomas, 1743-1826 Career in architecture.	LC subject headings
2	Jefferson, Thomas, 1743-1826 Career in law.	LC subject headings
2	Jefferson, Thomas, 1743-1826 Childhood and youth.	LC subject headings for children
3	Jefferson, Thomas, 1743-1826 Childhood and youth Juvenile literature.	LC subject headings
1	Jefferson, Thomas, 1743-1826 Collectibles Exhibitions.	LC subject headings
1	Jefferson, Thomas, 1743-1826 Commemoration.	not applicable
4	Jefferson, Thomas, 1743-1826 Contributions in architecture.	LC subject headings
1	Jefferson, Thomas, 1743-1826 Contributions in civil-military relations.	LC subject headings
1	Jefferson, Thomas, 1743-1826 Contributions in paleontology.	LC subject headings
1	Jefferson, Thomas, 1743-1826 Contributions in political science.	LC subject headings
1	Jefferson, Thomas, 1743-1826 Contributions in public administration.	LC subject headings
33	Jefferson, Thomas, 1743-1826 Correspondence.	LC subject headings
1	Jefferson, Thomas, 1743-1826 Correspondence Facsimiles.	LC subject headings

. . . [some index lines omitted here] . . .

3	Jefferson, Thomas, 1743-1826 Psychology.	LC subject headings
10	Jefferson, Thomas, 1743-1826 Quotations.	LC subject headings
1	Jefferson, Thomas, 1743-1826 Quotations.	not applicable
3	Jefferson, Thomas, 1743-1826 Relations with Afro-Americans.	LC subject headings
2	Jefferson, Thomas, 1743-1826 Relations with Brazilians.	LC subject headings
1	Jefferson, Thomas, 1743-1826 Relations with slaves.	LC subject headings
1	Jefferson, Thomas, 1743-1826 Relations with slaves Congresses.	LC subject headings
6	Jefferson, Thomas, 1743-1826 Relations with women.	LC subject headings
1	Jefferson, Thomas, 1743-1826 Relations with women Congresses.	LC subject headings
10	Jefferson, Thomas, 1743-1826 Relations with women Fiction.	LC subject headings
2	Jefferson, Thomas, 1743-1826 Relics	LC subject headings
6	Jefferson, Thomas, 1743-1826 Religion.	LC subject headings
1	Jefferson, Thomas, 1743-1826 Statues.	not applicable
1	Jefferson, Thomas, 1743-1826 Study and teaching (Elementary)	LC subject headings
1	Jefferson, Thomas, 1743-1826 Views on citizenship.	LC subject headings
1	Jefferson, Thomas, 1743-1826 Views on citizenship Congresses.	LC subject headings
1	Jefferson, Thomas, 1743-1826 Views on civil rights.	LC subject headings
1	Jefferson, Thomas, 1743-1826 Views on copying.	LC subject headings
1	Jefferson, Thomas, 1743-1826 Views on democracy.	LC subject headings
1	Jefferson, Thomas, 1743-1826 Views on economics.	LC subject headings
3	Jefferson, Thomas, 1743-1826 Views on education.	LC subject headings
3	Jefferson, Thomas, 1743-1826 Views on foreign relations.	LC subject headings
1	Jefferson, Thomas, 1743-1826 Views on France.	LC subject headings
1	Jefferson, Thomas, 1743-1826 Views on free thought.	LC subject headings
1	Jefferson, Thomas, 1743-1826 Views on freedom of religion.	LC subject headings
1	Jefferson, Thomas, 1743-1826 Views on Indians.	LC subject headings
1	Jefferson, Thomas, 1743-1826 Views on machinery.	LC subject headings

most students won't do it without being given prior examples of how useful the procedure is.

Note an important point: I said above that tracings are a good supplement, but a terrible substitute, for the red books. In the operation of the *total* subject heading system, that observation is very much a two-way street: The red books themselves cannot show researchers the information that they can find through tracings *or* subdivision browse displays. There's actually a four-way intersection involved: We need to teach all four ways of finding the right subject headings, because each of them is capable of showing us important information that the other three conceal. (And yes, there's a kind of fifth way, too: using individual word elements, taken from different *LCSH* strings, in Boolean combinations. But we can't teach that effectively until students first understand how to get the initial subject headings in the first place.)

There are several implications here, and I won't mince words. If we simply "put the red books out" without either drawing students' attention to them or volunteering instruction on *how to use* the system–including the *rule* of specific entry that goes with the list of headings–then we are not doing a good job of providing reference service. If we tell *ourselves* that we don't need the red books in paper format because the cross-reference structure is online, then we are also not doing a good job. The change in format of the same information effectively hides alphabetically adjacent terms that are outside the cross-reference structure, and which may be of crucial importance in any given inquiry. (Some screen display formats may also bury *LCSH* headings among many *titles* of books, and thereby effectively conceal both their difference and their importance from novice researchers.) Worst of all, if we *actually tell researchers not to use the controlled vocabulary system at all*, but to simply type in keywords and let the computer "relevance rank" them for us, we have abdicated all professional responsibility. And I'm not talking about saving catalogers' jobs here–I'm talking about providing lousy reference service. If we ourselves don't grasp how important the difference is between controlled vocabularies and keywords, and when to use *either* approach, then our schools of library and information science have utterly dropped the ball. Keyword searches–no matter how cleverly they are weighted, truncated, collocated, and ranked–cannot solve the basic problem that they draw upon only those words that happen to appear in the source works themselves. Keyword indexing does not *create and add retrievable points of commonality* among works on the same subject that do not already have words in common. Proper *cataloging* does create such groups of records, whose individual members may have wildly variant words that researchers could never specify in advance. (Further: Are we so naive as to think that only English-language records are worth finding in our research libraries? Subject headings, properly assigned, turn up all of the relevant books on their topics, regardless of the original languages of the books themselves.) There isn't space enough to argue the point here; at this point I must refer interested readers to the many examples given in *Library Research Models* (Mann, 1993) as well as in *The Oxford Guide to Library Research*.

The entire *LCSH* system uses *all* mechanisms that will get us from the words we think of to the proper category terms used by the library's retrieval system. In the real world, this system is much more than just the red books or their online equivalent network of cross-references. It is not a difficult system to use efficiently–even spectacularly. But it isn't obvious, and we need to cure ourselves of the affliction of assuming that it is, or even should be, "transparent" to users, and workable without any reference intervention or bibliographic instruction. Catalogs cannot explain themselves, and in the real world I truly think our profession needs to stop acting as though good research can be done in the complete absence of reference or Bibliographic Instruction assistance. Doing research efficiently is much too complicated a skill to be learned "transparently." I fully realize that most "distance education" eliminates the intervention of reference librarians. More's the pity for the dumbed-down research that will inevitably result. If researchers wish to achieve either a good overview of the materials available on their topics, or to zero in on the best material quickly, they simply must have help from the work of *both* catalogers *and* reference librarians. And they especially need help in having the *LCSH* system *taught* to them.

BIBLIOGRAPHY

Cutter, Charles A. *Rules for a Dictionary Catalog*. 4th ed., rewritten. Washington, D. C.: Government Printing Office, 1904.
Mann, Thomas. *The Oxford Guide to Library Research*. New York: Oxford University Press, 1998.
__Library Research Models_. New York: Oxford University Press, 1993.

LCSH Works!
Subject Searching Effectiveness at the Cleveland Public Library and the Growth of *Library of Congress Subject Headings* Through Cooperation

Louisa J. Kreider

SUMMARY. The nature of a library's collections determines what kind of subject access to provide to those collections. The collections of the Cleveland Public Library serve both the recreational and research needs of a large urban population. The Cleveland Public Library uses *Library of Congress Subject Headings* to describe its collections. A study of subject searches entered by library patrons over the course of one week reveals several patterns among the types of subject headings used most frequently, reflecting the characteristics of the population served. Other topics discussed include subject access to fiction, juvenile

Louisa J. Kreider, MLS, is Authority & Quality Control Coordinator, Catalog Deptartment, Cleveland Public Library, 17133 Lake Shore Boulevard, Cleveland, OH 44110 (E-mail: Louisa.Kreider@cpl.org).
The author would like to thank Margaret Shen, Head, Catalog Deptartment, for suggesting this study and assisting in the analysis of the data; Ann Palomo, Automation Deptartment, for generating the reports of search results used for this study; and Hiroko Aikawa, former Authority and Quality Control Coordinator for her pioneering work to establish authority control over the Cleveland Public Library's online catalog.

[Haworth co-indexing entry note]: "*LCSH* Works! Subject Searching Effectiveness at the Cleveland Public Library and the Growth of *Library of Congress Subject Headings* Through Cooperation." Kreider, Louisa J. Co-published simultaneously in *Cataloging & Classification Quarterly* (The Haworth Information Press, an imprint of The Haworth Press, Inc.) Vol. 29, No. 1/2, 2000, pp. 127-134; and: *The LCSH Century: One Hundred Years with the Library of Congress Subject Headings System* (ed: Alva T. Stone) The Haworth Information Press, an imprint of The Haworth Press, Inc., 2000, pp. 127-134. Single or multiple copies of this article are available for a fee from The Haworth Document Delivery Service [1-800-342-9678, 9:00 a.m. - 5:00 p.m. (EST). E-mail address: getinfo@haworthpressinc.com].

literature, and specialized collections. *[Article copies available for a fee from The Haworth Document Delivery Service: 1-800-342-9678. E-mail address: <getinfo@haworthpressinc.com> Website: <http://www.haworthpressinc.com>]*

KEYWORDS. OPACS, public libraries, SACO, subject headings

The choice of subject headings assigned to the bibliographic records in a library's catalog terminates a progression which begins with the population that the library serves. The characteristics of the library's clientele largely determine the scope of the library's collections. In turn, the nature of the collections drives the selection of subject headings for providing thematic access to those collections. Therefore, it follows that different types of libraries, serving patrons whose purposes differ in their use of library materials, generally have divergent requirements for providing subject access to their respective collections. The subject catalog of a public library serving a large urban population is likely to differ in particular ways from that of a large university library, for example.

The Cleveland Public Library is a case in point of how the subject catalog reflects the peculiarities of the collection, which itself is determined by the constituents served. While technically still the school district library for the Cleveland Public Schools, the Cleveland Public Library serves the city of Cleveland, Ohio, whose population numbers approximately 500,000[1] and embraces about 80 different ethnicities.[2,3] In addition to the centrally-located Main Library, CPL has 28 branches to serve the city. CPL is also the anchor of the CLEVNET consortium of 27 libraries in nine counties of northern Ohio, together serving nearly a fifth of the state's population.[4] CPL's general collection is somewhat atypical of a large urban public library system, insofar as it comprises not only materials intended for the general public but also research-level materials, as well as many specialized collections with a narrower focus.

In order to understand how *LCSH* is used by patrons at CPL, a sampling of about 1,250 subject searches was analyzed. The searches chosen for study were those entered on the public terminals in both CPL and the CLEVNET libraries over the course of seven days in September 1999. This analysis, combined with a review of subject headings recently contributed to the *LCSH* via LC's Subject Authority Cooperative program (SACO), yields several conclusions about the nature of subject headings used at CPL and CLEVNET libraries on a frequent basis. Such subject headings tend to fall into one of five categories: (1) subjects of popular interest; (2) subjects relevant to CPL's special collections; (3) subjects of local interest; (4) subjects of works of fiction; and (5) subjects of juvenile works.

Upon examination of the headings for subjects of popular interest, several patterns emerge. Such headings tend to fall within a few broad categories, in particular medicine, business and finance, animals, sports, language, home improvement, cooking, crafts, and collectibles. The largest such category encompasses headings of a medical nature, and most such headings searched are for specific diseases or conditions (**Hemophilia; Panic attacks; Insulin resistance; Asperger's syndrome**), while some center on diet and nutrition (**Reducing diets; Low-carbohydrate diet**). Some of the searches demonstrate a remarkable level of sophistication, evincing an understanding of the nature of such headings and the use of subdivisions, at least among some catalog users (**Endometriosis–Treatment–United States; Dentistry–Aesthetic aspects; Fertilization in vitro, Human**). Relatively few of the searches for medical topics fail to match an established heading or a *see also* reference, and such failures are due mostly to typographical errors rather than an incorrect formulation of the search.

As with the medical-oriented headings, most searches for headings in the area of business and finance correspond to a heading or a *see* reference, and several searches include subdivisions. However, one search including subdivision demonstrates a shortcoming of the subject authority structure in general, at least in the online environment. The search TAXES OHIO results in no hits in the catalog. Had the patron searched TAXES with no subdivision, the reference to *see* **Taxation** would have displayed. Unfortunately, a search including a subdivision along with a term that appears as a *see* reference in the authority record for the parent heading precludes the display of the *see* reference, at least in CPL's catalog. The patron is then led to believe, in this case mistakenly, that the library holds no materials for the topic in question. Indeed the catalog shows 81 titles attached to the subject string **Taxation–Ohio**, with another 27 subject strings beginning with **Taxation–Ohio** and including further subdivision.

Another subset of popular-interest topics includes headings related to current events and trends. A significant number of searches corresponds to headings that have been established only within the last five years. Such headings include **Teletubbies (Fictitious characters); Beanie Babies (Stuffed animals); Pokémon (Game); Endangered ecosystems; HTML (Document markup language); Web sites; Year 2000 date conversion (Computer systems);** and **Cellular telephones**. These types of searches indicate the necessity of establishing headings in a timely manner in order to provide access to new topics as soon as such topics gain currency in published materials, and LC generally completes this charge.

While *LCSH* succeeds in addressing topics of general interest, it is largely lacking in its coverage of specialized topics and local interest. Since earlier editions of *LCSH* reflected only subjects relevant to works in LC's collections, CPL resorted to using overly-broad, imprecise, or sometimes plainly inaccurate headings for items in the library's special collections, in accordance with the library's policy to adhere strictly to *LCSH* for all cataloging. However, the implementation of the SACO program, permitting libraries to contribute headings to *LCSH*, has enabled CPL to construct specific headings for topics not already represented in *LCSH*. By proposing headings for inclusion in *LCSH*, CPL has greatly improved subject access to these collections. Moreover, catalogers are assured that the headings and references they construct are fully in accordance with the guidelines set forth in LC's *Subject Cataloging Manual: Subject Headings*, a benefit which could not be guaranteed by maintaining a local authority file for headings not covered by *LCSH*.

Arguably the most renowned of CPL's special collections, the John G. White Collection of Chess, Folklore, and Orientalia suffers from the lack of relevant subject coverage in *LCSH*. The chess and checkers collection, the largest in the world, is particularly ill-served by *LCSH*. For example, until recently the names of individual chess openings were not established as subject headings. Therefore, the broad heading **Chess–Openings** was assigned not only to works about more than one opening but also to works that discussed one specific opening. As a result of this lack of specificity in the subject terminology, CPL's catalog shows nearly 2,700 titles containing the subject heading **Chess–Openings**. In early 1998, however, LC permitted the establishment of headings for individual openings. At the time of this writing, CPL has established two such headings (**Nimzo-Indian defense (Chess)** and **Spanish opening (Chess)**), as well as six headings for individual gambits, and continues to submit proposals for individual openings and gambits. To date CPL has contributed over 30 headings relating to the games of chess and checkers.

CPL's special collections are not limited to the research materials housed in the John G. White Dept. Many of the subject departments contain substantial collections of circulating materials with a particular focus. One such collection, which sees a great deal of use, is the collection of automobile maintenance manuals in the Science and Technology Dept. Most car manuals in the collection cover only one or two specific models of automobiles. While *LCSH* contains a fair number of headings for individual models of automobiles, many have not yet been established, especially for the most recent models. Before the library began contributing to SACO headings for models not yet established in *LCSH*, CPL had assigned headings for the general class of automobile based on the manufacturer's name, e.g., **Cadillac automobile**. While such a heading was accurate, it was hardly precise. CPL now establishes headings for individual models, allowing much greater specificity in the subject access and consequently eliminating irrelevant titles from subject searches. Patrons seem to be gradually absorbing the change from general to specific, as searches for car manuals recorded during the week of study ranged from AUTOMOBILES MAINTENANCE AND REPAIR to NISSAN and YAMAHA to MERCURY TRACER.

Another unique collection at CPL merits a department unto itself, the Foreign Literature Dept. Heavily used by members of Cleveland's myriad ethnic communities, this department collects and circulates books, periodicals, and audiovisual materials in over 45 languages, covering a full range of subjects, not solely language and literature. Since subject headings, apart from those related to specific languages and literatures, are assigned irrespective of the language of the text, it was not possible to track the desired language in the study of subject searches, for the most part. However, a considerable number of searches were entered for materials on the study of certain languages. Generally such searches were entered using only the name of the desired language, omitting the term, "language," from the search, e.g., FRENCH; GERMAN; SPANISH. In all of these cases, the patron would have to page down many screens before encountering the appropriate heading. In the case of the FRENCH search, **French** is an established heading representing French people; this apparent conflict could easily mislead and confuse the patron. Most of the headings that CPL has proposed for foreign-language materials revolve around a certain genre of literature in a given language (**Nature stories, Ukrainian; Bible stories, Serbo-Croatian**). Occasionally, however, the need also arises for a topical heading not yet covered in English-language publications (**Konotop (Sums'ka oblast', Ukraine), Battle of, 1659**).

The third category of widely-used subject headings at CPL and CLEVNET overlaps to some degree with the special collections category. Subject headings for topics of local interest pertain to materials in not only the general collections but also the Public Administration Library, a department of CPL located in Cleveland City Hall whose clientele includes both the public and city officials, the Photograph Collection within the History Dept., containing photographs of many local structures, and Special Collections, where rare and unique items, often with local flavor, reside. By far the majority of headings needed for topics of local interest are those for structures and for geographic features, such as **University Hall (Cleveland, Ohio); Kossuth Monument (Cleveland, Ohio); Superior Viaduct (Cleveland, Ohio); Allegheny Quarries (Ohio); and Chippewa Lake Park (Chippewa Lake, Ohio)**. Searches for topics of local interest reported in the study attest to the usefulness of both specific headings for local entities and geographic subdivisions for general subjects. Searches of the former type include OHIO AND ERIE CANAL HISTORY; searches of the latter type include MAFIA OHIO CLEVELAND HISTORY, ETHICS OHIO, and EXAMINATIONS OHIO.

Whereas the aforementioned three categories deal with headings for works of nonfiction, as a library serving readers with both research and recreational pursuits, CPL has a strong need for subject headings covering works of fiction. Interestingly, of the subject searches related to fiction entered during the week under scrutiny, only one is a topical heading subdivided by *Fiction*, and that one is for the name of a fictitious character: ROBICHEAUX DAVE FICTITIOUS CHARACTER FICTION. All of the other searches focus on the genre, not the subject. Because of the large collections of fiction, held in both the Literature and the Foreign Literature Depts., CPL contributed to the now-defunct OCLC/LC Fiction Project, wherein participating libraries enriched bibliographic records for works of fiction with both subject and genre headings and proposed subject headings for fictitious characters and places.[5,6] The quantity of genre searches bears out the value of CPL's participation in this project.

One genre search in particular illustrates a weakness in the current array of genre headings in use, viz., the lack of consistency among genre headings. The searches CHRISTIAN FICTION and HISTORICAL FICTION match established genre headings and therefore result in a successful search. The search SPY NOVELS, however, is unsuccessful, as the established genre heading is **Spy stories**. No cross reference to *see* **Spy stories** from *Spy novels* is recorded on the authority record for **Spy stories**, however, because Spy stories is a narrower term under **Fiction** in the *LCSH* hierarchy, and the term *Novels* is recorded as a *see* reference on the authority record for **Fiction**. While efforts are underway to revise genre headings for greater consistency and to create separate authority records for genre headings with a 155 tag,[7] until those efforts are complete, readers will have little help in navigating the catalog, short of knowing the exact genre heading in use, or stumbling upon it. In spite of this drawback, genre headings have proven to be worthwhile and helpful to patrons.

The last category of subject headings in greatest use in CPL's catalog concerns headings for juvenile works. Unfortunately, the local OPAC does not differentiate between subject headings used on bibliographic records for adult works (6xx with second indicator "0") and standard LC Annotated Card (AC) subject headings used on bibliographic records for juvenile works (6xx with second indicator "1"). In order to bring out the distinction, in the local system CPL copy catalogers change the second indicator from "1" to "0" in the 6xx fields and add an appropriate subdivision (**–Juvenile literature;–Juvenile software**). Modified and unique AC subject headings, however, are left unchanged. Subject searches recorded during the week of study indicate that patrons are aware of this pattern and enter searches for juvenile materials accordingly. Some searches, using the term *Juvenile* alone or a truncated form thereof as a subdivision, bring up all types of juvenile materials in that area (SUBSTANCE ABUSE JUVENILE; VEGETABLES JUV);

others specifically target the genre of material desired (BIRDS NESTS JU-VENILE FICTION; ARCHITECTURAL PRACTICE JUVENILE LITERA-TURE).

About eight years ago, the Catalog Dept. carried out a project to link modified and unique AC subject headings to their adult counterparts, when applicable, in the local database. Until 1996, when LC created online authority records for AC headings, CPL used locally-created authority records for the AC headings. CPL has since replaced those local authority records with LC AC authority records from the online subject authority file. The records for **Luck** (an AC subject heading) and **Fortune** (a standard LC subject heading) provide an example of how CPL linked authority records for corresponding juvenile and adult subject headings. In their unmodified forms, the record for **Luck** contains a *see* reference to **Fortune**, while the record for **Fortune** contains a *see* reference back to **Luck**. In order to break this circular *see*-reference pattern, CPL has suppressed the display of the *see* reference in the AC subject authority record and added two 680 fields that display in the OPAC. The first 680 field contains the text JUVENILE SUBJECT HEADING to indicate that bibliographic records containing this heading represent works aimed at a juvenile audience. The second 680 field contains the text FOR ADULT MATERIAL–and displays immediately above the *see* reference recorded on the authority record for **Fortune**. Thus, when a patron enters the search LUCK, the following display results:

Luck

JUVENILE SUBJECT HEADING

FOR ADULT MATERIAL–

Search under **Fortune**

Similarly, in the authority record for **Fortune,** a 680 field is added, containing the text FOR JUVENILE MATERIAL, *see* **Luck**, thereby bringing out and clarifying the see reference that is suppressed on the authority record for **Luck**. The following display results for subject searches using FORTUNE:

Fortune

FOR JUVENILE MATERIAL, See **Luck**

CPL keeps a detailed list of the AC authority records used in this way and updates the list annually. The database is kept current for both AC and standard headings by consulting *Library of Congress Subject Headings Weekly Lists*.

Overall, *LCSH* serves the needs of the Cleveland Public Library well. CPL's ongoing participation in the SACO program fills in the gaps where

LCSH does not adequately represent the library's specialized materials. The historic authoritativeness of *LCSH*, combined with its recent acceptance of headings beyond those in use only at the Library of Congress, ensures that *LCSH* will likely remain the standard for subject cataloging at CPL for the next 100 years and beyond.

NOTES

1. Northern Ohio Data Information Service, *1990 Census of Population & Housing: Profile Report (Summary Tape File 1A), Characteristics of the Population. Area: Cleveland City.* (Cleveland, Ohio: The Urban Center, Maxine Goodman Levin College of Urban Affairs, Cleveland State University, 1990), 4.

2. U.S. Dept. of Commerce, Economics and Statistics Administration, Bureau of the Census, *Population and Housing Characteristics for Census Tracts and Block Numbering Areas: Cleveland-Akron-Lorain, OH CMSA (Part), Cleveland, OH PMSA.* (Washington, D.C.: U.S. Dept. of Commerce, Economics and Statistics Administration, Bureau of the Census, 1993), 304-319.

3. "Cleveland, the New American City," *<http://www.cleveland.oh.us>*.

4. "Cleveland Public Library," *<http://www.cpl.org>*.

5. "OCLC/LC Fiction Project," *<http://lcweb.loc.gov/catdir/pcc/fictioninfo.html>*.

6. Susan Westberg, "OCLC/LC Fiction Project Discontinued September 2, 1999," Message posted to GSAFD listserv (GSAFD@listserv.uta.edu), Sept. 15, 1999.

7. "Authority Data Elements Implementation," *<http://lcweb.loc.gov/catdir/cpso/authimp.html>*.

LCSH for Music:
Historical and Empirical Perspectives

Harriette Hemmasi

J. Bradford Young

SUMMARY. The development of LC music headings is traced by reviewing the contributions and practices of the LC Music Division, the NYPL Music Division, and individual members of the Music Library Association. Cooperative efforts between LC and the Music Library Association are a hallmark of this development. Prospects for continuing and expanding this partnership continue today in the foundation provided by the Music Thesaurus Project. *[Article copies available for a fee from The Haworth Document Delivery Service: 1-800-342-9678. E-mail address: <getinfo@haworthpressinc.com> Website: <http://www.haworthpressinc.com>]*

KEYWORDS. Subject headings, *LCSH*, music libraries, Library of Congress Music Division, Music Thesaurus Project

LCSH FOR MUSIC BEGINS

Subject headings show diversity in language and form, and the manner by which they are interrelated. Music subject catalogs are more varied in these

Harriette Hemmasi, BM, MM, MLIS, is Acting Associate University Librarian for Technical and Automated Services, Technical and Automated Services Building, 47 Davidson Road, Busch Campus, Rutgers University, Piscataway, NJ 08855-1350. J. Bradford Young, BMA, MMA, MLS, is Music Technical Services Librarian, University of Pennsylvania, Van Pelt Library, 3420 Walnut Street, Philadelphia, PA 19104.

[Haworth co-indexing entry note]: "*LCSH* for Music: Historical and Empirical Perspectives." Hemmasi, Harriette and J. Bradford Young. Co-published simultaneously in *Cataloging & Classification Quarterly* (The Haworth Information Press, an imprint of The Haworth Press, Inc.) Vol. 29, No. 1/2, 2000, pp. 135-157; and: *The LCSH Century: One Hundred Years with the Library of Congress Subject Headings System* (ed: Alva T. Stone) The Haworth Information Press, an imprint of The Haworth Press, Inc., 2000, pp. 135-157. Single or multiple copies of this article are available for a fee from The Haworth Document Delivery Service [1-800-342-9678, 9:00 a.m. - 5:00 p.m. (EST). E-mail address: getinfo@haworthpressinc.com].

135

respects than any other.[1] Historically, subject headings for music materials in the United States have come from just a few unified systems. They are the result of leadership from the Library of Congress (LC) and cooperative efforts by music librarians working together through the Music Library Association (MLA) to achieve standardized access to what at first were predominantly research-oriented collections.[2] These efforts date back to 1933 when the MLA, founded in 1931, aware of diversity of practice, and concerned about the lack of a generally accepted system, produced the first of two provisional lists of subject headings based on LC practice. From this point, three lines departed in different directions: the general dictionary catalog of the LC printed cards, the classed catalog of the LC Music Division based on the Library of Congress Classification (LCC) and the specialized dictionary catalog of the New York Public Library (NYPL). They would not converge again for fifty years, in the *LCSH* for music we know today.[3]

Early editions of *Subject Headings Used in the Dictionary Catalogs of the Library of Congress* included headings to be used for books about music but did not include headings for musical compositions. However, access to music requires a vigorous vocabulary to address works of both types. In response to this need, MLA issued a "provisional list" of music headings in 1933 for both books and works of music based on the LC music card catalogs.[4] This list was largely the work of the former chief of the Music Division, Oscar G. T. Sonneck. Sonneck derived the list from the index to his 1902 classification for music and books on music.[5] The headings were in effect alphabetico-classed headings, a compromise between classification and subject headings in the strict sense of the word. While they were much appreciated by music librarians, the headings did not comfortably fit into the LC dictionary catalogs.

Chamber music. Quartets Violins (2), viola & violoncello.
Arrangements for clarinet. Solos.
National Music. Armenia.

illustrate the alphabetico-classed character of the provisional list.

MLA continued efforts to establish a generally accepted list that would serve as the basis for cooperation with other LC dictionary catalogs. While the LC general list of headings for books was recognized as the most complete, MLA found these headings to be inadequate and unsatisfactory in arrangement. MLA preferred avoiding **Music** with a long line of subdivisions; instead they chose to use the subdivisions as main headings. After considerable review of the 1933 provisional list, MLA issued its first separate list of subject headings for the literature of music in 1935. This list was based on 3rd *LCSH* 1928[6] and contained 424 headings and 236 references; 36 of the headings had subdivisions. The compiler reported that "We may have added to your mirth by including the heading **Semimelodeon**. It sounds musical, but what it is we don't know. There must be a book about it in the Library of Congress !"[7]

While the MLA list served a very practical use outside LC, practices began to change in the LC Music Division that would have impact on the *LCSH* for music. In 1943 the LC Music Division changed the subject portion of its divided catalog into a classed catalog based on the LCC M schedule. From this time until the closing of the card catalogs in 1981, the music headings listed in *LCSH* represented terms authorized for use on LC printed cards, but not terms used at the institution devising them. This may be a principal reason for the many long-unresolved problems which existed in the *LCSH* for music. When the LC subject catalog for music was converted to a classed catalog, the entries were re-filed by class number without any change being made on the cards. The organization of the M classification schedule is, in general, based on medium of performance. This meant that the first approach in the classed catalog was by medium. For each musical work processed, a card was filed under the class number. The numbers in the classification schedule were also used as reference numbers, serving as an access point to the alternative medium of performance. A work for violin or flute and piano was classified in M219 (violin and piano) with the reference number M242 (flute and piano). But a further approach by musical form, not provided by the classification schedule, was also needed. To solve this problem, the Subject Cataloging Division developed a scheme of reference numbers, "imaginary numbers" in that they were not used for shelving material. As a part of the scheme, a pattern of decimal numbers was set up. These numbers were added to class numbers as reference numbers wherever such subdivisions were not included in the schedule:

1. Sonatas
2. Suites
3. Variations
4. Fugues
5. Marches, etc., etc.

Beethoven's Fugue, op. 137 was classified in M552 because the medium of performance is 2 violins, 2 violas, and violoncello. A card was filed in the classed catalog under M552.4, providing the necessary approach to the work as a fugue, as well as the medium of performance.[8]

The Descriptive Cataloging Division continued to expand the list of reference numbers as needed. M1105 was a case in point. Separate numbers for solo instruments with string orchestra were not provided in the M schedule as they were for solo instruments with full orchestra in M1005-M1041. These compositions continued to be classified in M1105, but they were also as-

signed appropriate reference numbers in M1108-M11419. Reference numbers had been established in the M5000's when they could not be fitted
logically into the printed schedule. M5700, for example, represents funeral
music.[9] LC headings were used as index entries only when they provided the
most direct approach to the material, such as **Folk-music, Swedish** or **Violin
and piano music**. Cross references were not used. They were replaced by
index entries in uninverted form (Swedish folk-music) or in reverse form
(Piano and violin music).[10] The classed catalog analyzed the music collections by medium of performance, subject, and musical form. This analysis
paralleled that provided in *LCSH* and replicated the manner in which LC
provided subject access to its music collections.

Through time, other large music libraries adapted the classed catalog for
music by converting their shelflists into a partially classed catalog while
retaining *LCSH* in the dictionary catalog. This practice addressed a problem
encountered daily in music libraries: the request for the literature of a particular medium of performance, such as violin and piano. It was and continues to
be difficult to respond to this frequent request in any music library that uses
LCSH. The problem, as viewed by the MLA committee, was that in LC
subject headings "form, an element of secondary importance, is given prece-
dence over medium of performance, thereby denying direct access to the
library's collection by medium."[11] Under **Violin and piano music**, rather
than all the library's holdings for that combination, is found a long list of
"see also" references of the pattern <form of composition> (Violin and
piano), such as **Sonatas (Violin and piano), Suites (Violin and piano)**, etc.

Knowing from experience the shortcomings of *LCSH*, a librarian would
go to the section of the shelflist where most, though not all, of the library's
violin and piano music was listed: M217-M223.[12] This use of the shelflist for
improved access by musical medium was built on the fact that what *LCSH*
scattered, the M schedule frequently brought together. A series of guide cards
were inserted in the catalog, directing readers to appropriate sections of the
shelflist for particular musical media. A violinist looking for violin and piano
music would find in the main catalogs only a single guide reading: *Violin and
piano music see M217-M223 in the shelflist*. In order for this approach to
work in terms of providing complete medium coverage, the shelflist had to be
supplemented with "dummy" cards for music not classed according to medium. For example, a work for violin and piano may be classed in M2 as a
member of a series. In such an instance, a dummy shelflist card would be
made for the work, to be filed in the violin and piano section of the shelflist,
M217-M223. At the Cornell University Music Library when use of the shelflist as a partially classed catalog was first implemented, it was found that
93% of the entries under the subject **Symphonies–Scores** were classed in
M1001. That meant that 721 subject cards could be eliminated since they

were, in effect, duplicating the work of the shelflist. The remaining 7%, or 57 cards, not classed in M1001 were re-filed in the shelflist as dummy cards.[13]

The idea of using the shelflist as a partially classed catalog was derived to some extent from the LC practice of a classed catalog based on the M schedule. While LC maintained a complete classed catalog separate from its shelflist, use of the shelflist as a partially classed catalog involved using portions of the shelflist while continuing to use *LCSH* for the control of certain topics. The important difference between using the shelflist as a partially classed catalog and the LC system was that LC relied entirely on a classed catalog for subject control of its music collection, without the use of *LCSH*. There were a number of instances in which the *LCSH*, usually because of their more specific formulation, provided a superior means of access. An outstanding example was the detailed access given by *LCSH* to specific chamber music combinations. The M schedule tended to and still does lump materials together by broad categories. Music for four recorders may be easily surveyed under **Woodwind quartets (Recorders (4))**. In the shelflist at M457.2, the number for woodwind quartets, recorder quartets are a minority combination mixed in with many other works for four woodwinds.[14] A complete classed catalog becomes so complex, so filled with non-shelving numbers, that it can no longer serve as a shelflist but must be maintained separately.

After the publication of 4th *LCSH* 1943, music headings–especially those for work of music–underwent a great expansion. Form headings for music were first included in *Subject Headings Used in the Dictionary Catalogs of the Library of Congress* with 5th *LCSH* 1948.[15] Their inclusion was not exhaustive, but an effort was made to give the main headings and to include the references and subdivisions under a representative selection of them as guides. Subjects chosen for full treatment were: **Music; Orchestral music; Piano music; Operas**. The name of Richard Wagner was also included in order to show by example the subdivisions, which may be used under names of composers.[16]

LCSH FOR MUSIC MATURES

A milestone in *LCSH* for music was *Music Subject Headings Used on Printed Catalog Cards of the Library of Congress*.[17] This first comprehensive list of form headings for music based on LC practice was developed in response to the expressed need of the MLA for a list that was more appropriate for use in a dictionary catalog than its own provisional lists of the 1930s. MLA's preliminary list in 1933 was never found to be totally acceptable because the alphabetico-classed headings did not fit into a dictionary catalog. Neither was the second list in 1935 adequate because it was limited to books on music. Recognizing these problems, MLA appointed a committee for the compilation of a more satisfactory, combined list. Because LC had already begun the preparation of such a list, as it turned out not for use in its own catalog, but for libraries maintaining dictionary catalogs, MLA waited for the LC results. LC's new list was not a revision of the two provisional lists published by the MLA, but it included all valid headings found in the 1935 list as well as all newly devised subject form headings. Due to the considerable acceleration in subject cataloging of music, many new headings for both books about music and works of music were added.[18]

The merger in 1952 of the earlier MLA lists with the music subject headings used by LC on printed cards formed the basis of our current practice. David J. Haykin's introduction to this volume of *LCSH* remains the most cogent statement of its fundamental principles.[19] Even though these principles were not dependent upon LC practice, the headings were chosen from the first integrated system of music subject headings LC had prepared. The distinction Haykin points out, "used on printed catalog cards" rather than "used in the dictionary catalogs," was significant. As stated earlier, over the next forty years these *LCSH* for music, although used in the catalogs of most other American libraries, would not be used at LC.

Although the headings were designed for either a general dictionary or a subject catalog, it was realized from the beginning that some headings required modification if used in a catalog exclusively for music. The major group was those beginning with "music" and "musical." Instead of **Musical pitch, Pitch** would be adequate. The qualification **Musical** was omitted where it appeared inverted. **Paleography** would displace **Paleography, Musical**. Omission was not practiced if it would lead to ambiguity such as the reference under "Musical glasses," or in the heading **Musical temperament**.[20] The qualification **(Music)** following the same term used in several senses in a general catalog could be omitted in a music catalog. Among such are the heading **Composition (Music)** and the reference at "Transcription (Music)." Subdivisions under the heading **Music** could be used as main headings. Their application to music is obvious as in the case of **Bibliography, Biography**, and **Thematic catalogs**.[21] Inverted adjectival phrases used in a general catalog brought music headings together. The inverted qualifying term might be a descriptive, ethnic or geographical adjective such as **Music, Incidental; Music, Jewish; Music, Oriental; or Music, Popular (Songs, etc.)**. In a music catalog such headings would be direct: **Incidental music; Jewish music;** and **Popular music (Songs, etc.)**. Where music was juxtaposed with another concept in phrase headings, the two concepts were reversed such as **Literature and music** rather than **Music and literature, War and music** rather than **Music and war**.[22] The reference structure had to be adjusted to such changes in adapting the headings for use in a music catalog.

In most instances, a "see" reference from the heading given in the list to the adapted heading would be needed. The additions that appeared regularly in the cumulative supplements to *LCSH* would also need to be adapted to the local catalog. Given the difficulties involved in adapting the headings and references it was usually found preferable to use the headings as they stood.[23] The rapidly growing availability of LC printed cards for printed music and later for sound recordings was a further administrative factor contributing to widespread use of *LCSH* for music in most American libraries.

If the printed headings themselves were not adapted, the filing often was. In a general catalog, unless the music collection was very small, the subject headings could be filed unaltered. In a separate music catalog, since the entire catalog pertained to music, it was not necessary to have a large block under **Music**, especially where it was followed by a subdivision, or under headings beginning with the word **Musical**. Common procedure was to drop **Music**, or **Musical**, and file directly under **History and criticism, Instruction and study**, and similar subdivisions, or in the case of such headings as **Musical fiction** under **Fiction**.[24] Inverted headings were filed under the direct form except where this would impair meaning. **Music, French** was under **French music**, although **Music as a profession** would file in its original form.[25] Where applicable, complete cross references were needed from the original heading as it appeared in the list of subject headings to the filing heading as it appeared in the catalog. Cross-references were rarely made, however.

Because of the size of the LC music collection, it had always been necessary to divide music subject headings very minutely. Therefore other adjustments were advisable for a small music collection. In many cases only the first part of the heading needed to be used. If it made little difference whether the available music for piano was original or arranged, all material was filed under **Piano music** and the remaining, **Arranged**, was omitted. If the library's holdings of choral music for men's voices was insufficient to warrant the separation into specific number of parts, the heading **Choruses, Secular (Men's voices, 4 pts.) with piano** could become **Choruses, Secular (Men's voices) with piano**, or even **Choruses (Men's voices)** which combined sacred and secular choruses for any number of men's voices both accompanied and unaccompanied.[26] A smaller or specialized library was able to build on the basic work done by LC and adapt the headings to the particular need.

Another innovation of the 1950s was caused by the widespread introduction of sound recordings into music libraries. LC commissioned a study of the applicability of its subject headings on printed cards for sound recordings.[27] Apparently by 1953 this study had indicated that existing headings would be appropriate with a few minor modifications. The major decision was whether to develop a form subdivision for "Phonorecords." Without this subdivision many headings would have been used for the first time without a format subdivision such as **Scores and parts**. It was decided not to develop such a form subdivision. The unsubdivided headings for recordings could have co-existed in front of the subdivided headings for printed music. This was considered undesirable and was one factor in the creation of separate sound recording catalogs in many libraries. They were designed to prevent the intermingling of subject cards for scores and recordings.[28]

Many of the headings in *LCSH* were influenced by the subject headings used by the NYPL Music Division. A list of these NYPL headings was published in 1959.[29] These two lists were produced for use by the nation's two largest and most complex research music collections and thus were similar in many ways. However, they also had several basic differences. One major difference was that the Library of Congress list chose form of composition modified by medium of performance as its primary access point, whereas the New York Public list chose medium of performance as its primary access point. A more subtle difference was that of audience. *LCSH* was intended for use in a general dictionary catalog while the NYPL list was intended for use in a catalog of music only. Often differing forms in headings resulted. Many headings beginning with **Music** and **Musical** in *LCSH* were entered directly under the secondary term in the NYPL list. The NYPL list, more appropriate for research collections in many ways, was dropped in 1978 when NYPL automated its cataloging operations. At that time, NYPL adopted LC standards for all aspects of its cataloging.

Much can be learned about *LCSH* by its comparison to and contrast with the NYPL list. The path not chosen for the one is more clearly seen in the other, sometimes revealing a rut unwittingly dug. Wilma Reid Cipolla investigated fundamental subject heading theory as exemplified in the practice of these two largest American music libraries.[30] Because both lists were based on Cutter's principles, she compared their practices from the point of view of these basic principles. Significant differences in terminology and form were identified. She concluded that NYPL's variation from *LCSH* subdivision and inversion resulted in more specific and direct subject entry. The principle of user convenience points back to the basic contrast in orientation: the NYPL list was intended for use only within the music catalog. Since *LCSH* had a dual purpose for general dictionary catalogs as well as music catalogs, it compromised some distinctly musical features. In the principle of common usage, Cipolla identified differences in the use of technical rather than popular terms, and foreign-language as opposed to English language terms. Since the layman was familiar with theoretical terms such as **Counterpoint, Modulation**, and **Transposition**, and many foreign words, such as **Cantata, Concerto**, and Sonata, such terminology appeared in both. The NYPL list also included a far greater number of more highly specialized terms such as **Conductus, Fauxbourdons**, and **Hocket**.[31]

The principle of specific entry was a major concern for Cipolla as she compared the NYPL and LC lists. Cutter had emphasized that specific entry was the difference between the dictionary catalog and the alphabetico-classed catalog. *LCSH* was intended for a dictionary catalog, but appeared to have been a compromise because of its heavy use of subdivided and inverted headings, as well as compound forms. The resemblance of LC headings to an informal faceted classification scheme owed its existence to Sonneck's provisional list of 1933 based on his LCC M schedule of 1902. Cipolla recognized how this flexible but inconsistent application of faceting, with its subarrangement of the broad term by means of punctuation marks, the dash and the comma, treated equivalent facets in different ways. Specifically, she found nothing inherent in the structure of language to require the arbitrary differentiation between the geographic subdivision, **Music–France**, and the linguistic or ethnic adjective, **Music, French**.[32]

General principles for choice and the form of terms are equally applicable to the special library. Being limited to a single subject makes certain deviations from these principles desirable. Haykin identified five common points which can best be demonstrated by contrasting examples of NYPL and

LCSH:[33]

1. Omission of the initial noun designating the subject: e.g., **Bibliography**, not **Music–Bibliography** and **Printing**, not **Music printing**.
2. Omission of subject qualifiers: e.g., Impressionism, not **Impressionism (Music)**.
3. Direct, rather than inverted, order: e.g., Popular music, not **Music, Popular**.
4. Reversal of terms in compound headings: e.g., **Literature and music**, not **Music and literature**.
5. Use of geographic subdivisions as main headings; e.g., **United States**, not **Music–United States**.

Due to NYPL's use of geographic places as main headings, it was possible to apply chronological subdivisions, which varied from one heading to another. This allowed a comprehensive term such as **History and criticism** to be subdivided according to the commonly accepted historical periods, rather than the less specialized designation by century, as employed by *LCSH*.[34] Lastly, the most obvious difference between NYPL and *LCSH* was in their use of form subdivisions. *LCSH* identified over a hundred subdivisions. Some are true form subdivisions, a particular literary form or form of publication; most were really aspects of the main heading. Because NYPL virtually eliminated the initial subject word **Music** from its catalog, form subdivisions were also virtually eliminated. Instead, the various aspects of the subject assumed entry word position in direct order.[35]

LCSH FOR MUSIC CONTINUES

Further developments in *LCSH* for music consisted primarily of extending existing LC headings or the rules for their application into the uncharted waters beyond Western classical music. MLA had a strong hand in these developments. In 1971 Sanford Berman, Head of the Hennepin County, Minnesota Library Catalog Department, issued a ringing complaint that *LCSH* terminology was obsolete and prejudicial.[36] The headings for popular music were his primary concerns. Among the responses to his prose poem "Cataloging philosophy"[37] was a letter from Ruth Henderson, at that time editor of *Music Cataloging Bulletin*, published monthly by MLA. (One of the purposes of the *Music Cataloging Bulletin* was to communicate to LC when its cataloging for music was failing to meet the needs of library patrons, and Henderson did just that.) Because of this communication, the headings **Bluegrass music, Country music, Ragtime music, Rock music,** and cross-references for **Gospel music** and **Soul music** were established. Broader issues were also taken up by MLA for consideration and appropriate action. Henderson stated that, "Music catalogers do have a voice in determining the cataloging acceptable to their own libraries and accepted by most libraries in this country. It is their responsibility to use it."[38] Clearly this was and continues to be the MLA cataloging philosophy regarding *LCSH*.

Based on further recommendations by MLA, major changes were also made in the application of subject headings to the music of ethnic and national groups.[39] The problem of subject access to recordings of non-Western music had long been a major concern of music librarians. In a field where there were few written transcriptions and even fewer opportunities to hear the music performed live, recordings were the most important resource. Yet it was much more difficult to identify recordings of non-Western music than to find recordings of Western art music. Titles of works and names of composers and performers were usually unknown. Many music libraries did not place their recordings on open shelves for browsing. Subject headings were the only means of access to non-Western music. Since *LCSH* was the most commonly used subject headings in academic libraries, a compilation of all of the headings that LC had used for recordings of non-Western music in the years 1973 through 1976 was arranged by country, culture, tribe, instruments, language, etc. The resultant lists clearly indicated some problems with *LCSH* practices.

The one overriding problem which emerged was that for each culture there were and still are many different types of *LCSH* which serve to scatter the music of that culture. Even where there are adequate cross-references, it is necessary to search in far too many places for the music of a particular culture. Japanese music is used below to demonstrate the variety of headings, which must be consulted to find the music of just one culture.

1. Term followed by inverted cultural modifier: **Buddhist hymns, Japanese; Children's songs, Japanese; Dance music, Japanese;** etc.
2. Term followed by cultural modifier in parentheses: **Chants (Buddhist)**
3. Term preceded by cultural modifier: **Buddhist hymns**
4. Genre without cultural modifier: **Bagaku; Gagaku; Jruri; Kouta; Shigin**
5. Names of instruments, singly or combined, followed by music: **Koto music; Shakuhachi and biwa music; Shakuhachi and koto music; Shamisen music**
6. Term or names of instruments followed by accompaniment: **Koto with orchestra; Monologues with music (Shamisen); Songs with koto**
7. Ensemble or form followed by instrumentation in parentheses: **Concertos (Koto); Quartets (Shakuhachi, kotos (2), shamtsen); Trios (Shakuhachi, koto, shamisen)**
8. Non-musical heading followed by musical subdivision: **Kabuki plays–Incidental music; Noh plays–Incidental music.**[40]

It was apparent that there was no simple solution to the subject access problems relating to non-Western music. The two most popular methods used for subject access were *LCSH*, which provided access by instruments, genres, cultures, countries, etc., but scattered culturally-related terms, and the *Outline of World Cultures*,[41] which brought together culturally-related music but did not provide any other type of access. A list in the *Outline* of the *LCSH* appropriate to each culture was recommended as a temporary solution for combining the advantages of both systems.[42] MLA appointed a committee, working closely with LC and with ethnomusicologists, to propose a nationally uniform, permanent solution for the cataloging of non-Western music which would bring together the music of each culture, relate music of similar cultures and allow for retrieval by a variety of facets. In 1981 LC announced sweeping changes in *LCSH* policy for subject treatment of ethnic and national music which in essence implemented most of the recommendations made by the 1977 MLA report.[43]

In addition to non-Western music, there was a growing increase in Western *non*-classical recordings in libraries and archives calling attention to the limitations of *LCSH* for this music. Most public libraries had large collections of popular music. Courses in jazz and rock music had become a normal part of academic music curricula. As a step toward improving subject access in this area, a report was undertaken by MLA to study the subject headings and their application.[44]

The study results indicated that access by provenance is important for most music, especially folk music. Of the three aspects of provenance–place, ethnic or national group, and language–*LCSH* had a large number of Western non-classical music subject headings for places but only a small number for ethnic or national groups and languages. One of the changes LC adopted in 1981 was the policy of always assigning to ethnic and national music, when possible, a heading for musical genre or style with local subdivision. Unfortunately, the many different headings for musical genre or style available for the music of each place resulted in dispersed access to the music of that place. Similar to the earlier example of Japanese music, music from Germany was expressed by many different subject headings, for example: **Bluegrass music–Germany; Blues (Songs, etc.)–Germany; Children's songs–Germany; Country music–Germany;** and many others.[45]

Until 1977, only a small number of qualifiers used in inverted subject headings referred to ethnic groups:, **Cajun;, Creole;, French-Canadian, Gypsy;, Pennsylvania German**. In 1977, LC established several new headings under a policy of preferring "the uninverted form . . . , when establishing new headings for ethnic groups of the United States. . . . "[46] These were: **Afro-American music; Afro-American songs; Hispanic American folk-music; Hispanic American folk-songs; Mexican American ballads; Polish-American music; Romanian American ballads; Ukrainian-American music**. While giving limited access to music by ethnic or national group, this policy served to further scatter non-classical music. In 1981, LC canceled all of the above headings and adopted a new policy of always assigning, when possible, headings of the type [ethnic or national group]–[local subdivision, if appropriate]–Music, e.g.: **Germans–Hungary–Music; Afro-Americans-Louisiana-Music;** and French-Canadians-Music. Headings of this category are not assigned to individual nationalities within their own country.[47]

Before 1981 the qualifier following **Ballads, Folk-songs** or **Songs** referred to place, not to language. **Folk-songs, Portuguese** did not apply to Brazilian folk-songs in the Portuguese language. **Ballads, American–North Carolina** was used for English language ballads originating in North Carolina. This policy prevented retrieval of non-classical music by language. From 1981 on, the qualifier following **Ballads, Folk-songs** or **Songs** referred instead to language. All qualifiers in this category that did not correspond to a language were canceled and headings with language qualifiers were established as needed. As a result of the new policy **Folk-songs, Scottish-North Carolina** and **Ballads, Scottish–North Carolina** became: **Folk-songs, English–North Carolina; Ballads, English–North Carolina; Scottish Americans–North Carolina–Music**; and, **Folk music–North Carolina**.[48]

LCSH provided access to medium of performance for Jazz, country, folk and national music through application of various types of headings: **Banjo** music; Fiddle tunes; Guitar music (Blues); Banjo and guitar music; Appalachian dulcimer music (Appalachian dulcimers (2)); Saxophone with Jazz ensemble; Songs with banjo; Songs with Jazz ensemble; Concertos (Jazz quintet with string orchestra).[49] However, these subject headings were only applied when the recording consisted exclusively of solo, duet, or concerto-like performances, rather than as part of a group. Despite the prominence of the dulcimer, searching **Dulcimer music** did not retrieve the album Pacific Rim Dulcimer Project, for which only the headings **Music, Popular (Songs, etc.)–United States** and **Folk music–United States** were applied.[50] These problems resulted from LC's having borrowed from the headings for Western classical music, where the distinction between unaccompanied solos, duets, trios, etc., is the norm. In Western non-classical music this distinction is less important. The most sought performances are buried within large ensemble recordings, especially in Jazz performances.[51] *LCSH* for medium of performance in Western classical music did not transfer successfully to Western non-classical music and the need for access to jazz, folk, country and national music by medium of performance was not being filled because *LCSH* failed to index the aspects appropriate to non-classical music as well as it did classical music.

The MLA study indicated that genre was a highly desired access point for Jazz, blues, folk, rock and other popular music. Although *LCSH* did provide some genre subject headings for this music, there were problems which severely limited their effectiveness. The most frequently applied genre subject headings had huge files that were not further subdivided in any way. The subject headings beginning with the word **Jazz** did not further delineate style in any way, nor did **Rock music** and **Music, Popular (Songs, etc.)**, which also had unwieldy files. As well as establishing headings for the well identified sub-genres of Jazz and popular music, there was a need to subdivide these genres by decade of performance.[52] Many Jazz subject headings provide inadequate access to genre because the genre term does not appear as an entry word. The few *LCSH* for Jazz and blues which did have a genre as entry word, such as **Big band music, Dixieland music** or **Ragtime music,** were only applied if one of the medium of performance subject headings was not applicable. The genre term most often appeared as a qualifier such as **Piano music (Boogie Woogie)**. A recording of solo ragtime guitar playing was not given a subject heading with the entry word "ragtime" but rather, **Guitar music (Ragtime)**,[53] thus reducing the already limited access by genre. In 1985, following consultation with MLA, review of its 1983 report and the distribution of questionnaires, extensive changes were made to *LCSH* for Jazz and popular music.[54]

It is important to realize that *LCSH* was developed by musicologists working in a tradition of Western art music as it was understood at the dawn of the twentieth century. As musical practice expanded, demand for more flexible indexing methods and less xenophobic terminology increased. In recent times more sweeping changes have been proposed. Many of these changes, long demanded by music librarians but rejected by LC in earlier times, are now made possible because LC began using *LCSH* in its online catalog in 1981.[55] As with other disciplines, the subject headings for music were created as they were needed by the catalogers. Revised lists with additions and changes were compiled from time to time. They were never developed as a comprehensive or internally consistent system such as would be found in a thesaurus constructed according to modern principles of vocabulary control. In fact, the LCC M schedule, first devised by O. G. T. Sonneck in 1902, effectively provided a more rigidly structured form of access that was central to the operation of the Music Division in the period during which the headings for music were first created. The M schedule with its index provided a more hierarchically syndetic control than did *LCSH*. These two core tools cannot be fully understood in isolation.

The inclusion of music and sound recordings in the LC printed card program had led to widespread use of *LCSH* for music in other American libraries. The emergence of OCLC and other bibliographic utilities and the rapid growth in the use of shared cataloging have heightened interest in consistency and cooperation in the use of *LCSH* for music. Previously an exceptional degree of local practice was found in most large music collections. Development and use of the MARC format for subject authority records led to widespread display of cross-references for subject headings, which were rarely provided comprehensively in card catalogs for music, and to the use of automated techniques to support verification of subject headings used in online public access catalogs. Distinctive features of the headings for music caused these systems to function less well for music than for some other subjects. These problems can be attributed to an emphasis on form rather than topical access, the frequent need to construct specific headings beyond those found in the subject authority file, and, above all, the multi-faceted character of *LCSH* for music. Inherent inconsistencies in the form and structure of headings and most especially in the hierarchies of narrower, broader, and related term cross-references became more apparent when viewed online.[56]

By 1992 the Subject Authority Cooperative Program for *LCSH* proposals by catalogers from outside LC had been established.[57] A compilation, revision, and index of various LC subject cataloging memoranda had made available for the first time important information about the creation and use of *LCSH*.[58] There has been a growing interest in form and genre access, as distinct from topical access, to various library materials including art, literature, folklore, and legal, religious, philosophical texts, as well as music. The validation of field tags and a subfield code for form data in MARC biblio-graphic and authority records has brought some of the distinctive concerns of music subject cataloging further into the mainstream of bibliographic con-trol.[59] Increasingly, the library community is turning to contemporary con-cepts of faceted access and hierarchical thesaurus construction as models for reforming and enhancing the subject cataloging tradition established in the last century. Serious consideration of alternatives to *LCSH* in MARC records for indexing of music and musical sound recordings took place within LC. This is an indication of a profound rethinking among American librarians of subject access techniques following the 1991 Airlie House conference.[60] The subsequent decision to retain *LCSH* for music confirms LC's continuing commitment to its development and its increasing international use. Begin-ning in 1984 MLA has investigated the potential of conducting a music thesaurus project, the early goal of which was considered to be the develop-ment of an indexing protocol. [61] This commitment to continued development of music subject headings is also reflected in the work being carried out at Rutgers University towards the establishment of a Music Thesaurus Project along the lines of the *Art and Architecture Thesaurus (AAT)*.[62] Both the AAT and the Music Thesaurus Project support better development and use of *LCSH*. The Music Thesaurus Project constitutes a modern vocabulary track-ing tool that comprehensively incorporates *LCSH* terms among those from other sources. The development of *LCSH* for music has been shaped by such unique factors as the classed catalog of the LC Music Division, the influence of the NYPL specialist catalog, and above all the continuous involvement of the MLA. Indeed, cooperation has distinguished its entire history and appears poised to continue to do so in the future.

EMPIRICAL OBSERVATIONS ON *LCSH* FOR MUSIC

In response to a call for volunteers at an MLA meeting in the early 1990s, Hemmasi began work with Anderson and Rowley at Rutgers University to create a prototype music thesaurus based on LC music headings. This prelim-inary work was designed as a tool by which LC music headings and their relationships could be displayed, analyzed, and evaluated. While preserving the original structure of the music headings, the thesaurus provided new ways of searching and viewing the LC music subject headings, individual terms within those headings, and heading/term relationships. In the new thesaurus format, the subject headings could be viewed and searched in three standard projections–in an alphabetical index, in separate thesaurus records, and in a hierarchical tree display. This new format has revealed the incomplete and inconsistent syndetic structure of LC music headings and has provided access to their domain-specific vocabulary in ways that the printed and online versions of *LCSH* are not able to do.[63]

The prototype thesaurus was based on LC music headings contained in the 1988 edition of *Music Subject Headings Compiled from the Library of Congress Subject Headings*, to which were added updated headings through September 1991.[64] The data set resulted in about 12,000 entries, including preferred, non-preferred (i.e., use for), broader, narrower, and related term headings. Roughly two-thirds of the entries were preferred headings and one-third non-preferred, broader, narrower and related terms. In total, 3,200 unique words were identified within the headings.

Of the approximately 8,000 preferred headings, more than two thousand were top terms, meaning that they were not part of a larger syndetic framework; they had no broader term. Some of these were single-concept headings, such as: **Artists, Canticles, Doxology, Lute, Libretto,** or **Sonatas**. More frequently, multi-faceted headings were found in the top term list, such as: **Dance music–Africa, West; Folk-songs, Russian; Guitar and concerto music; Horns (3), violin with chamber orchestra; Islamic hymns; Music–20th century; Sacred songs (Low voice with continuo); Singers in literature.**

Because of the multi-faceted nature of these headings, it is difficult, even impossible to satisfactorily place the headings within a single syndetic structure. Understandably, LC has not attempted to provide broader terms for these headings. However, LC has offered changes to some of the multi-faceted music headings, such as:

HEADING	BROADER TERM 1988	BROADER TERM 1998
Afro-American composers	none	**Composers–United States**
Political ballads and songs	none	**Ballads**
		National songs
		Political poetry
		Songs

Likewise, LC has systematically improved the syndetic structure of certain categories of music subject headings since the early 1990's. Among these categories are headings for musical instruments, musicians, and topical headings relating to musical form. Examples of these improvements are:

HEADING 1998	BROADER TERM 1998	BROADER TERM 1998
Brass instruments	none	**Wind instruments**
Cantatas, Secular	none	**Vocal music**
Gong	none	**Percussion instruments**
Libretto	none	**Dramatic music**

Percussionists	none	**Instrumentalists**
Popular music	none	**Music**

Despite these efforts, the fact remains that the majority of LC music headings are multi-faceted strings set within a framework plagued by omissions of key concepts and links, and as long as they remain such, a comprehensive and meaningful syndetic structure is not possible.

One of the results of Hemmasi's early work was to identify single-concept terms contained in the LC music headings and to begin categorizing that vocabulary into broad, primary facets representing the discipline of music. A set of general categories or tentative facets were selected (agents, events, forms/genres, geo-cultural attributes, sound devices, texts; other topics) and were used as temporary groupings for the rich vocabulary contained in the LC music headings. The process of isolating and reorganizing core vocabulary from the headings for use in the music thesaurus proved to be quite challenging as the "real" meaning of a term was sought. When considered within the broader context of the discipline of music, some headings clearly have meanings or uses beyond those provided in *LCSH*. For example, does **Sonatas** belong to vocal or instrumental forms/genres, or both; is **Agnus dei (Music)** a form/genre, a text, part of the liturgy, or all three; does another entry for "ballades (instrumental)" need to be made to represent the 19th century piano piece, whereas *LCSH* only contains **Ballades (Polyphonic chanson)**? As the pursuit continued, questions mounted. Their resolution will require extensive research and ultimately a review by music scholars before any publication of the thesaurus project can be attempted.[65]

Because of its widespread usage, *LCSH* cannot and should not be tossed aside to make room for new developments. As early as 1981 Cochrane encouraged the development of subject specific thesauri to act as supplements to *LCSH*.[66] The Music Thesaurus Project promises to be this type of supplement. To this end, the music thesaurus maintains verbal and conceptual ties with LC music headings and has as its fundamental goals to develop:

1. a standard vocabulary for the discipline of music
2. a hierarchical arrangement of that vocabulary
3. a faceted terminology
4. a rich lead-in vocabulary
5. a complete syndetic structure[67]

Recognizing the need to continue tracing the LC music headings even as efforts to create a separate music thesaurus were underway, in 1994 Hemmasi and Rowley began a project that used the core music vocabulary found in the original set of headings to search against the whole of *LCSH* as represented in CDMARC Subjects, 1992, issue 1. The truncated keyword searches retrieved more than 50,000 headings that matched the core vocabulary. While this wide-cast net brought in many non-relevant headings, it also uncovered thousands of headings that are pertinent to music that might have otherwise been missed. Subsequent searches through the *LCSH* hierarchies associated with the retrieved headings produced hundreds of other germane headings. A critical part of the project was the determination of which headings should be included in the updated collection. In total the project, including manually entered heading updates through December 1997, rendered a new data set of about 15,000 entries. Results were published by Soldier Creek in 1998 as the second edition of *Music Subject Headings*.[68]

This data set contains approximately the same ratio as the 1991 data of two-thirds preferred headings to one-third non-preferred. Of the 10,500 preferred headings, more than 8,500 are form/genre headings. Due to the predominance of form/genre headings among all music headings and their relative familiarity, MLA appointed a Form/Genre Vocabulary Working Group to provide assistance to the Music Thesaurus Project. To further the work of this group, Hemmasi identified form/genre headings contained in the 1998 publication and analyzed them according to content and syntactical pattern. Analysis reveals the following patterns.

1. FORM/GENRE w/o MEDIUM OF
PERFORMANCE
a. <forms/genres>
Anthems
Fandangos
b. <forms/genres> (<qualified>)
Ballades (Instrumental music)
c. <forms/genres>, <geo-cultural
qualifier>
f. < > (Music)
Blues (Music)
Agnus dei (Music)
g. <style, forms/genres> music
Belly dance music
Computer music
h. <forms/genres> with music
Monologues with music

2. FORM/GENRE WITH MEDIUM
OF PERFORMANCE
a. <forms/genres> (<instrument/ensemble>)

Ballads, Irish
d. <forms/genres>, <inverted heading>
Solo cantatas, Sacred
e. <forms/genres>, <forms/genres>,
<forms/genres>, etc
Glees, catches, rounds, etc.

i.<forms/genres> with music, <inverted>
Pantomimes with music, Sacred
j. Music for <topic>
Music for meditation
k. <forms/genres> and <topic>
Street music and musicians
l. <topic> and <forms/genres>
Drugs and popular music

**Variations (Bassoon and oboe
with wind ensemble)**
e. <forms/genres> (<instrument/
ensemble>)

or <forms/genres>(<instrument>(2)), etc.
Canons, fugues, etc. (Accordion)
Minuets (Band)
Concertos (Harps (2))
b. <forms/genres> (<instrument>,
<instrument>, <instrument> <+>)

**Suites (Harpsichord, flute, violin,
violoncello)**
c. <forms/genres> (<instrument> and
<instrument>)
Rondos (Flute and continuo)
d. <forms/genres> (<instrument> and
<instrument> with <ensemble>)
   Choruses, Sacred, with orchestra

3. MEDIUM OF PERFORMANCE AS
FORM/GENRE
a. <ensembles>
<instrument> ensembles
Symphonies
Tuba ensembles
b. <instrument> with <ensemble>
Clarinet with chamber orchestra
c. <instrument>, <instrument>, <+> with
<ensemble>
Piano, clarinet, violin with orchestra
d. <ensemble> with <ensemble>
Instrumental ensemble with orchestra
<ensemble> and <ensemble>
e. <ensemble> (<instrument>,
<instrument>, <+>)
**Piano and electronic organ with Jazz
ensemble**
j. <instrument> music <instrument> and
<instrument> music

with <ensemble.)
**Concertos (Dulcimer with string
orchestra)**
Concertos (String quartet with band)

f. <forms/genres> (<instrument>,
<instrument>, <+> with <ensemble>)
**Passacaglias (Guitar, unspecified
instruments (2) with Orchestra)**
g. <vocal forms/genres> (<voice(s)>) with
<instrument/ensemble>
Songs (Low voice) with piano
h. <vocal forms/genres> with
<instrument/ensemble>

**Nonets (Bassoon, clarinet, flute, horn,
oboe, trombone, trumpet, percussion)**
f. <ensemble> (<instrument>
and <instrument>)
Symphonies (Piano and organ)
g. <ensemble> (<instrument> with
<ensemble>)
**Symphonies (Organ with string
orchestra)**

h. <instrument> and <instrument>
Bugle and drum corps
Rhythm bands and orchestras
i. <instrument> and <instrument> with
<ensemble>

Bugle music
Bass clarinet and percussion music

FUTURE OF LCSH FOR MUSIC

The task of improving subject access to music is an ongoing process that involves many participants. Its success or failure has not and will not rest singly on LC's development of *LCSH* and LCC, volunteer efforts within and beyond MLA, commercial music indexing services, use of metadata, nor research and technological improvements in database design, retrieval methods, text analyses, automatic indexing or automatic classification. As important as each of these efforts is, the successful future of music subject access depends on a combination and coordination of these efforts in ways not previously experienced. As outlined in the preceding pages, LC has provided diligent (if somewhat sporadic) revision of *LCSH* and significant leadership in music subject analysis and access issues has emanated from the MLA membership. LC and MLA have worked both jointly and independently through the years to help bring about changes in music subject access. But their work has lacked consistency; it has lacked the vision and direction of a comprehensive plan.

The Music Thesaurus Project based, in part, on LC music headings provides this fundamental guideline, a pivotal point of departure, for improved subject access to music. To the project's strong conceptual foundation, a strong practical implementation must be initiated and sustained. Funding is critical to the continuation of this broad-scale project, as is a centralized administration of the project that would facilitate coordination of efforts among all groups who would commit to jointly improving subject access for music.

With the rapid, escalating production and distribution of music and information about music, we must extend our partnerships to include and to be included among commerce and industry, to offer and participate in cutting-edge research and technological advances, to join forces with national and international efforts. By combining and focusing our efforts, we have the potential to shape and coordinate the future of music subject access, indeed, all subject access.

NOTES

1. David Judson Haykin, "Introduction," *Music Subject Headings Used on Printed Catalog Cards of the Library Of Congress.* (Washington: Library of Congress, 1952), p. iii.

2. Richard P. Smiraglia, *Music Cataloging: The Bibliographic Control of Printed and Recorded Music in Libraries* (Englewood, Colo.: Libraries Unlimited,1989), p. 74.

3. Ibid.

4. *A Provisional List of Subject Headings for Music Based on the Library of Congress Classification* (Rochester: Music Library Association, 1933).

5. *Library of Congress Classification. Class M. Music, Class ML Books on Music Class MT Musical Instruction Adopted December 1902.* (Washington, DC: Government Printing Office, 1904).

6. *Subject Headings Used in the Dictionary Catalogues of the Library of Congress*, edited by Mary Wilson McNair. 3rd ed. (Washington, D.C.: United States Government Printing Office, 1928).

7. Eva J. O'Meara, "Music Subject Headings," *Notes* 3 (1935): 16.

8. Virginia Cunningham, "The Library of Congress Classed Catalog for Music," *Library Resources & Technical Services* 8 (1964): 285.

9. Ibid., p. 286.

10. Ibid., p. 287.

11. Donald C. Seibert, *SLACC: The Partial Use of the Shelflist as Classed Catalog* (Ypsilanti, Mich.: University Library, Eastern Michigan University, 1973) Music Library Association. Technical reports: Information for music media specialists,; no. 1. Prepared for the Music Library Association. Cataloging and Classification Committee, p. 1.

12. Ibid., p. 2.

13. Ibid., p. 3.

14. Ibid., p. 51.

15. Marguerite Rebecca Vogeding Quattlebaum, "Introduction," *Subject Headings Used in the Dictionary Catalogs of the Library of Congress*. 5th ed. Ed. by Nella Jane Martin. (Washington: [s.n.], 1948), p. iv.

16. Ibid.

17. *Music Subject Headings Used on Printed Catalog Cards of the Library Of Congress*. (Washington: Library of Congress, 1952).

18. Haykin, *Introduction*, p. iii.

19. Haykin, *Introduction*.

20. Ibid., p. v.

21. Ibid.

22. Ibid.

23. Ibid.

24. Helen E. Bush and David Judson Haykin, "Music Subject Headings," *Notes* 6 (1948): 44.

25. Ibid.

26. Ibid., p. 45.

27. Richard S. Angell, "Subject Headings," *Notes* 10 (1953): 198-200.

28. Smiraglia, p. 75.

29. New York. Public Library. Reference Department, *Music Subject Headings Authorized for Use in the Catalogs of the Music Division* (Boston: G. K. Hall, 1959).

30. Wilma Reid Cipolla, "Music Subject Headings: A Comparison," *Library Resources & Technical Services* 18 (1974): 387-97.

31. Ibid., p. 390.

32. Ibid.

33. David Judson Haykin, *Subject Headings: A Practical Guide*. (Washington: Library of Congress, 1951), p. 73-74.

34. Cipolla, p. 392..

35. Ibid.

36. Sanford Berman, *Prejudices and Antipathies: A Tract on the LC Subject Heads Concerning People* (Metuchen: Scarecrow Press, 1971).

37. Sanford Berman, " Cataloging Philosophy," *Library Journal*, 99 (Sep. 1, 1974): 2033-2035.

38. Ruth Henderson, "Subject Heads: A Rebuttal," *Library Journal*, 99 (Dec. 15, 1974): 3156-3157.

39. Judith Kaufman, *Recordings of Non-Western Music, Subject and Added Entry Access* (Ann Arbor, Mich.: Music Library Association, 1977). MLA technical reports; no. 5.

40. Ibid., p.

41. George Peter Murdock, *Outline of World Cultures*. 5th ed. (New Haven: Human Relations Area Files, 1975).

42. Kaufman, *Recordings of Non-Western Music*.

43. "Music of Ethnic and National Groups," *Music Cataloging Bulletin* 12/5 (1981): 2-5.

44. Judith Kaufman, *Library of Congress Subject Headings for Recordings of Western Non-Classical Music* (Philadelphia: Music Library Association, 1983) MLA technical reports, no. 14.

45. Ibid.

46. "Ethnic Qualifiers," *Music Cataloging Bulletin* 8/8 (1977): 2.

47. *Music of Ethnic and National Groups*.

48. Kaufman, *Library of Congress Subject Headings for Recordings of Western Non-Classical Music*, p. 16.

49. Ibid., p. 18.

50. Ibid., p. 20.

51. Ibid.

52. Ibid., p. 22.

53. Ibid., p. 24.

54. "Subject Headings for Jazz and Popular Music," *Music Cataloging Bulletin* 16/5 (1985): 2-4.

55. Smiraglia, p. 75.

56. J. Bradford Young, "Introduction," Harriette Hemmasi, *Music Subject Headings, Compiled from Library of Congress Subject Headings*. 2nd ed. (Lake Crystal, MN: Soldier Creek Press, 1998), p. 1.

57. *SACO Program Description* <http://lcweb.loc.gov/catdir/pcc/sacopara.html>.

58. *Subject Cataloging Manual: Subject Headings*. Rev. ed. (Washington: Library of Congress. Cataloging Distribution Service, 1985).

59. *Proposal 95-11. Definition of X55 fields for genre/form terms in the USMARC authority format*. <http://lcweb.loc.gov/marc/marbi/1995/95-11.html>.

60. Martha O'Hara Conway, "Library of Congress Subject Subdivisions Conference. Recommendations," *Cataloging & Classification Quarterly* 15/4 (1992): 126-9.

61. Mark McKnight and others, "Improving Access to Music: A Report of the MLA Music Thesaurus Project Working Group," *Notes*, 45 (1989): 714-721.

62. Harriette Hemmasi, "The Music Thesaurus: Function and Foundations," *Notes*, 50 (1994): 875-882

63. Harriette Hemmasi, "ARIS Music Thesaurus: Another View of *LCSH*," *Library Resources & Technical Services*, 36/4 (October, 1992): 487-503.

64. Perry Bratcher and Jennifer Smith, *Music Subject Headings, Compiled from Library of Congress Subject Headings* (Lake Crystal, MN: Soldier Creek Press, 1988).

65. Harriette Hemmasi, Fred Rowley, and James D. Anderson. "Isolating and Reorganizing Core Vocabulary form Library of Congress Music Headings for Use in the

Music Thesaurus," *Advances in Classification Research*, vol. 4: Proceedings of the 4th ASIS SIG/CR Classification Research Workshop, ed. By Philip J. Smith et al. published by Information Today, Inc. for the American Society for Information Science, 1995, p. 67-79.

66. Pauline A. Cochrane and Monika Kirtland, *Critical Views of LCSH–the Library of Congress Subject Headings: A Bibliographic and Bibliometric Essay and an Analysis of Vocabulary Control in the Library of Congress List of Subject Headings* (Syracuse, N.Y.: ERIC Clearinghouse on Information Resources, ED208 900, 1981).

67. Harriette Hemmasi, "The music Thesaurus: Function and Foundations."

68. Harriette Hemmasi, *Music Subject Headings, Compiled from Library of Congress Subject Headings*, 2nd ed., (Lake Crystal, MN: Soldier Creek Press, 1998).

LCSH and Periodical Indexing: Adoption vs. Adaptation

Joseph Miller
Patricia Kuhr

SUMMARY. The *Library of Congress Subjects Headings* (and author-ity lists derived from *LCSH*) are used by the H. W. Wilson Company to index a wide variety of peridocials, including the most popular news-stand magazines, children's materials, trade magazines, professional journals, scholarly academic journals, and technical and scientific jour-nals. The simple syndetic structure and subject-string grammar of *LCSH* are practical, pragmatic, and readily adaptable to periodical in-dexing. Some modifications are necessary, however. Not only does the material being indexed require specialized headings, but the various user groups, from children to lawyers, require various levels of lan-guage in subject access. Furthermore, because periodical articles are often on very narrow (or new) topics, periodical indexing requires much greater specificity (or currency) than *LCSH* usually provides. *[Article copies available for a fee from The Haworth Document Delivery Service: 1-800-342-9678. E-mail address: <getinfo@haworthpressinc.com> Website: <http://www.haworthpressinc.com>]*

KEYWORDS. Indexing, periodicals, subject headings, periodical lit-erature, articles

---

Joseph Miller, BA, MLS, PhD, is editor of the *Sears' List of Subject Headings*, H.W. Wilson Company, 950 University Avenue, Bronx, NY 10452 (E-mail: jmiller@ hwwilson.com). Patricia Kuhr, BA, MLS, is editor of the Subject Authority Files, Indexing and Abstracting Services Division, H.W. Wilson Company, 950 University Avenue, Bronx, NY 10452 (E-mail: pkuhr@hwwilson.com).

[Haworth co-indexing entry note]: *"LCSH* and Periodical Indexing: Adoption vs. Adaptation." Miller, Joseph, and Patricia Kuhr. Co-published simultaneously in *Cataloging & Classification Quarterly* (The Haworth Information Press, an imprint of The Haworth Press, Inc.) Vol. 29, No. 1/2, 2000, pp. 159-168; and: *The LCSH Century: One Hundred Years with the Library of Congress Subject Headings System* (ed: Alva T. Stone) The Haworth Information Press, an imprint of The Haworth Press, Inc., 2000, pp. 159-168. Single or multiple copies of this article are available for a fee from The Haworth Document Delivery Service [1-800-342-9678, 9:00 a.m. - 5:00 p.m. (EST). E-mail address: getinfo@haworthpressinc.com].

Because the *Library of Congress Subject Headings* (*LCSH*) is the largest and most complete subject authority list that is readily available to the public and familiar to librarians and library users, it is understandable that many people are interested in using it, in so far as possible, for indexing things other than books, for which it is primarily intended. Cataloging materials such as films, recordings, curriculum materials, etc., for subject content is one use of *LCSH* that is already widespread. In this article we intend to explore the use of *LCSH* for indexing the subject content of a wide range of periodical literature, with special reference to the indexing operations of the H. W. Wilson Company.

The first attempts at a systematic index of diverse periodical materials was that of William Frederick Poole, who began indexing periodicals while he was still a student at Yale and published his first efforts as a 154-page booklet in 1848 under the title *Index to Subjects Treated in the Reviews and Other Periodicals*. A second edition, six times as large, appeared in 1853, but a third edition was not published until 1882, after Poole had solicited the cooperation of the American Library Association (ALA) in what was quickly becoming an overwhelming task. From 1883 to 1899 a *Cooperative Index to Periodicals* was published under the aegis of ALA, but that enterprise suffered severe organizational and financial problems. It was only in 1901, when the young Halsey William Wilson in Minneapolis launched his *Readers' Guide to Periodical Literature* as a commercial venture, that prompt, reliable, and consistent periodical indexing became a reality. Wilson also took advantage of the then new technology of linotype to offer cumulated indexes, which proved a boon to librarians and researchers.

Apart from its erratic publication, the most serious shortcoming of Poole's index was its lack of consistent subject authorities. It does not diminish the historical importance of Poole's achievement to recognize this fault. In his instructions to the cooperating indexers, who were scattered across the country without access to a central authority file, Poole advised them to use the words of the title as the best guide to an article's subject content: "In most instances the author's own title best expresses the subject of his paper; but if the author has given his article an obscure or fanciful title, the indexer will give it a better one and place it under the heading where it naturally belongs, and where it will be looked for" (*LJ*, 287). This faith in the power of indexers to know where something naturally belongs or where it will be looked for seems wonderfully naive today to anyone who has grappled with the complexities of subject authorities. Many of Poole's critics demanded cross-references, and Poole himself encouraged the use of cross-references on a limited basis, but not from unauthorized terms to authorized terms. By having the indexing in his *Readers' Guide* done in one place by a single staff of trained professionals, Wilson was able to institute subject authorities, and in so doing accomplished a breakthrough in the bibliographic control of periodical materials.

While the *Cumulative Book Index* was the first Wilson publication, it was with the introduction of *Readers' Guide* that the Wilson Company found the need to establish a vocabulary tailored expressly for the purpose of indexing magazine and journal materials. Both *LCSH* and the vocabulary of *Readers' Guide to Periodical Literature* had their beginnings in the American Library Association's publication *A List of Subject Headings for Use in a Dictionary Catalog*, published in 1895. Both vocabularies were based on the same initial list, and both followed the principles set forth in Charles A. Cutter's *Rules for a Dictionary Catalog* (1876-1904). Since the first Library of Congress list was not published until 1909 the expansion of the ALA list for *Readers' Guide* occurred simultaneously with that of *LCSH*. John Lawler's history of the Wilson Company points out that even then there was disagreement among the editorial staff on the form that subject headings should take. A notable example was the disagreement about **Child labor** versus "Children–Employment": "During the early days of the company, the editors had few guides to subject-entry form. The American Library Association had published a slender list of generalized headings, and the Peabody and Athenaeum catalogs were available; but they did not always agree. The result was a friendly dispute among the staff members of the indexes. Miss [Anna L.] Guthrie, then editor of *Readers' Guide*, preferred the straight Peabody headings ("Child labor"), while Miss [Marion E.] Potter [editor of *Cumulative Book Index*] favored the Athenaeum's subdivisions ("Children–Employment"). The discussion continued until in time the two editors had converted each other. Then it was resumed with Miss Guthrie defending Miss Potter's former position and Miss Potter advocating Miss Guthrie's discarded theories" (Lawler, 101). Even today, nearly a century later, the issue remains unresolved. Five Wilson indexes use **Child labor** and five use "Children–Employment."

Unlike the early days, when vocabularies were still developing, indexing services today have a wealth of choices, such as *Medical Subject Headings* (MESH), *Public Affairs Information Service* (PAIS), *Art and Architecture Thesaurus* (AAT), as well as *LCSH*, to draw upon in developing headings. The advantages of using *LCSH* as a starting point in developing indexing vocabularies are considerable. The first and most obvious is its broad scope. *LCSH* has been establishing terminology according to high scholarly standards over a long period of time, based upon subject analysis of quantities of materials in many fields by established experts in those fields. The authority of *LCSH* is profound, and in establishing its own terminology an indexing service can ignore *LCSH* only at the expense of replicating immense amounts of work. Furthermore, *LCSH* is public property and can be used by anyone who likes.

Another advantage of using *LCSH* in developing indexing vocabularies is that the structure of *LCSH* (i.e., the grammar of precoordinated strings and the references to and from broader, narrower, and related terms) is a structure very familiar to library users. Some indexing services, of course, prefer discrete terms for postcoordinate searching, and that requires a greater divergence from *LCSH* terminology, but many indexing services, including those of the H. W. Wilson Company, feel that precoordination and the standard syndetic structure of references is not only in itself the best means of arriving at accurate and complete retrieval on the part of the user, but is also the form that best merges with bibliographic records for books that have been cataloged according to LC practice. Given the basic assumption that *LCSH* will be the "ground zero" of vocabulary, the job of indexing services is to adapt and expand *LCSH* to their own needs.

Indexing services have a number of options when terms they need are not readily available from *LCSH* for copying or adapting. Some useful sources include an unabridged dictionary and other reference books, particularly specialized dictionaries such as *The McGraw Hill Dictionary of Scientific and Technical Terms*. The Wilson indexes each maintain collections of hundreds of reference works in their specialties. Sometimes thesauri or subject heading lists other than *LCSH* have established a heading that can be borrowed or adapted. The Library of Congress also borrows and adapts headings established elsewhere, and "cross breeding" can be seen in the source notes for *LCSH* where other thesauri and indexes, including the Wilson indexes, are often cited. Where no other source exists the indexer falls back on the usage in the literature itself, and the term used in the article to represent a concept becomes the indexing term of choice. Ideally, indexing terms should never stray too far from the words used in the material indexed.

In using and adapting terms from *LCSH* to describe the subject content of articles, the first consideration is the wide variety of materials being indexed. Despite the broad coverage of *LCSH*, the subject authority needs of the various periodical indexes can never be met by any single subject list designed for book cataloging. The Wilson indexes alone include at least seven distinct kinds of materials, all with special vocabulary needs. They are (1) popular newsstand magazines, which are indexed in *Readers' Guide to Periodical Literature*; (2) children's materials, indexed in *Readers' Guide for Young People*; (3) scholarly and academic journals, indexed in *Humanities Index* and *Social Sciences Index*; (4) professional journals, indexed in *Education Index, Library Literature & Information Science*, and *Index to Legal Periodicals & Books*; (5) technical and scientific journals, indexed in *General Science Index, Biological & Agricultural Index*, and *Applied Science & Technology Index*; (6) art, architecture, archaeology and design materials (some professional and some of general interest), indexed in *Art Index*; and (7) trade magazines, indexed in *Business Periodicals Index*. Each of these seven kinds of materials requires special adaptation, although *LCSH* is a suitable starting point for their indexing vocabularies.

The first way in which *LCSH* must be adapted for use in periodical indexing is seen in the case of *Readers' Guide to Periodical Literature*. Both *LCSH* and *Readers' Guide* establish terms only on the basis of literary warrant, but the literary warrant of the two databases involved are immensely different one from the other. General interest magazines contain articles on things that no one is ever likely to write an entire book about. Travel magazines yield a wealth of headings for tiny towns and regions subdivided by **–Description and travel**. Cooking and lifestyle magazines have articles devoted to "Tonic water," "Pastry bags," "Napoleons," "Skiboards," and "Post-It notes." Many web sites are the subject of individual articles, for which subject headings need to be established, such as "Stamps.com". Some topics, like "Perfume allergy" or "HE200 (Drug)," are likely to be dealt with in serious books, but no entire book would be devoted to the topic, hence there are no such headings in *LCSH*. Although the Library of Congress has established hundreds of headings for single words like **Praos (The Greek word)** and some headings for phrases like **Extra Hungariam non est vita (The Latin phrase)**, they are usually erudite and definitively less colorful that those generated by William Safire's column in the *New York Times*, which has required the formulation of headings of the type: "Oomph (Term)" and "What am I, chopped liver? (Phrase)." In other cases, narrower terms are drawn out of the periodical literature that *LCSH* subsumes under broader terms with upward *see* references. For example, *Readers' Guide* has established "Nephritis," which *LCSH* has as a *see* reference to **Kidney–Diseases**, and "Extraterrestrials," which *LCSH* has as a *see* reference to **Life on other planets**.

Children's materials, such as those indexed in *Readers' Guide for Young People*, present another kind of adaptation that is needed, according to the age level of the users. While *Readers' Guide for Young People* is not aimed exclusively at children and indexes reviews and professional materials for elementary teachers, it aims nonetheless to keep the level of vocabulary as close as possible to that of children. The *LCSH* heading **Swine** becomes "Pigs," and **Arachnophobia** becomes "Fear of spiders." The popular names for animals, plants, rocks, etc., are particularly important in indexing children's literature, much of which is devoted to animal stories and nature study. Children's materials also bring up topics for toys and games, e.g., "Pog (Game)" that are not elsewhere discussed.

A special kind of adaptation of *LCSH* is necessary in indexing the professional journals found in *Education Index, Library Literature & Information Science*, and *Index to Legal Periodicals & Books*. Each of these indexes is narrowly focused on a particular discipline. As a result, the heading "Admin-

istration" in *Library Literature & Information Science* means Library administration, and "Surveys" in *Education Index* means Educational surveys.
Without adapting the headings according to the focus of the index, nearly
every article in *Education Index* would be under "Education [this or that]" or
"School [this or that]." Furthermore, in *Education Index* headings are further
narrowed in scope by creating subdivisions for academic levels. For example,
the heading "Student achievements" is subdivided by "–High school,"
"–Elementary school," "–Fifth grade," etc. (These three subdivisions under
this heading have postings of 494, 434, and 30, respectively.) *Education
Index* also establishes terms that are upward *see* references in *LCSH*, such as
"Flash cards," which is a reference to **Word recognition** in *LCSH*. In *Index
to Legal Periodicals & Books*, all terms from *LCSH* qualified by **(Law)**
remain unqualified for obvious reasons. In the Wilson megathesaurus, on the
other hand, terms that are unqualified in *LCSH* are often qualified because of
variant usage in the different disciplines, e.g., "Miners (Birds)," "Arrow-
heads (Plants)," "Baths (Chemical apparatus)," and "Mosaics (Biology)."
There are probably better ways of constructing some of these qualified terms
such as "Chemical baths," as the NISO standard recommends. (NISO, 3).

In technical and scientific journals, such as those indexed in *Biological &
Agricultural Index* and *Applied Science & Technology Index*, a special kind
of extension of the basic vocabulary is needed. It is not so much new topics
that require additional headings, although there are indeed new topics all the
time in those journals, but topics much narrower than any that books are ever
written about. These indexes, for example, have subject headings for thousands of individual species of plants and animals, individual chemicals, and
laboratory phenomena. Some terms in *LCSH* are considered to be lay terms in
such indexes as *Applied Science & Technology Index*, which prefer more
technical language. Examples include "Stochastic fields" for LC's **Random
fields**, "Dichloroethyl sulfide" for **Mustard gas**, and "Seismic hazard analysis" for **Earthquake hazard analysis**. Even among the scientific indexes,
however, the age and academic level of the intended audience is important.
General Science Index, which is aimed at a broader audience, mostly of
students, uses less technical terms than *Biological & Agricultural Index*, such
as "Slipper spurges" rather than the more scientific "Pedilanthus," or
"Moles (Dermatology)" rather than "Nevi." Reflecting both audience and
need for disambiguation is the term "Angel's trumpet." While *General Science Index* has "Angel's-trumpet, " a popular term for more than one species, *LCSH* has a *see* reference from "Angel's-trumpets (Plants)" to the more
scientific term for one species, **Brugmansia**. In *Biological & Agricultural
Index*, however, two types of Angel's-trumpets are differentiated as "Angel's-trumpet (Brugmansia)" and "Angel's-trumpet (Datura inoxia)."

Every type of business and industry has its own trade literature, and those journals are indexed for the benefit of the business community in *Business Periodicals Index*. Here again many new topics are introduced, since new ideas for products and services and new ideas in business and management are the focus of much of this literature. Long before books were written about topics like "Internet selling" and **Mortgage brokers**, these topics were discussed extensively in the periodical literature. **Mortgage brokers** was established in *Business Periodicals Index* before 1982 but not in *LCSH* until 1996. Likewise, new topics in the humanities and social sciences are first introduced in the scholarly and academic journals indexed in *Humanities Index* and *Social Sciences Index* before books are written on those topics. Another example of the need for "fast action" on the part of indexing services involved the break-up of the Soviet Union. The Library of Congress created an authority record for **Russia (Federation)** on May 22, 1992. By that date *Readers' Guide* had indexed 179 articles about the new Russia, and this before they had begun indexing the *New York Times*.

Art Index also produces large numbers of subjects that are dealt with in articles but seldom in entire books, such as "Predellas," which is a see reference in *LCSH* to the broader term **Altarpieces**. There are roughly four hundred headings for archaeological sites in *Art Index* that have never found their way into *LCSH*. Headings for archaeological and ethnological artifacts are also plentiful, such as "Yoruba costume," "Yoruba ivories," "Yoruba iconography," "Yoruba metalwork," etc. Two subdivisions alone,**–Exhibitions** and **–Collectors and collecting**, have generated thousands of subject authority records in *Art Index*. The subject headings and their variants established by *Art Index* since 1985, when it went online, are only about two-thirds of those that have been used since the index began. The recently completed Art Retro project, a retrospective conversion of *Art Index* from 1985 back to the index's beginnings in 1929, turned up an additional 26,000 subjects.

Some of the principal ways, then, that periodical indexing vocabularies vary from *LCSH* include:

1. establishing terms for newer and narrower concepts that have not been established in *LCSH*;
2. lifting narrower terms out of the upward *See* references in *LCSH* and establishing them as headings;
3. varying the level of language according to the age and academic level of the intended audience;
4. defining the meaning of a heading according to academic level; and
5. limiting the meaning of a heading according to the limited scope of an index.

In spite of the need for adaptation and exceptions, the vocabularies of both *LCSH* and the Wilson indexes have expanded remarkably along the same lines. Because *LCSH* contains fewer authority records as a result of allowing for free-floating subdivisions (the Wilson indexes establish authority records for all strings), direct comparison of numbers are impossible. If we limit our comparison to single segment subject terms, i.e., terms having a 150 $a field only, *LCSH* has just over 133,000 as of mid-July 1999 and the Wilson indexes have about 147,500 in the collective file. This collective file, a merger of the eleven periodical subject authority files, contains approximately 675,000 authority records dating back only to about 1980. Earlier records for topics used infrequently between 1901 and 1979 were not converted into the subject authority databases in 1984. Of the current records about one-third have been reviewed for *LCSH* mapping: 58,000 have no *LCSH* equivalent; 125,000 would have an *LCSH* match if *LCSH* had authority records for terms with free-floating subdivisions; and 76,000 records have a corresponding *LCSH* term. Unfortunately there is no way of knowing how many are exact matches. At the time the Wilson collective file was created in 1993, sixteen thousand records were programmatically mapped, but many thousands more are the same term, differing only in inversion or singular/plural. Many others differ not in words but in construction, i.e., subdivision vs. phrase, e.g., **Music–Publishing** vs. "Music publishing."

In general the Wilson indexes use headings directly from *LCSH* when those subject headings do not need to be adapted for the special needs of the individual indexes as noted above. In the collective file, which is being used to create a megathesaurus for merged indexes such as the new OMNI database, conficting headings between and among individual indexes will be overwritten with a more uniform and broad-based vocabulary like that of *LCSH*, at the same time allowing for the current customization of terms in the individual specialized indexes. This megathesaurus will follow the NISO standard for thesaurus construction and LC's *Subject Cataloging Manual: Subject Headings* for subject structure, including the indirect form of geographic subdivision, when these terms do not conflict with other priorities for updating and streamlining the terminology to allow for easier search capabilities in the electronic environment. These priorities include:

1. uninverting inverted headings;
2. revising terms when it becomes apparent that the literature has changed, e.g., **Congresses and conventions** to "Conferences," and **Pregnant schoolgirls** to "Pregnant teenagers;"
3. revising subdivisions when the usage varies, e.g., the revision of LC's **Law and legislation** to "Laws and regulations" to include administrative and municipal regulations, which is a wider topic in periodical literature; and
4. varying the form subdivisions when necessary. For example, when LC canceled the form subdivision **–Anecdotes, facetiae, satire, etc.,** in

favor of the two subdivisions–**Anecdotes** and–**Humor**, the Wilson indexes, which had had the same subdivision, kept it as a single subdivision and revised it to "–Humor, satire, etc.," since individual non-humorous anecdotes in periodicals, as opposed to collections of anecdotes in book form, are indistinguishable from any other articles on a topic.

The varying use of form headings and form subdivisions points out a further difference between cataloging books and indexing periodical literature. Only books can be dictionaries, encyclopedias, atlases, etc., while periodical literature can take the form of feature articles, individual book reviews, interviews, obituaries, recipes, etc. In indexing periodical literature, each item in a periodical is assigned one of a number of codes before any subject analysis is done. These codes correspond conceptually to the form headings and form subdivisions allowed by MARC in the 655 field. These codes identify not the subject content but the form of the material itself. As a result of this preliminary identification of material by form in a separate field, all headings and subdivisions that would seem to be forms (with the exception of the subdivisions–**Bibliography** and–**Reviews**), when they are used in indexing an article, are used not as forms but as topics. The string **United States–Atlases**, for example, always indicates an article about atlases of the United States rather than an atlas itself.

CONCLUSION

Because the simple syndetic structure and subject-string grammar of *LCSH* are practical and pragmatic, *LCSH* is a reliable starting point for developing more detailed subject authorities for periodical indexing. The adaptations needed, however, can be extensive and profound. They depend upon three basic considerations: (1) the peculiar nature of the materials being indexed; (2) the scope and focus of the individual index; and (3) the age or academic level of the intended users of the index. No single subject authority list can be perfectly suitable for more than one periodical index, but if the authority lists of a number of indexes are all derived ultimately from a single parent list, in this case *LCSH*, they should be as similar and compatible as is possible given the above three considerations.

BIBLIOGRAPHY

Cutter, Charles A. *Rules for A Dictionary Catalog*. 4th ed., rewritten. Washington, D.C.: Government Printing Office, 1904.

Lawler, John. *The H. W. Wilson Company: A Half Century of Bibliographic Publishing*. Minneapolis: University of Minnesota Press, 1950.

Library of Congress. *Library of Congress Subject Headings.* 22nd ed. Washington, D.C.: Library of Congress, 1999.

Library of Congress. Cataloging Policy and Support Office. *Subject Cataloging Manual: Subject Headings.* 5th ed. Washington, D.C.; Cataloging Distribution Service, Library of Congress, 1996.

National Information Standards Organization (U.S.). Guidelines for the Construction, Format, and Management of Monolingual Thesauri. Rev. ed. Bethesda, Md.: NISO Press, 1993. [ANSI/NISO Z39.19-1993].

Poole, William Frederick. *An Alphabetical Index to Subjects Treated in the Reviews and Other Periodicals to Which No Indexes Have Been Published.* New York: G. P. Putnam, 1848. "Poole's Index Committee–Second Report." *Library Journal,* v.1, no. 8 (April 1877).

Out from Under:
Form/Genre Access in *LCSH*

David P. Miller

SUMMARY. The provisions for access to genres and forms of library materials in *LCSH* are examined through a survey of Library of Congress policy over the century. This article focuses on main headings for literature and moving-image materials, and form subdivisions. Policy documents in this area have become steadily more elaborate and explicit in their instructions, indicating an increased awareness of the importance of form and genre to the library community at large. Nevertheless, there remain doubts as to whether a general subject vocabulary is best suited to provide the full spectrum of form/genre access as well. *[Article copies available for a fee from The Haworth Document Delivery Service: 1-800-342-9678. E-mail address: <getinfo@haworthpressinc.com> Website: <http//www.haworthpressinc.com>]*

KEYWORDS. Form headings, genre headings, form subdivisions, subject subdivisions, literature headings, moving-image materials, *Library of Congress Subject Headings, LCSH*

INTRODUCTION

Providing access to the forms and genres of library and research materials has been a practice of catalogers and indexers since at least the sixteenth

David P. Miller, MSLIS, MA, BA, is Associate Professor and Head of Technical Services, Levin Library, Curry College, Milton, MA 02186.

[Haworth co-indexing entry note]: "Out from Under: Form/Genre Access in *LCSH*." Miller, David P. Co-published simultaneously in *Cataloging & Classification Quarterly* (The Haworth Information Press, an imprint of The Haworth Press, Inc.) Vol. 29, No. 1/2, 2000, pp. 169-188; and: *The LCSH Century: One Hundred Years with the Library of Congress Subject Headings System* (ed: Alva T. Stone) The Haworth Information Press, an imprint of The Haworth Press, Inc., 2000, pp. 169-188. Single or multiple copies of this article are available for a fee from The Haworth Document Delivery Service [1-800-342-9678, 9:00 a.m. - 5:00 p.m. (EST). E-mail address: getinfo@haworthpressinc.com].

century. In his study, *General Subject-Indexes since 1548*, Archer Taylor
provides numerous instances, beginning with Conrad Gesner's *Pandectae*,
the second volume of his *Biblioteca universalis*. In the fourth section (or
liber) of this work, published in 1548, Gesner listed writers of bucolic poetry,
comedy, tragedy, satire, lyric, and other literary genres (Taylor 1966, 42-44).
Similar examples can be easily found throughout Taylor's book, as indexes
and library catalogs into the twentieth century indicate where examples of
forms and genres as varied as abbreviations, hymns, musical invective, jest-
books and "last words of famous men" may be found. The more recent
developments in form/genre access are therefore not, as is sometimes maintained, innovations cooked up by the theoretically obsessed, but are rather
steps in the direction of untangling it from subject analysis proper. One of the
fundamental assumptions behind this effort is that while library users of all
kinds may incidentally be interested in both *works about* or *examples of* a
given form or genre, they rarely are so indiscriminately. That is, at any given
time–in any given catalog search or research trip–one need or the other is
likely to predominate, and it is the part of good service to make the distinctions as clear as possible.

The provision of explicit form/genre access is dependent not only on
vocabulary development (including guidelines for application), but on developments in MARC and other forms of database coding, and the file structure,
indexing and display practices of differing types of catalogs and databases.
While the latter two topics are outside the scope of this journal issue, a recent
article by Hemmasi, Miller, and Lasater provides background on the changes
in MARC coding practice relevant to form/genre during the 1990s. Also out
of scope, but worth remembering, is that form considerations have also
entered into descriptive cataloging codes, from Panizzi's *Rules* of 1841 (especially Rules 80 and above), to *AACR2R*'s provisions for uniform titles for
literary and musical works (Brault 1972, 89). The fury sometimes aroused by
these issues in the descriptive realm can be sampled in the mid-century
debate between Werner B. Ellinger (1954), subject cataloger in law at the
Library of Congress, and Seymour Lubetzky (1954), renowned cataloging
theorist and reformer, over "non-author headings."

This article is primarily concerned with the Library of Congress's *public*
documentation of form/genre analysis and access, as provided in various
publications throughout the century. The emphasis on public documentation
is intended to provide an overview of how LC has provided guidance for one
of its constituencies–practicing catalogers outside the Library–in this often-
ambiguous area. This overview provides a look at what the Library has found
important to communicate outside its walls, as well as the changing status of
form/genre access in the *LCSH* system. The problematic relationship with

subject analysis *per se* will also be touched on, as will other form/genre vocabularies separate from, but related to, *LCSH*.

In modern cataloging practice, the mandate for separate form/genre access can be traced back to Charles Cutter, and an often-neglected element of his stated objectives of the catalog. All four editions of Cutter's *Rules for a Dictionary Catalog* include this as the complete text of the second objective: "2. To show what the library has

> D. by a given author
> E. on a given subject
> F. in a given kind of literature." (Cutter 1904, 12)

There is no doubt here that form headings for kinds of literature–and by extension, form/genre/medium headings for pieces of music, types of reference sources, film genres, or even examples of realia such as toys and clothing–are regarded as conceptually distinct from topical headings. Indeed, as Francis Miksa writes: "[Cutter's] subject rules do not include form entry. Cutter theoretically conceived of the dictionary catalog as the interfiling of four separate catalogs–author, title, subject, and form. . . [H]is subject rules are not only separate from author and title rules, but also from form entry rules. The latter differentiation sets his rules apart from modern subject cataloging where subject and form entry are normally intermixed" (Miksa 1983, 124).[1] However, with all entries filed together in the dictionary catalog, and given that a physically separate "form catalog" seems hardly to have existed in practice, the distinction between subject and form entries became difficult to sustain. This is particularly true since the same, or similar terminology is generally used (possibly *must* be used in some cases) to designate both instances of works about, and examples of, a "kind of literature." Although name and title entries may be confused with subject entries in a dictionary catalog in limited instances, the subject/form confusion is far more likely to occur. The two concepts thus became mired in a not-the-same, not-different state of incomplete fusion, expressed best by the curious locution, "form subject headings." Recent developments in vocabulary and application (as well as catalog technology and MARC coding) are devoted to resolving this ambiguity to the greatest extent practicable.

This review of *LCSH*'s expression of form and genre across the century will look first at the provision of main headings in certain fields, and then at form subdivision policy, as expressed in its public documentation. This will mean, to a limited extent, a redundant chronological march through the editions of *LCSH* and its related publications. However, main headings and subdivisions present different sets of issues in vocabulary and application, as they serve distinct functions in precoordinated subject heading strings. Main headings, such as **Biochemistry, Community policing, American drama,** or **Magnets,** must address a searcher's primary concern. The searcher look-ing for works about Gertrude Stein may know in advance (or discover at the catalog) that she wants to read a biography, would like periodical articles about Stein, or would benefit from a production history of Stein's theater pieces, but she is not approaching the catalog looking for biographies, period-icals, or theatrical production histories in general. The questions involved in provision of form/genre access via either main headings or subdivisions are therefore sufficiently distinct that separate chronological examinations seem necessary.

MAIN HEADINGS

In the public documentation of *LCSH* practice–the editions of the list itself, those of *Subject Cataloging Manual: Subject Headings*, and related documents–provision of access to genre and form for works of literature and music are most prominent. The reasons for this should be obvious. Works of literature and music, published separately and in collections, have long been important and popular elements of library collections. They are frequently sought by library users precisely because their genres and forms, as compared with subject content (where that can even be analyzed). They are easily collected and circulated in quantity by libraries of many types and sizes, as compared, for example, with original artworks–for which genre/ form access could also be provided. Again, although a wide variety of types of discursive writing, such as research reports, dissertations, exposés, futurist predictions and grant proposals are in fact genres in and of themselves, they are rarely thought of as such by the majority of librarians and library users. Finally, a great many LC headings, such as **Magnets, Beads,** or **Socks,** may serve as form headings for curriculum libraries or special collections, where the objects themselves (realia) are collected, but this is clearly an adaptation of headings in the list for a purpose outside the *LCSH* system proper.

One piece of evidence, demonstrating literature and music as "subjects" for which main headings are prominent, was supplied almost incidentally by Jessica Lee Harris in 1969. In her dissertation, published in 1970 as *Subject Analysis: Computer Implications of Rigorous Definition*, she used a 10 per cent sample of the headings in the 7th *LCSH* (1966) as the basis for several types of analysis (Harris 1970, 220). Of that sample, four hundred (400) headings were selected as possibly, though not necessarily, indicating the form of a work. Of that four hundred, three hundred and twenty-three (323) represented concepts in literature and music. One hundred and ninety-four (194) of these, just under half of her total sample, were headings for "specific instruments and instrument groupings" for individual musical works, or headings for musical forms, "sometimes also followed by designation of instruments used" (Harris 1970, 119).

The field of music is well covered by Hemmasi and Young, in their contribution to this volume. To avoid duplication, and for reasons of space, the following discussion will concentrate on headings for works of literature. Access to works on film and video will also be discussed, although these artforms are dealt with less extensively by the Library of Congress in its documentation.

Literature

The 1st *LCSH* was published between 1909 and 1914. The first "issue" of the *Preliminary List of Literature Subject Headings* (*PLLSH*), a publication extracted from the subject list proper, was published in 1913 (Library of Congress 1913).[2] *PLLSH* included headings, such as **Gipsy poetry** and **Literature, Immoral,** which could serve either for form or subject access, as well as headings such as **Children as authors** and **Meistersinger** which would serve as subject headings. The distinction is not explicitly made, though practice can be inferred from explanatory notes and definitions. The headings **American wit and humor**, and **French wit and humor**, for instance, have the note, "Here are entered collections from several authors, but not works of individual authors." Subdivisions, such as **–Hist. & crit.– -Period.,** are provided under many of the headings, although "under minor literatures subdivisions by form or period are limited to the more important ones, or are entirely omitted" (3). It is also noted that "[h]eadings and subdivisions are more fully developed under English than under the other literatures, and should be consulted for explanatory notes and references" (5). Indeed, five pages are given to heading-subdivision notations and usage notes from **English ballads and songs** to **English wit and humor, Pictorial**. Here we note the probable origin of the pattern heading, **English literature**, documented as such for the first time in the 8th *LCSH* (1975).

An important issue in access to literary works arises in *PLLSH*, although it is not discussed explicitly. This is the question of direct vs. inverted word order for ethnic or national literatures, a question related to the notion of "major" vs. "minor" literatures. The pattern of practice in this area has remained essentially consistent across the many editions of *LCSH*, and has been documented most explicitly in the *Subject Cataloging Manual: Subject Headings* (*SCM:SH*). In the 5th *SCM:SH* (1996), the most pertinent instruction sheets are H306, "Natural Language in Topical Subject Headings," H320, "Headings Qualified by Nationality, Ethnic Group, Language, Etc.", and H1156, "Pattern Headings: Literatures."

The issue of establishing a heading such as **English poetry** in direct (uninverted, natural language) order, or as an inverted heading (Poetry, English) is related to two other issues: (1) that of which facet, nationality or form, is likely to be of primary interest to the so-called "user," and (2) that of enabling reasonably sized retrieval sets. The latter issue is particularly acute for management of card catalogs, where working through multiple drawers of cards headed **Drama** is at least as discouraging as paging through multiple screens in an online catalog. However, the overall question is pertinent for catalogs of all types which lack adequate display of cross references–as, inexplicably, many online catalogs still do. In that situation, the division of form/genre headings between entries for nationality or language and those for the form/genre itself is likely to equate to a stark difference between search success and failure. It also requires the user to decide whether or not she *cares* about nationality when approaching the catalog in a search for kinds of literature; it may be an irrelevant criterion. Where catalogs provide the appropriate references, at least between the direct and inverted forms of headings, this problem will be mitigated to a great extent.

The decision of whether or not to establish a heading for a type of literature in natural language form is essentially, although not exclusively, referred to the status of the form as "major" or "minor." Headings for major forms are established in direct order, whereas those for minor forms or genres are established in inverted order. In this way, what would be potentially excessive retrievals for headings such as **Drama** and **Poetry** are made comparatively manageable, assuming the provision of *see* references to **American drama, English drama, Japanese drama,** etc. The countervailing consideration, of course, is that retrievals for lead terms such as American, English, and French also have the potential for excess. However, since one must choose some word to lead a multiterm heading, this may be regarded as the lesser of two evils. In this light, a potential advantage of a separately maintained genre/form index is that headings beginning with national or linguistic adjectives are more likely to concentrate headings for desired materials together, removing intervening subject headings such as **American elm, American Eskimo dog, Japanese Red Army** or **Japanese tea ceremony**. This is reminiscent of Lois Mai Chan's comment, that "[i]f we have a separate subject heading list for each discipline, consistency would be more easily achieved and discerned. As it exists now, the dictionary catalog contains a conglomerate of disciplines and subject areas. The forms of the subject headings have to adapt to the needs of individual subject matter, resulting in a great number of inconsistencies and irregularities" (Chan 1973, 339).

There is not absolute consistency in the current edition of *SCM:SH* regarding what is considered a major or minor form of literature. Instruction sheet H320, section 2, makes reference to H306, sec. 2.a.(1) for a list of what constitute "major literary forms" (Aug. 1998, 1).[3] H306, however, does not explicitly address the question of major vs. minor, but rather simply lists those headings that are to be established in "normal word order":

"[. . .] diaries
[. . .] drama
[. . .] drama (Comedy)
[. . .] drama (Tragedy)
[. . .] drama (Tragicomedy)
[. . .] essays
[. . .] farces
[. . .] fiction
. . .
[. . .] letters
[. . .] literature
[. . .] newspapers
[. . .] periodicals
. . .
[. . .] poetry
[. . .] prose literature
[. . .] wit and humor
[. . .] wit and humor, Pictorial" (Aug, 1998, 2)

It seems odd here that farces and diaries, for example, are implicitly defined as major literary forms. Indeed, instruction sheet H1156 provides, via a negative definition of what is not "minor," a much more restricted set of major forms for the purposes of providing period subdivisions: "[. . .] **fiction,** [. . .]**drama,** [. . .] **poetry,** [. . .] **essays, and** [. . .] **prose literature**" (February 1999, 2).

Despite this disparity in what is considered major or minor, the instructions for providing natural language vs. inverted forms of headings are explicit enough in individual instances. Those listed presently in H306 are to be established in natural language form when used with adjectives denoting language, nationality, ethnic group or religion. Returning now to *PLLSH*, we find that in fact headings for every kind of literature denoted in H306 were established in natural language form in that early list. The practice of relating major or minor form of literature to form of heading is not discussed, but is evident through a perusal of the list. *See* references from direct to inverted headings for "minor" forms are sometimes provided ("Italian satire, *see* **Satire, Italian**"), as are general *see also* references from headings for unqualified major forms to qualified headings ("**Letters,** *see also* **English letters; French letters,** etc."). It should be noted, however, that natural language order is also established for other forms not included in current practice, such as **American ballads and songs** and **American orations**.

Headings for these two forms were established in natural language order through the 8th *LCSH* (1975). With the 9th edition (1980), [. . .] **ballads and songs** was split into the separate, inverted headings **Ballads, American [English, French, etc.]** and **Songs, American [English, French, etc.]**. With the 10th *LCSH* (1986), [. . .] **orations** was both inverted and changed to **Speeches, addresses, etc.**, with national adjectives as qualifiers established separately.

The fifth edition of *Literature Subject Headings* (Library of Congress 1926) was referred to as the source for such headings as late as the 6th *LCSH* (1957), although in fact literary headings were already included in the main list. The literature heading list proper had expanded from sixty-one to eighty-five pages by 1926, and Library of Congress Classification numbers were frequently provided. There was still, however, minimal discussion of principles of application, and no explicit discussion of the principles underlying forms of headings.

The next major step in public documentation for literary form/genre headings was taken with the official establishment of pattern headings in the 8th *LCSH* (1975). As noted, **English literature** was and is the pattern heading for literatures, building on its comparatively thorough treatment in the early lists. However, beginning with its preliminary edition in 1984, *SCM: SH* has provided a continually more thorough exposition of policy and practice, separating this discussion from the vocabulary itself. The phrase "continually more thorough" means just that; in the Preface to the 5th *SCM:SH* (1996), Barbara Tillett wrote, "Many cataloging practices that had been observed at the Library of Congress as part of its 'oral tradition' are now documented in writing for the first time" (Preface, 2). It might seem surprising, to those who had become used to wielding the hefty *SCM:SH* volumes, that there was anything left to say!

Besides the instruction sheets already mentioned, the 5th *SCM:SH* includes H1775,"Literature: General," H1780, "Literature: Drama," H1790, "Literature: Fiction," and H1800, "Literature: Poetry." H1775, new in the fifth edition, summarizes the instruction sheets used throughout *SCM:SH* for works of and about literature, and outlines the "most commonly expressed concepts in subject headings for literature" as well as the "most commonly found types of works in literature cataloging." From the perspective of form/genre access, the two latter concepts are related to each other in that "form or genre" is one of the concepts that may expressed to different extents in three "commonly found types": collections of works by several authors, collections of works by a single author, and single literary works.

LC's policies for assigning form/genre headings to collections and individual works are closely similar for fiction, drama, and poetry. For collections by more than one author, form headings such as **American dra-**

ma-20th century, Epistolary fiction, or **College verse** are used. Phrase headings which "combine both form and topical aspects into one heading," such as **Christmas plays,** are used when needed; however, if the collection is of works on a specific subject that can be expressed by a heading in the form **[topic]-Drama,** such phrase headings are not to be used (H1780, August 1998, 1). Instead, the topical heading with subdivision, such as **Santa Claus-Drama,** will be assigned along with a *"broader, nontopical,* form heading", such as **One-act plays,** English (emphasis in original). This policy tends to enforce the separation of subject from form/genre access where possible. The problem of subject and genre indications combined in phrase headings such as **Detective and mystery plays** will be discussed further in the conclusion to this paper. For collections by a single author, form headings are assigned if they are of the topical/form phrase type, or if the works "are of a highly specific form and the form is an essential point of the collection," such as **Carnival plays, Allegories,** or **Concrete poetry, German** (H1780, August 1998, 2). No guidance is provided as to what is to be considered highly specific—indeed, specialists are likely to regard any candidate terms as generalities—but the examples seem to stand at the opposite end of a conceptual spectrum from the "major forms," as least as far as the average member of the literary public is concerned. The third type of collection discussed is of works for children, by one or several authors. These receive, in addition to any other headings required, headings such as **Children's poetry** or **Children's plays, Japanese.**

Individual works of drama and poetry receive the same treatment as collections by a single author: phrase headings with a topical aspect are assigned, as well as those for works in a "highly specific" form. Individual works for children also receive headings expressing their intended audience. Fiction is treated differently, however. Although the preliminary *SCM:SH* (1984) specified that individual works of children's fiction should receive headings in the form **Children's stories, Italian,** this was disallowed in the revised edition (1985). Current policy is to "assign no form headings to individual works of adult fiction, children's fiction, or young adult fiction" (H1790, August 1996, 3). This policy, despite being of long standing, has created dissatisfaction for many librarians, particularly those who serve the many consumers of genre fiction. These patrons, making up a diverse demographic group, have indeed always wanted access to individual works precisely because of the genres they represent.

To meet this need, the first edition of *Guidelines to Subject Access to Individual Works of Fiction, Drama, Etc. (GSAFD)* was published in 1990 (Subcommittee 1990). *GSAFD* was the result of work by a subcommittee of the American Library Association's Resources and Technical Services Division, Subject Analysis Committee (SAC). The publication was intended "to enable libraries to improve access to individual works . . . in all formats" (2). Headings not present in *LCSH* (e.g., **Edwardian novels, Superhero radio programs**) are included. For collections of works, the reader was referred back to the practices documented in *SCM:SH*. *GSAFD* has proved to be a very popular resource, and many bibliographic records are now populated with headings drawn from it. As of this writing, a revised edition is in press.

Although the Library of Congress does not use *GSAFD* in its own literature cataloging, H1790 does refer to it, and to the OCLC Fiction Project which made use of it until the formal ending of the Project in 1999. In a section titled "Special provisions for increased subject access to fiction," LC catalogers are instructed not to "remove or change headings added under this program unless they are formulated incorrectly or are clearly in error." More significant, perhaps, is that headings added under the program "may be used on new editions being cataloged," a means by which form/genre access to individual literary works may be propagated through cataloging at LC itself, albeit to a limited extent (August 1998, 5-7). In addition, the revision of at least some literary form/genre headings in *LCSH*, and the revision process for *GSAFD*, have proceeded somewhat in tandem, each with an eye on the other. In the introduction to the revised *GSAFD* edition, the SAC subcommittee in charge of revision emphasizes that "application of these guidelines is not in conflict with the spirit" of *SCM:SH*, "particularly Section H1790" (Subcommittee on Revision, [2]). By the same token, a set of recent *LCSH* changes, from headings beginning with the word "Fantastic" as a designation of fantasy literature to the more current "Fantasy" (e.g., **Fantasy fiction, Fantasy films**), is in line with the expressed desires of *GSAFD* users. These attempts at confluence raise the issue of whether or not the *LCSH* system overall can really be made to serve the needs of more specialized user groups. Efforts to harmonize vocabularies, and develop compatible, if differing, policies for application, will go a long way toward preventing explicit conflicts or introducing ambiguous usages into library catalogs. But should the *Library of Congress Subject Headings* really be asked to serve as an in-depth form/genre list? Or might the careful combination of multiple vocabularies, along with indexing that explicitly indicates form/genre vs. subject access, actually be simpler and more effective in the long run?

Moving-Image Materials

The question of how best to serve the needs of genre consumers is raised rather more sharply where moving-image materials (films, videotapes, full-motion video via the Web, etc.) are concerned. As compared with the generous documentation that the Library has provided for literary works and Western art music, the main public statement regarding treatment of these materials is to be found in *SCM:SH* instruction sheet H2230, "Visual Materials and Non-Music Sound Recordings." For "fiction films," the instructions provide for assignment of "[f]orm headings that express either genre (for example, **Comedy films, Western films**) or technique (for example, **Silent films, Experimental films**)" where appropriate, and require assignment of either **Feature films** or **Short films**, depending on the item's running time (August 1996, 2). Form headings indicating accessibility for particular audiences, such as **Films for the hearing impaired** or **Video recordings for the visually handicapped**, should also be assigned. The subject subdivisions **–Drama and –Juvenile** films are mandated for topical headings. For juvenile materials, catalogers are further referred to H1690, "Juvenile materials," which primarily provides guidance on subdivision policy.

Beyond these instructions, however, assignment of main form/genre headings to moving-image works is not the relatively straightforward situation faced by the cataloger of music or literature. Several difficulties will be suggested here. To begin with, there is the problem of scope. Most pertinent LC headings refer explicitly to the film medium (e.g., **Erotic films, Puppet films**), suggesting manifestations of works on film *per se*. While one might generically describe a re-release of *Citizen Kane* on videotape as being a "film," this won't apply to works which have never seen celluloid, including those which only exist as full-motion video over the Web or on CD-ROM/ DVD. Additionally, this wording connotes that a given library's moving-image collection actually consists of film reels, which is decreasing the case. To avoid that connotation, catalogers sometimes resort to awkward and unauthorized constructions such as **Children's films–Videorecordings**. A second difficulty lies in the lack of guidance available, via authority records, regarding the appropriate use of these headings for either subject and/or genre access. In an earlier study, Miller (1995) examined the authority records for twenty-three LC headings for moving-image materials. In only one instance did a scope note indicate that the heading (**Animal films**) was to be used for genre access. Elements such as classification numbers and reference terms, in the authority records for thirteen other headings indicated subject use. These thirteen headings were nevertheless used for genre access for between 16% and 91% of all records including them in OCLC's Online Union Catalog (now WorldCat). Clearly, such headings are needed for genre access, regardless of their official use by the Library. The third major difficulty lies with vocabulary: either the absence of headings in *LCSH* for a number of moving-image forms and genres, or headings with wording that is considered not to reflect common usage. These problems are similar to some of those addressed by *GSAFD*.

To meet these difficulties, two alternative thesauri have been developed: *Moving-Image Materials: Genre Terms* (*MIM*) and the *Moving Image Genre-Form Guide* (*MIGFG*). (*GSAFD* itself includes some useful headings for moving-image materials, though that is not its focus.) *MIM*, published in 1988, was developed by the National Moving Image Database Standards Committee of the National Center for Film and Video Preservation at the American Film Institute. Its stated purpose is "to standardize terms used to designate genres and forms of moving image materials," and is considered "a general list, best-suited to collections which contain many different types of moving-image materials" (Yee 1988, 11-13). *MIM* is inclusive with regard to media; headings such as **Detective films and programs** and **Scientific films and** video are typical.[4] Its use for form/genre access is obvious, and it includes a number of concepts with no equivalents in *LCSH*, such as **Made for TV movies and Pin screen animation**. Unfortunately, there are no plans for an updated edition of *MIM*.

MIGFG was developed and is used by the Motion Picture/Broadcasting/ Recorded Sound Division at the Library of Congress. It is a faceted thesaurus, in that it includes separate lists of approximately 150 genre and form terms, to be combined as necessary for a particular work. The genre term list includes, for example, the single words **Animal, Children's**, and **Yukon**, and the briefer form list includes terms such as **Feature, Serial**, and **Television pilot**. Physical format terms are also provided but are optional. Thus one can construct headings as needed, without requiring that they be specifically established. The resulting headings may be familiar in appearance (**Western–Television series**) or less so (**Musical–Feature–Animation**), but they will in any case be quite specific to the work cataloged. *MIGFG* includes scope notes, multiple examples, and *see* references for its terms. It should be clear, though, that for all its interest and potential, *MIGFG* lies quite outside the *LCSH* system, in structure, terminology, and application. This is hardly a fault, of course, but between the unusual characteristics of *MIGFG*, and *MIM*'s gradual obsolescence, the cataloger who must work with *LCSH* or a compatible vocabulary is still left without a useable, comprehensive source of form/genre headings for moving-image materials.

SUBJECT SUBDIVISIONS

A Preliminary List of Subject Subdivisions was first issued by the Library of Congress in 1906. The "third issue" of 1910 includes a single page of sixteen "General Form Subdivisions Under Subjects" (Library of Congress 1910, 19). The persistence of this group of subdivisions over the next several decades justifies listing it here:

–Addresses, essays, lectures	**–Handbooks, manuals, etc.**
–Bibliography	**–History**
–Bio-bibliography	**–Outlines, syllabi, etc.**

-Collected works
-Collections
-Congresses
-Dictionaries
-Exhibitions

-Periodicals
-Societies
-Statistics
-Study and teaching
-Year-books

Besides this brief list, some of the subdivisions listed elsewhere, as "used under special classes of subjects" (21-30), are easily recognized as form subdivisions that later became free-floating. For example, the subdivision **-Charts, diagrams, etc.** was authorized for use only with astronomy and music headings; **-Fiction** was authorized for "historical and biographical headings," and **-Poetry** was restricted to headings about musicians and aspects of United States history. (A particular bias of American librarianship during this period is evident in the subdivision **-Juvenile and popular literature**.) In the "fourth issue" of 1916, the list of "General Form Subdivisions Under Subjects" was expanded to two pages (19-20) with eighteen entries (Library of Congress 1916). While only two subdivisions were added, usage notes for several others were new. There is a certain poignancy to some of these instructions in the light of the post-Airlie House reforms undertaken by the Library in the 1990s.[5] In 1916, while the single word Dictionaries serves as a general form subdivision, the usage note instructs us, "cf. **Dictionaries, indexes, etc.**, on p. 33." The latter form is to be used "under literature headings (e.g., **Fiction, Literature, English drama**)," and is flanked on the same page 33 by **-Dictionaries and encyclopedias**, to be used only for the heading **Jews** (!), and **-Dictionaries, vocabularies, etc.**, which is reserved for **Library science**. Returning to the list of "General Form Subdivisions," the difference between sixteen subdivisions in 1910 and eighteen in 1916 is due to the addition of **-Directories**, and **-Societies, etc.**, as well as the already-existing **-Societies**. The two "society subdivisions" have quite distinct applications, and again, a usage note for the latter directs us to "**Societies, periodicals, etc.**, on p. 60." We cannot resist turning to page 60, whereupon we find that this latter subdivision is authorized "under names of *certain* authors, artists, etc., e.g., Shakespeare" [emphasis added]. Present-day complaints about the supposed hairsplitting involved in determining subdivision order, or even distinguishing form/genre from subject, might be well-informed by considering the finesse our predecessors found necessary!

The preface to the 2nd *LCSH* (1919) refers to the fourth issue of the *Preliminary List* as a guide to the use of form subdivisions, and the introduction to the third edition (1928) refers to the "sixth edition of Subject Subdivisions" of 1924 as the current guide to subdivision practice. Thus we have, at the early stage of *LCSH* documentation, separate publications for main headings and subdivisions. However, as with the lists for literature (and music) headings, the next phase of subdivisions documentation will see a merging of instructions. The 4th (1943) and 5th (1948) *LCSH* still refer to the 1924 subdivision publication (reprinted in 1936). It is with the 6th (1957) that guidance on general form subdivision usage is incorporated into the introductory matter of *LCSH* itself for the first time (vi-vii). These are still the same eighteen subdivisions, with similar usage notes, as in the *Preliminary List* of 1916.

The 7th *LCSH* (1966) drops the reference to "form" in its introductory list, "Subdivisions of General Application," used "under any subject heading as required" (p. vii-viii). This list, somewhat revised from the canonical list of fifty years earlier, is nevertheless devoted primarily to matters of form. The subdivisions **–Abstracts, –Case studies, –Film catalogs** and **–Indexes** make their appearance. The "society headings" split is resolved in favor of **–Societies, etc**.

The 8th *LCSH* (1975) marks a great step forward in documenting form subdivision practice. The introductory matter contains a paragraph describing form subdivisions in general terms, and fifty-five pages of "Most Commonly Used Subdivisions." The general paragraph distinguishes form from subject in an indirect fashion: "Form subdivisions are used to specify the particular form in which the material on a particular subject is organized (e.g., congresses, dictionaries, periodicals, etc.) and as such are added as the last element to any heading, after main heading or subdivision. In general, a heading without special form subdivision should be interpreted as designating general discussions or treatises on the subject" (p. xii). In this definition, it seems that the *absence* of a form subdivision is the significant factor, indicating in essence that the work belongs to a default genre of "general discussion or treatise."[6]

The section on "Most Commonly Used Subdivisions" (xviii ff.) is the first effort made by the Library to provide more extensive guidance on in-house LC policy and practice. The 1924 edition of *Subject Subdivisions*, the last printed guide to practice, "represented a complete transcript of the LC subdivision file as it existed at the time" (xviii). Since a transcript of the same greatly enlarged file fifty years later would be of little value, the Library took a different approach: listing the most commonly used subdivisions, providing general statements about the types of headings to which each subdivision is applicable rather than listing every specific heading, and providing expanded usage notes. These notes explicitly indicate form use where authorized for each subdivision. **–Abbreviations**, for example, is to be used "as a form subdivision under topical headings for lists of abbreviations of words or phrases, e.g., **Engineering–Abbreviations**." This list also features an elaborated form of the "cf." references of 1916. *See, See also,* and *See from* references are provided between subdivisions; for example, the entry for Abstracts concludes with:

"sa   Bibliography
                   Book reviews
                   Digests
x   Summaries of publications" (xix).

The introductory apparatus to the 8th *LCSH* proved to be of such value that it was reprinted separately. *An Introduction to Library of Congress Subject Headings* (Library of Congress 1975) in turn became *Library of Congress Subject Headings: A Guide to Subdivision Practice* (Library of Congress 1981), combining introductory material from the 8th and 9th *LCSH* (1980). Correspondingly, "Most Commonly Used Subdivisions" dropped out of the 9th *LCSH*. Thus we can see that a significant expansion in documentation of practice coincided with a very brief period of providing that documentation in the body of *LCSH* itself. Movement back out into a separate publication, an enlarged successor to the 1906 *Preliminary List*, took place almost immediately.

The introduction to the 9th *LCSH* is also notable for its more direct statement of the nature of form subdivisions. In place of the 8th edition's " . . . a heading without special form subdivision should be interpreted as designating general discussions or treatises on the subject," we have the terse, "Form subdivisions represent what a work is, rather than what it is about" (x). This is the first appearance in the *LCSH* context of a phrase which has become something of a mantra for form/genre access advocates (including this writer). It also implies a binary opposition between subject and form access which, while helping prepare the way for more recent developments in vocabulary development, indexing and coding, has the unfortunate dualistic effect of implying that a given heading or subdivision can only be used for one purpose or the other. This is not the case; a difference in access to *aspects of a work* (form/genre vs. subject, in this case) does not demand that specific words or phrases be dedicated, acolyte-fashion, to those different modes of access.

Prior to publication of the 10th *LCSH* (1986), the "preliminary edition" of *SCM:SH* (1984) made its appearance, and with this, guidance on subdivision practice was once again greatly reduced in *LCSH* itself. The introduction to the 10th edition states that the 1981 *Guide to Subdivision Practice* should be "consulted with caution" (xii), and the 12th *LCSH* (1989) declares that the *Guide* was generally superseded "in H1095 and elsewhere" in the 3rd *SCM:SH* (1989). With regard to form subdivisions in particular, the 10th *LCSH* included an expanded general "Form Subdivisions" statement, which has remained in place with minor variations to the present. The additional material points out that "most form subdivisions are indicated in the list [i.e., the body of *LCSH*] by a general *see also* reference under the heading representing the form as a whole." As an example, the heading for **Periodicals** as a subject in itself makes a *sa* reference to the same term as a subdivision, neatly stating in this way the use of the same term for different types of access. The "Form Subdivisions" statement also refers the user to the *SCM:SH* for "guidance on the use of many specific form subdivisions" (xii).

The general guidance on use of form subdivisions in *SCM:SH*, as later supplemented by *Free-Floating Subdivisions: An Alphabetical Index* (*FFS*), can be described more briefly. The H-numbered instruction sheets in *SCM:SH* for "Special Subdivisions, Materials, Themes, etc." (H1205-2400 in the 5th edition) specify authorization for form use when relevant. H1075, "Subdivisions," provides a summary of the appropriate usage and coding of form subdivisions (August 1998, 2). The 3rd *SCM:SH*, which, as noted, absorbed the *Guide to Subdivision Practice*, introduced instruction sheet H1095, "Form and Topical Subdivisions of General Application," the latest descendent of the 1906 *Preliminary List*. H1095 provides references to other instruction sheets for specific guidelines on usage of particular subdivisions. It is worth noting that, in contrast to the sixteen form subdivisions listed in the 1906 publication, the latest iteration of H1095, as of this writing, lists over one hundred and forty (140) subdivisions that may be used to indicate form. It is true that many of these subdivisions, such as **–Rules**, are authorized for use in a limited number of subject areas, and other subdivisions, such as **–Poetry**, were present in other sections of the *Preliminary List*. This expansion is nevertheless indicative of a greatly enlarged, and more explicitly indicated, conception of the forms that library materials may take, in addition to sociological factors such as increased publishing activity in a greater variety of media.

Also in the service of greater specificity is the explicit MARC tagging introduced in updates to the 5th *SCM:SH* (1996). As of the second 1998 update to this edition, examples are provided with appropriate subfield codes, including $v for form subdivisions. *FFS* is, as its subtitle states, an index to sections H1095-H1200 and H1600 of *SCM:SH*. In the 9th *FFS* (1997), subdivisions which can be used for form access were tagged with a diamond symbol. The 11th *FFS* (1999) replaces the diamonds with a "Subfield Code(s)" column, where a letter v, x, or y is provided to show even more directly how these subdivisions are tagged. With compound free-floating subdivisions, the "Subfield Code(s)" column indicates the appropriate combination of tags, e.g., for **–Committees–Indexes**, the combination x-v is shown. (It is also possible for subdivisions given a "v" tag to be tagged "x" where they actually function topically in a particular instance.) Thus, in the guidance provided by *SCM:SH* and *FFS* combined, verbal instructions are supplemented with symbolic notation, making the significance of form as an element of subject analysis almost impossible to miss or ignore.

SOME ISSUES, AND A CONCLUSION

Provisions for access to form and genre have been available in *LCSH* or its related publications since the beginning of its public documentation early in this century. However, as the title of this paper implies, documentation of form/genre-related policies have become steadily more extensive and explicit over time. At first, both the policy statements and major vocabulary subsets (for literature, music, and form subdivisions) were published in separate documents. After a comparatively brief period in which major policy statements were added to the introductory matter of *LCSH,* it was soon found that separate publications were again necessary, culminating at present in the four volumes of *SCM:SH* and the annual *FFS* editions. The main headings, of course, are no longer confined to separate publications, but we have seen, in the cases of literature and moving-image materials, that separate thesauri addressing perceived deficits in *LCSH* have recently been produced by other bodies (sometimes within the Library itself). The question remains, therefore, as to whether *LCSH* proper is the best medium for form/genre access in library catalogs, or whether other vocabularies should be more actively developed and maintained for this purpose.

One issue that persists, although only touched on here, is that of the ambiguous relationship between subject and form/genre access, particularly given that the same or very similar headings are used for each. As Chan notes, where identical headings are involved, "the failure to make the distinction between form and topic is a violation of the principle of unique headings." Fortunately, this difficulty may "possibly be solved through application policy rather than the vocabulary per se," and with the increased use of MARC21 Bibliographic field 655 this is becoming a quite practical possibility (Chan 1995, 397-398).

A more complicated problem arises with certain classes of genre headings, particularly for literature and moving-image materials. Genre headings such as **Western films**, which incorporate the genre's major subject concern into the wording of the heading, may seem functionally indistinguishable from subject headings such as **West (U.S.)–Drama**. In cases like this, is there any useful purpose served by providing genre headings? One answer to this question (apart from the fact that the headings are not actually identical) is that those genres which make use of standard subjects (detectives, courtrooms, love) nevertheless treat those subjects in a manner distinct enough to be sought separately. Not all works which might validly have the heading **West (U.S.)–Drama** assigned will be "Westerns," or even films for that matter. As the introduction to *MIGFG* states, "Genres contain conventions of narrational strategy and organizational structure, using similar themes, motifs, settings, situations, and characterizations. In this way, the makers of moving image works use recognizable patterns of storytelling that are readily understood by audiences" (Library of Congress, Motion Picture/Broadcasting/Recorded Sound Division 1998, Introduction, par. [2]). The fact that genre headings frequently name their typical subject content does not make them redundant with form-subdivided topical headings which name the same or similar content.

This distinction is nevertheless confounded in *LCSH* by the presence of headings which, though semantically similar to genre headings, do not indicate real genres. Headings such as **Golf stories**, which do not really name a "highly specific" genre, should probably be changed to form-subdivided topical headings (**Golf–Fiction**). It might be established, through consulting the any critical literature that exists, that stories about golf do in fact possess genre qualities (as do horror stories, which are not simply stories about people feeling horror). Otherwise, it is difficult to explain why **Legal stories** (from *GSAFD*) should be indexed as a genre, whereas **Fishing stories** should not, when the headings share the same semantic structure.

The final issue to be raised here is that of the use of national and linguistic qualifiers in headings for literature. The practice of including these terms in main headings, or in subdivided headings for genres at all, has been repeatedly questioned, as has the confluence of language and nationality. In the first instance, it should be established, again by consulting the relevant critical literature, whether actual subgenres exist which vary according to national origin. English and French farces may in fact differ significantly enough to be so named, but do, say, Australian and Canadian science fiction? It is also sometimes stated that providing geographical subdivisions for form/genre headings "splits the file" and requires multiple, frustrating lookups. While this might be true for a library with an demographically homogeneous publication, the reverse may be true for library systems, such as Queens (New York) and Los Angeles, which serve extremely diverse populations. In these cases, geographic subdivision, or linguistic qualifiers, may in fact be of great service. In any event, providing a consistent means to distinguish between language and national origin is a question which should be further considered. As one example, the heading **English drama** is probably misleading when applied, as it was on many older catalog records, to a translated collection of plays from around the world.

The larger picture, fortunately, shows that these and other issues can now be discussed in a context in which form/genre access in *LCSH* is no longer semi-obscure, to be teased out through hints and inferences. Whether or not *LCSH* is the best venue for providing this access to a broad range of materials (including expository genres such as press conferences and opinion polls) remains to be seen, but its prominence as part of the *LCSH* system is more evident now than ever before.

NOTES

1. I am grateful to Arlene Taylor for drawing my attention back to this passage in Miksa's discussion.

2. The following discussion uses the third issue of *Literature Subject Headings* (Library of Congress 1917) as the basic text.

3. Unless otherwise noted, *SCM:SH* references are to the fifth edition (1996). As this edition is regularly updated, the date of the pertinent update page, as well as the page number, is given for each instruction sheet.

4. The base text of *MIM* must be used in conjunction with updates published in two issues of *Cataloging Service Bulletin*: no. 46 (Fall 1989), and no. 49 (Summer 1990). The wording of many headings was changed, some added, and others eliminated, in these updates.

5. An invitational conference, held in May 1991 at Airlie House in Virginia, examined subdivision practice in *LCSH* from a number of perspectives. Several recommendations for simplification resulted from the conference; the Library's implementation of those recommendations throughout the 1990s has been documented in issues of its *Cataloging Service Bulletin*.

6. See Wilson and Robinson (1990) for an interesting discussion of the idea of a nonliterary (or expository) "default genre."

REFERENCES

Brault, Nancy. 1972. *The great debate on Panizzi's rules in 1847-1849: The issues discussed*. Los Angeles: The School of Library Service and The University Library, University of California.

Chan, Lois Mai. 1973. "American poetry" but "Satire, American": The direct and inverted forms of subject headings containing national adjectives. *Library Resources & Technical Services* 17:330-339. — 1995. *Library of Congress Subject Headings: Principles and application*. 3rd ed. Englewood, Col.: Libraries Unlimited.

Cutter, Charles A. 1904. *Rules for a dictionary catalog*. 4th ed. Washington, D.C.: Government Printing Office.

Ellinger, Werner B. 1954. Non-author headings. *Journal of cataloging and classification* 10:61-73.

Harris, Jessica Lee. 1970. *Subject analysis: Computer implications of rigorous definition*. Metuchen, N.J.: Scarecrow Press.

Hemmasi, Harriette, David Miller and Mary Charles Lasater, ed. by Arlene G. Taylor. 1999. Access to form data in online catalogs. *ALCTS Newsletter* 10. <http://www.ala.org/alcts/alcts_news/v10n4/formdat2.html> (viewed October 15, 1999).

Library of Congress. 1910. *Preliminary list of subject subdivisions*. Washington, D.C.: Government Printing Office.

— 1913. *Preliminary list of literature subject headings*. Washington, D.C.: Government Printing Office.

— 1916. *Preliminary lists [sic] of subject subdivisions*. Washington, D.C.: Government Printing Office, Library Branch.

— 1917. *Preliminary list of literature subject headings, with a tentative list for Shakespeare collections.* 3rd issue. Washington, D.C.: Government Printing Office, Library Branch.

— 1926. *Literature subject headings, with list for Shakespeare collections, and Language subject headings.* 5th ed. Washington, D.C.: Government Printing Office.

— 1975. *An introduction to Library of Congress Subject Headings.* Washington, D.C: Library of Congress.

— 1981. *Library of Congress Subject Headings: A guide to subdivision practice.* Washington, D.C.: Library of Congress.

— Motion Picture/Broadcasting/Recorded Sound Division. 1998. *The moving image genre-form guide.* <http://lcweb.loc.gov/rr/mopic/migintro.html> (viewed September 17, 1999).

Lubetzky, Seymour. 1954. Non-author headings, a negative theory. *Journal of Cataloging and Classification* 10:147-154.

Miksa, Francis. 1983. *The subject in the dictionary catalog from Cutter to the present.* Chicago: American Library Association.

Miller, David. 1995. Ambiguities in the use of certain *Library of Congress Subject Headings* for form and genre access to moving image materials. *Cataloging & Classification Quarterly* 20:83-104.

Subcommittee on Subject Access to Subject Access to Individual Works of Fiction, Drama, etc. 1990. *Guidelines on subject access to individual works of fiction, drama, etc.* Chicago: American Library Association.

Subcommittee on the Revision of the Guidelines on Subject Access to Individual Works of Fiction. In press. *Guidelines on subject access to individual works of fiction, drama, etc.* Rev. Chicago: American Library Association.

Taylor, Archer. 1966. *General subject-Indexes since 1548.* Philadelphia: University of Pennsylvania Press.

Wilson, Patrick and Nick Robinson. 1990. Form subdivisions and genre. *Library Resources & Technical Services* 34:36-43.

Yee, Martha M., comp. 1988. *Moving-image materials: Genre terms.* Washington, D.C.: Cataloging Distribution Service, Library of Congress.

Survey on Subject Heading Languages Used in National Libraries and Bibliographies

Magda Heiner-Freiling

SUMMARY. Surveys conducted during the last four years under the auspices of the International Federation of Library Associations and Organizations (IFLA) reveal that the *Library of Congress Subject Headings* is heavily used in national libraries outside of the United States, particularly in English-speaking countries. Many other countries report using a translation or adaptation of *LCSH* as their principal subject heading language. Magda Heiner-Freiling presents an analysis of the IFLA data, which also includes information on the classification schemes used by the libraries and whether or not the libraries have produced a manual on the creation and application of subject headings. The paper concludes with an Appendix showing the complete data from the

Magda Heiner-Freiling is Senior Reference Librarian, Die Deutsches Bibliothek, Adickesallee 1, D-60322 Frankfurt, Germany (E-mail: heiner@dbf.ddb.de).

The author wishes to thank Dorothy McGarry and Julianne Beall for their help and advice on this paper.

[Haworth co-indexing entry note]: "Survey on Subject Heading Languages Used in National Libraries and Bibliographies." Heiner-Freiling, Magda. Co-published simultaneously in *Cataloging & Classification Quarterly* (The Haworth Information Press, an imprint of The Haworth Press, Inc.) Vol. 29, No. 1/2, 2000, pp. 189-198; and: *The LCSH Century: One Hundred Years with the Library of Congress Subject Headings System* (ed: Alva T. Stone) The Haworth Information Press, an imprint of The Haworth Press, Inc., 2000, pp. 189-198. Single or multiple copies of this article are available for a fee from The Haworth Document Delivery Service [1-800-342-9678, 9:00 a.m. - 5:00 p.m. (EST). E-mail address: getinfo@haworthpressinc.com].

189

88 national libraries that responded to the surveys. *[Article copies available for a fee from The Haworth Document Delivery Service: 1-800-342-9678. E-mail address: <getinfo@haworthpressinc.com> Website: <http://www.haworthpressinc. com>]*

KEYWORDS. Subject heading languages, IFLA, library surveys, national libraries, *LCSH*

INTRODUCTION

In 1994 the IFLA Section on Classification and Indexing discussed plans for an IFLA funded research project concerning the state of the art in the field of subject heading languages used in national bibliographies or catalogues of national libraries. A first questionnaire was sent to the national libraries in July 1995 asking for information on the kinds of verbal subject access offered in their bibliographies, the underlying rules or manuals used for the indexing process and a person responsible for the coordination who could be contacted for further inquiries. This project was planned as a follow-up to work done on *Principles Underlying Subject Heading Languages (SHLs)*[1] which had been started by a working group of the Section on Classification and Indexing in 1990. After the Working Group on Principles Underlying Subject Heading Languages reached agreement on nine construction and two application principles underlying subject heading languages in general, a practical analysis of eleven real existing systems used in national bibliographies verified these principles. Since the systems were mainly representing countries connected with the Section because of personal membership on its Standing Committee or countries represented at a satellite meeting held in Lisbon in 1993,[2] a broader survey of subject indexing systems worldwide seemed desirable.

Originally the proposal for a state-of-the-art project was intended to provide for a consultant to look at various written documents related to subject cataloguing codes, to see if they provided for the principles identified. Funding was not found for a consultant, so it was decided to begin by obtaining information from national libraries on what systems were used and whether a subject cataloguing code existed for the library. The letter to national librarians was prepared by Dorothy McGarry (University of California, Los Angeles) and Donna Duncan (McGill University), who were then the officers of the Section. The responses received were tallied to determine the number of libraries, the number from each continent, and totals for the subject systems used.

Unfortunately the responses to the first questionnaire were limited to a total of 44 countries only, yet the results and the contacts established with a number of developing countries were interesting and promising enough to encourage proceeding with gathering information. The Standing Committee decided in August 1997 to send out a second questionnaire to those who had not answered the first one, this time not only in English, but also in French, Spanish and German, which offered the opportunity to answer in a language perhaps more familiar to the respondents than English. Indeed this led to additional responses from another 44 countries and a final total of 88 national libraries or national bibliographic agencies. The questionnaire was sent, and the responses tallied, by Magda Heiner-Freiling (Die Deutsche Bibliothek). The responses were from

> Europe: 37 countries
> Africa: 18 countries
> Asia: 15 countries
> The Americas: 15 countries (Latin America: 11)
> Others: 3 countries (Australia, New Zealand, Papua New Guinea)

Results

The responses to the survey show a very clear predominance of use of the *Library of Congress Subject Headings (LCSH)*. Twenty-four national libraries use *LCSH* in their national bibliographies (of course mainly in the anglophone world) or at least for their titles in foreign languages (mainly countries with an important book production in their own language, but with English as a second language for academic exchange, such as China, Egypt or Malaysia). Another group of countries use translations or adaptations of *LCSH* into their own languages, in total 12 countries; however, it is difficult to decide how far national adaptations of *LCSH* should be counted here without a thorough study of manuals and subject authority files. The French subject heading system RAMEAU, for instance, goes back to *LCSH* in its beginnings and its underlying structure, as does RVM (Répertoire des vedettes matière) used by the National Library of Canada for the Canadian titles in the French language, but they are counted as independent systems here.

RAMEAU and the German subject heading system RSWK (Regeln für den Schlagwortkatalog) are gaining a prominent role in the countries sharing French or German as the common language. Whereas RSWK is used in all three German-speaking countries (Germany, Austria, Switzerland, and also, although not for bibliographic purposes, in the German-speaking part of Italy), the importance of RAMEAU is increasing in the francophone countries of Northern Africa and the Middle East, such as Tunisia, Algeria or Lebanon.

The importance of the *Sears List of Subject Headings* as a second English-language subject heading system is obvious. It is used in ten countries, especially those with English as the first or second language and a rather small book production (e.g., the Bermuda Islands, Belize, Barbados, Ethiopia, Zambia, and Bangladesh); among them are also those that use Sears only for special purposes (e.g., juvenile literature) or have given it up lately for *LCSH* (Trinidad and Tobago). In India both systems are used; *LCSH*, however, is preferred by the national library.

It was not the aim of this study to gain detailed information on the classification systems used by the national libraries or in the national bibliographies. Yet it was asked if classification is used instead of or in addition to a verbal indexing system, and many countries answered this question. The predominant role of DDC is not surprising after the results of Barbara Bell's study on DDC in national bibliographies.[3] It is also striking that a combination of *LCSH* and/or the *Sears List* together with DDC is used in nearly twenty national bibliographies or national library catalogues. There is a strong tendency to use an international classification such as DDC or UDC in addition when an in-house system or a national subject heading system is applied–countries such as Portugal, Macau, Poland, Croatia, Hungary, Spain and Andorra are typical examples of the use of UDC in combination with national subject authority files. Instead of a subject heading language, DDC is used in countries with a huge book production like Israel or Denmark, as well as in developing countries like Swaziland; UDC as a single instrument for subject analysis is typical for some countries Eastern Europe such as Romania, Latvia or Moldavia. Two interesting cases, which might contradict some general expectations, are the Netherlands and Yugoslavia. The Netherlands, with a polyglot population and strong international contacts, developed a national subject authority file (Gemeenschappelijke Trefwoorden-thesaurus) as well as a national classification (Basisclassificatie), whereas Yugoslavia with a tradition of national independance in politics and culture uses international systems like *LCSH* (since 1948) and UDC. The German-speaking countries have agreed to use a common subject indexing system (RSWK), but none of them uses a classification; however, plans for the application of DDC in the near future are being discussed.

Not all libraries indicated the year in which they started with their present subject heading system, but more than half of those who gave this information began in 1989 or after, i.e., in the last ten years. Of course this item is connected with the fundamental political changes in East and Southeast Europe, which led to a break with former traditions in subject indexing and classification in already existing countries like Poland, but above all with the coming into existence of a considerable number of independent new states. Their newly created national bibliographies usually started on a high level concerning the standards of bibliographic description, which includes classification and indexing. It is obvious that many of these countries adopted or translated *LCSH* (the Czech Republic, Estonia, Lithuania, Macedonia, Slovakia, Slovenia, planned in Ukraine) or started very soon with their own national subject authority files (Croatia). Nearly all of them decided to use an international classification in addition, and in most cases it was the UDC with its long tradition and high reputation in the eastern part of Europe.

Many developing countries started with their present system of subject cataloguing during the 1990s or had already begun between 1980 and 1989. The organisation of IFLA conferences, workshops and publications connected with topics like bibliographic control[4] and the development of guidelines for subject authorities[5] probably influenced this process and helped to establish a system of recommendations and instructions for national bibliographies.

The existence of national subject authority files without direct connection with *LCSH* and their implementation into national bibliographies are typical characteristics of the 1990s; the large and widely accepted systems like RAMEAU (France), RSWK (Germany) and SIPORBASE (Portugal) were developed in these years, a product of the increasing importance of nationwide central services in subject indexing based on the progress in information technology and the rise of OPACs.

The question concerning a published manual for the creation and application of subject headings was answered by fewer than half of the participants, which probably can be translated into a "no" for all those who did not answer this question. Printed manuals exist especially in the industrialized countries of the world (including Japan and South Korea), but also in some countries like Iran, Malaysia, Yugoslavia and China. Among those who plan a printed manual in the near future are several countries in Eastern and Southeast Europe.

Further Inquiries

Some of the results presented here go back to information sent in three years ago and may no longer be correct or complete. Early in 1999 a second letter accompanied by a first draft of the survey was sent by Heiner-Freiling to all participants in the survey asking them to verify or correct the items concerning their own countries. Though this was also written in four languages (English, French, German and Spanish), only 21 participants responded. Their comments were integrated into the survey. The Working Group also discussed an online publication of the survey via IFLANET with a regular update and web addresses of the participating national libraries and, if possible, of their thesauri, manuals or bibliographic information in the web. As only eight libraries mentioned a homepage or any other website connected with these features, an online presentation of the survey can offer the information found, but only a very small number of helpful links. It may be of little practical value except as a snapshot in time against which a later survey could be compared.

NOTES

1. IFLA Section on Classification and Indexing, Working Group on Principles Underlying Subject Heading Languages, *Principles Underlying Subject Heading Languages (SHLs)*, Maria Inês Lopes and Julianne Beall, eds. (München: K.G. Saur, 1999).

2. The countries represented were the USA, Germany, Portugal, Iran, Canada (both English and French), Norway, Spain, Poland, France, and Russia. Proceedings of the satellite meeting were published as: Robert P. Holley, ed., *Subject Indexing:Principles and Practices in the 90's* (München, K.G. Saur, 1995).

3. Barbara Bell, "The Dewey Decimal Classification System in National Bibliographies." In: *Dewey Decimal Classification: Edition 21 and International Perspectives*, Lois Mai Chan and Joan S. Mitchell, eds. (Albany, N.Y.: Forest Press, 1997), pp. 43-58.

4. Winston D. Roberts, ed., *Proceedings of the National Bibliographies Seminar, Brighton, 18 August 1987* (London: IFLA Universal Bibliographic Control and International MARC Programme, 1988).

5. IFLA Section on Classification and Indexing, Working Group on Guidelines for Subject Authority Files, *Guidelines for Subject Authority and Reference Entries* (München: K.G. Saur, 1993).

Last update: July 1999
(An asterisk *LCSH**, indicates a translation and/or adaptation of *LCSH*)

Country	Library	System of Subject Heading Language	Used since	Classification used instead or additionally	Publication of manual
Albania	National Library of Albania	---		UDC	planned
Andorra	Biblioteca Nacional www.andorra.ad/bibnac.	Llista d'encapçalaments de matèria en català	1989	UDC	planned
Australia	National Library of Australia	*LCSH*	1961	DDC	
Austria	Österreich. Nationalbibliothek	RSWK	1989		
Bangladesh	National Library Dakar	Sears List			
Barbados	National Library Service	Sears List, Macrothesaurus economy and social development. In-house list			
Belarus	National Library of Belarus	Combination of descriptors and uncontrolled vocabulary in Russian/Belorussian	1993	UDC, Rugasnti (Rubricator for Scientific and Technological Information	---
Belize	National Library Service	Sears List	1935		
Bermuda	Bermuda National Library	Sears List	before 1978		
Brazil	Biblioteca Nacional	*LCSH**	1948	DDC	yes
Burundi	Bibliothèque Nationale	---		DDC (planned)	---
Cameroon	Bibliothèque Nationale	Liste des vedettes matière BIBLIO	1971	DDC	
Canada	National Library Ottawa	*LCSH*, RVM	1967		yes
China	National Library	Classified Chinese Thesaurus, LCSH (for foreign literature)	1987	Chinese Library Class.	yes
Colombia	Biblioteca Nacional	planned		Mostly used in C.: Lista de encabezamientos de materia para bibliotecas	yes

APPENDIX (continued)

Country	Library	System of Subject Heading Language	Used since	Classification used instead or additionally	Publication of manual
Costa Rica	Biblioteca Nacional	*LCSH**			---
Croatia	National and University Library Zagreb	National subject authority file	1997	UDC	planned
Czech Republic	National Library	*LCSH**	1995	UDC (Top level)	
Denmark	Kongelige Bibliotek www.kb.dk			DDC	
Egypt	National Library	Arabic list of subject headings, *LCSH*	1995	DDC	
Estonia	National Library	National subject index	1991	DDC	
Ethiopia	National Archives and Library	Sears List			---
Finland	University Library Helsinki hul.helsinki.fi/hyk/hul/indexe.html	Finnish General Thesaurus hul.helsinki.fi/hyk/hul/kte/thesaur.html	1987		yes
France	Bibliothèque Nationale	RAMEAU	1980	UDC	yes
Gabun	Bibliothèque Nationale	Thesanrus + Ibiscus Macrothèsaurus DE	1998		---
Germany	Deutsche Bibliothek www.ddb.de	RSWK	1986		yes
Ghana	Research Library Accra				
Greece	National Library	*LCSH*	1978	DDC	
Guatemala	Biblioteca Nacional	*LCSH**	1985		
Guyana	National Library	Lista des encabezamientos		UDC	yes
Hungary	National Library	Sears List (only for juvenile literature)		DDC	planned
India	National Library Calcutta	National subject heading system planned	1951,1953	DDC	yes
Indonesia	National Library	*LCSH* (Nat. Libr.), Sears List	ca. 1965		yes
Iran	National Library	Sears List*	1984		
Ireland	National Library www.heanet.ie/natlib/	*LCSH*	ca. 1975		
Israel	National and University Library Jerusalem huji.ac.il/jnul.	Free-language English descriptors		DDC	
Jamaica	National Library www.nlj.org.jm	*LCSH* (BNB version)		DDC	---
Japan	National Diet Library www.ndl.go.jp	National Diet Libray Subject Headings	1949		yes

Country	Library	System of Subject Heading Language	Used since	Classification used instead or additionally	Publication of manual
Korea (South)	National Library	National Library of Korea Subject Headings (planned)	1999	Korean DC	yes
Latvia	National Library	---			
Lesotho	National Library	LCSH*	1978	UDC	
Libya	National Library	Arabic SHL between 1977 and 1986		DDC	
Liechtenstein	Liechtensteinische Landesbibliothek	---			
Lithuania	National Library	LCSH*	1992		planned
Luxemburg	Bibliothèque nationale				
Macau	Biblioteca Central Macau	SIPORBASE, Chinese Subject Headings	1996	UDC	---
Macedonia	National and University Library Skopje	LCSH*	1993	UDC	planned
Madagascar	Bibliothèque nationale	Choix de vedettes matières à l'intention des bibliothèques	1994	UDC	
Malawi	National Archives	LCSH (card catalog only)	1991		yes
Malaysia	National Library	LCSH, Local Subject Headings	1982 1993	DDC	yes
Malta	National Library	Sears List - LCSH included recently	1983	DDC	
Moldavia	National Library		planned	UDC	
Namibia	National Library	LCSH	1990	DDC	
Netherlands		Gemeenschappelijke Trefwoorden-thiesaurus	1991	Basisclassificatie	
New Zealand	National Library	LCSH, Maori Wordnet	1950		
Norway	National Library	MARC categories	1940/45,1950		
Pakistan	National Library	LCSH, National system of descriptors	1975		
Panama	Biblioteca Nacional	Encabezamiento de materia, Lista de materias del ICFES		DDC	
Papua New Guinea	National Library Service	LCSH	1981	DDC	
Peru	Biblioteca Nacional	National system			
Philippines	National Library	LCSH			
Poland	National Library	National system	1946/1956, etc.	UDC	
Portugal	Biblioteca Nacional	SIPORBASE	1987	UDC	

197

Country	Library	System of Subject Heading Language	Used since	Classification used instead or additionally	Publication of manual
Romania	Biblioteca Nationala Bucaresti		planned	UDC	
Russia	National Library St. Petersburg				
Scotland	National Library Edinburgh	LCSH	1968		yes
Seychelles	National Library	Sears List	1997	DDC	planned
Slovakia	National Library	LCSH	1995	UDC	planned
Slovenia	National and University Library	In-house system	1994	UDC	
South Africa	National Library Statelibrary.pwv.gov.za	LCSH	1992	DDC	no
Spain	Biblioteca Nacional	National subject authority file	1958	UDC	
Sri Lanka	National Library	LCSH	1986		
Swaziland	University Library Kwaluseni	---		DDC	---
Sweden	Kunglike biblioteket	MARC categories			planned
Switzerland	Schweizerische Landesbibliothek	RSWK, RAMEAU	1998		yes
Syria	Assad National Library	National system	1984	DDC	---
Togo	Bibliothèque nationale	Catalog of national library			---
Trinidad and Tobago	Library Division Office of Prime Minister	LCSH	1991 until 1990	DDC	---
Tunisia	Bibliothèque Nationale	Biblio, RAMEAU	1986-1997; 1998	UDC (DDC planned)	no
Turkey	National Library	LCSH*	planned		
Ukraine	National Parliamentary Library	In-house system LCSH*	1995 planned	BBK	
United Kingdom	British Library	LCSH (PRECIS) (COMPASS)	1994 1971-1991 1991-1996		yes (PRECIS and LCSH)
USA	Library of Congress	LCSH	1898		yes
Venezuela	Biblioteca Nacional	LCSH*		DDC	
Wales	National Library	LCSH	1985		
Yugoslavia	National Library of Serbia	LCSH	1948	UDC	yes
Zambia	National Archives of Zambia	Sears List	1970	DDC	
Zimbabwe	National Archives	LCSH		DDC	---

Crossing Language Barriers in Europe: Linking *LCSH* to Other Subject Heading Languages

Andrew MacEwan

SUMMARY. A study group representing four European national libraries (the Swiss National Library, Die Deutsche Bibliothek, the Bibliotheque nationale de France and The British Library) recently conducted a study on the possibility of establishing multilingual thesaural links between the headings in the *LCSH* authority file and the authority files of the German indexing system SWD/RSWK and the French indexing system RAMEAU. The study demonstrated a high level of correspondence in main headings, but also revealed a number of issues requiring further investigation. The study group's findings led to recommendations on the scope for the development of a prototype system for linking the three Subject Heading Languages (SHLs) in the databases of the four institutions. *[Article copies available for a fee from The Haworth Document Delivery Service: 1-800-342-9678. E-mail address: <getinfo@haworthpressinc.com> Website: <http://www.haworthpressinc.com>]*

KEYWORDS. Multilingual thesauri, Subject Heading Language, RAMEAU, SWD/RSWK, *LCSH*

INTRODUCTION

The *Library of Congress Subject Headings* has firmly established its predominance as the most widely used system for providing natural language

Andrew MacEwan is Cataloguing Manager, The British Library, Collection Management, Boston Spa, Weitherby, West Yorkshire LS23 7BQ, England.

[Haworth co-indexing entry note]: "Crossing Language Barriers in Europe: Linking *LCSH* to Other Subject Heading Languages." MacEwan, Andrew. Co-published simultaneously in *Cataloging & Classification Quarterly* (The Haworth Information Press, an imprint of The Haworth Press, Inc.) Vol. 29, No. 1/2, 2000, pp. 199-207; and: *The LCSH Century: One Hundred Years with the Library of Congress Subject Headings System* (ed: Alva T. Stone) The Haworth Information Press, an imprint of The Haworth Press, Inc., 2000, pp. 199-207. Single or multiple copies of this article are available for a fee from The Haworth Document Delivery Service [1-800-342-9678, 9:00 a.m. - 5:00 p.m. (EST). E-mail address: getinfo@haworthpressinc.com].

subject access in libraries in the English speaking world. Through the doorway provided by the Subject Authorities Cooperative Program (SACO) this extensivity translates into a certain amount of intercultural influence on the headings and references vocabulary as it continues to accommodate national differences in the use of English. By a process of degrees *LCSH* is becoming a more international subject language. The potential benefits of having such a single, predominant international subject headings system for interlibrary cooperation and user access are limited only by the bounds of the English speaking world. In contrast to a classification code, a natural language based system of subject access inevitably reaches this natural boundary. The idea of transcending this boundary through a system of multithesaural links has been the subject of a recent European study funded under the umbrella of Co-BRA+ (Computerised Bibliographic Record Actions), a concerted action of European national libraries and bibliographic agencies which supports a number of cooperative initiatives. The multithesaural study was undertaken jointly between the Swiss National Library (SNL), Die Deutsche Bibliothek (DDB), the Bibliotheque nationale de France (BNF) and The British Library (BL). This paper reports on that study.[1]

The initial impetus for undertaking the study is the European libraries' context. Where European unity on many levels brings multilingualism into politics, commerce, government and the law, it is natural for libraries to reflect user needs by providing access that can cross linguistic barriers. The ability to network between catalogues in different countries highlights the problem of providing comprehensive subject access where not only languages vary, but subject heading languages or systems vary, too. The problem with not providing multilingual subject access to documents, whatever the original language of the document, is brought sharply into focus where the context is a single country, such as Switzerland, where the national library itself serves a population speaking several languages. The same problem exists for networked access between national libraries across Europe, where technological improvements in access will soon highlight the need for better cooperation on subject access. The ideal would be for users to search comprehensively in their own native language but to be enabled by the catalogue to retrieve documents written and indexed in other languages. An English speaking user should be able to search the database of the Deutsche Bibliothek using English-language headings and retrieve documents which have been indexed using the German subject headings' list. The ability to do this depends upon establishing equivalence links between the terms in the different Subject Heading Languages (SHLs).

From the outset the partners in the project agreed to reject the alternative option: the adoption of one SHL by all the institutions by means of translating it into several languages and thereafter maintaining these in parallel. Just as *LCSH* has become the predominant SHL in the English speaking world by virtue of the fact that past investment in many catalogues makes the invention of a new system uneconomical, so much is also true for the German and French SHLs in their linguistic contexts. Access to documents already indexed would be impeded by the lack of continuity between the abandoned system and the new preferred system. Instead the study set out to investigate the feasibility of establishing equivalence links between the three SHLs used in the four institutions: RAMEAU[2] (France, Switzerland), SWD[3] (Germany), and *LCSH* (Great Britain, Switzerland). Models for this kind of approach already exist in other projects: the creation of equivalents between the *Art and Architecture Thesaurus* and other controlled vocabularies in the same field; and in the Unified Medical Language System (UMLS).

AIMS OF THE STUDY

The study focussed on four key objectives:

- to establish a methodology for the selection and linking of headings that would in principle be extensible to any other SHL if it proved valid in the context of the three SHLs studied;
- to link headings and analyse the results in two selected subject areas: Sports and Theatre;
- to demonstrate the practical applications of these linked headings by indexing 40 titles from the field of Theatre using each SHL being studied and then comparing the results; and,
- to compare the indexing of titles in other subject fields outside the linking study by examining a random selection of titles which had been indexed separately in all three of the SHLs.

These four key elements to the study were selected with the knowledge that the linking approach would be limited to establishing links between authority records. All three subject heading systems are characterized by the provision of rules for the construction of subject heading strings which generate a great many more assigned headings than there are authority records. In the case of RAMEAU and *LCSH*, headings established at the authority level are combined with qualifying subdivisions to precisely delineate a subject, whilst in SWD/RSWK different headings are combined with each other to form similarly more precise strings. There would be significant problems inherent in attempting to map across and establish links between these variant syntactical constructions. The scale of the task, issues in comparing syntax and meaning, and finally the need to identify a mechanism for recording links all pointed towards the advantage of first establishing links between authority records. This would mean that the fullest level of access to the searcher would come from using the language in which a document was indexed, but access through the other SHLs would at least provide a way-in to the host SHL. Although this would provide less than full, "ideal" multilingual access, it avoided syntactical complexities and focussed the study on the likely tool for establishing equivalence relationships–the authority record. In short the study opted for the feasible.

Having taken this decision the group felt that the comparative application of the headings in each system remained a key issue. It might prove possible to find a high level of equivalence in the vocabulary terms established in the authority file, but simultaneously to find a lack of correspondence in the choices made by cataloguers when assigning headings. In principle all the SHLs should be applied to the same level of specificity,[4] but would the practical application by cataloguers reveal differences in judgement on what is specific? The maintenance of inter-indexer consistency within the sphere of application of a single SHL is often a cause for concern, but in comparing separate SHLs we would be entering new territory.

METHODOLOGY: LINKING HEADINGS

The two subject areas Sports and Theatre were selected as manageable samples on which to develop the methodology. Both offered particular advantages for the purposes of testing the level of equivalences. Sports was adopted in the expectation that it would be relatively uncomplicated, with limited cultural or national bias affecting the types of headings, but terms would not be as international as those in a defined scientific field. Theatre was chosen for the opposite reason that cultural variations were to be expected and this would generate potentially interesting problems in matching terminology.

The aim of establishing a methodology was achieved in the process of studying the links between these fields. The process was broken down into a number of steps:

1. The subject field was defined by choosing corresponding generic main headings in the SHLs and from these tracing the Narrower Terms. Because *LCSH* is not a strictly controlled thesaurus this had to be backed up through additional searching for associated compound headings, usually by browsing the terms adjacent to those found in the hierarchical approach. The same adjustment was necessary for the other SHLs, too. The scope of the subject area was further limited by agreement in order to prevent unnecessary expansion into related fields, e.g., Theatre was defined to exclude Drama which meant that some headings origi-

nally picked up in the hierarchical approach were then eliminated, such as **Didactic drama**.
2. Monolingual lists were established in the chosen subject field from each SHL, and checked for consistency in scope.
3. The lists were then compared and matches made between equivalent headings. Methodological issues arose in the application of the third step. The process of looking for perfect one-to-one matches soon led to some more flexible solutions where one-to-two equivalents were also allowed at the heading level. The decision to include such matches was grounded in a structured view of the subject heading as part of a subject heading language. In the context of an SHL the meaning or use of a given subject heading is further defined by the equivalent *Used For* references added in the authority record. This "Synonymy Principle" was followed in all the SHLs in the study and so provided a valid basis for allowing one-to-two links in some instances, e.g., the UF reference **High jumping** in *LCSH* serves to validate the following two links to the SWD and RAMEAU:

Jumping = **Sprung** = Sauts (athletisme)
Jumping = **Hochsprung** = Saut en hauteur

The other major methodological issue that the study revealed was the impact of the syntactical variance between the three SHLs. A heading in one language would often be equivalent to a string created only at the point of assigning the headings in one or both of the other SHLs. At the indexing level there would be exact correspondence, but at the headings level there was only partial correspondence. For example, **Track athletics–Coaches** in *LCSH* matches with **Leichtathletiktrainer** in the SWD, but in RAMEAU it is only matched by adding a subdivision to the authority record at the point of indexing a document: **Athletisme–***Entraineurs*.

One possible solution to this would be to establish such strings as authority records in order to allow the linking to be possible. If authority records existed for all the terms used in a string then it would be possible to look at one-to-many relationships from a compound heading to equivalent parts which together make a match from a different SHL. Since authority records exist for all terms in the SWD and the establishment of an authority file for *LCSH* subdivisions is on the agenda, this was felt to be capable of a technical solution at some future date. For the purposes of the study in examining the level of linguistic mapping possible between the SHLs the decision was made to allow links between headings and strings in the results. This modified the original aim to the extent that the existence of an authority record in at least one SHL was required to initiate the search for a match, but an assigned string would be accepted in the results as an acceptable equivalence in any of the other SHL vocabularies.

One further modification was also introduced in the process of finding matches, although this only had a limited impact. Where comparison between the SHLs revealed an opportunity to improve one of the SHLs by the creation of a new heading this was done in order to create the match, provided there was literary warrant in the catalogue of the user institution.

METHODOLOGY–COMPARATIVE INDEXING

Two complementary samples were taken to compare the indexing of the same works using the different SHLs. Firstly a general comparison was made between titles which had already been indexed separately using all three SHLs. This sample was harder to study because it touched randomly on subject areas and involved a comparative analysis of headings assigned which had not been matched at the authority level in the first part of the study. It was included, however, to provide evidence for the general level of correspondence between the indexing of the four institutions in their application of the three SHLs. The second approach was to work specifically in the field of Theatre, which had been studied at the headings level, and independently index a selection of works in the three SHLs in order to compare the results. The advantage of this approach would be to test the meaningfulness of the matches being established between the headings. Would they be used in practice to index the same documents?

RESULTS–LINKING HEADINGS

Comparison of terms in the area of *Sports* (total sample 278 headings):

- 86% of headings matched across all the three SHLs
- 8% of headings matched across two SHLs
- 6% of headings remained unmatched

Comparison of terms in the area of *Theatre* (total sample 261 headings):

- 60% of headings matched across all three SHLs
- 18% of headings matched across two SHLs
- 22% of headings remained unmatched

These results were taken to be a positive outcome reflecting the expectations held at the outset concerning the two subject fields. In the case of Theatre the culture of the countries in which each SHL originated had a higher impact on the level of matching than was likely to be possible, since in many cases no translation was possible between culture-specific headings. Literary warrant simply had not occurred to generate the need for a heading. For instance the concept represented by **Kasperletheater** exists only in the SWD, and **Living newspaper** does not exist in RAMEAU. Another significant observation made in interpreting the results was that the most frequently used headings were most likely to find equivalences across all three SHLs. For the 50 most frequently used RAMEAU headings in the field of Theatre in the database of the Bibliotheque nationale de France, the level of trilingual equivalence rose to 86%.

RESULTS–COMPARATIVE INDEXING

The first approach of comparing indexing across a wide range of subjects revealed an overlap in the use of equivalent headings, which varied from between 29% to 56%. In more definitive subject fields correspondence was easier to find, e.g.,

Title: Using and understanding medical statistics

SWD/RSWK **Medizinische Statistik**
LCSH **Medical statistics**
RAMEAU **Statistique medicale**

In other fields differences ranged from relatively minor to more serious. For instance SWD/RSWK defined "early church" history as the period 30-325 AD, whereas *LCSH* and RAMEAU defined the period as 30-600 AD. But in terms of the study these differences only appeared in subdivisions, not at the level of headings to be matched. More serious differences occurred at the level of the main headings assigned:

Title: Bank guarantees in international trade: the law and practice of independent (first demand) guarantees and standby letters of credit in civil law and common law jurisdictions

SWD/RSWK **Bankgarantie/Aussenhandel/Internationales Privatrecht/ Rechtsvereinheitlichung**
LCSH **Suretyship and guaranty**
Letters of credit
RAMEAU **Garanties a premiere demande**

The second comparison of the indexing of 40 works was more focussed and produced a better result. However, allowance had to be made for the fact that a number of the titles studied involved the assignment of personal names, period subdivisions and form subdivisions which were not part of the authorities studied. Setting the titles aside which achieved specificity by the use of name as subject access gave a result of 23 out of 27 titles with at least one direct equivalence at the authority level–85%.

NEXT STEPS

The results of the study show that a high level of equivalence links can be established between the SHLs. These links do in many cases provide a potentially valuable pathway between the different systems in application, although the results of the comparative indexing suggest that this may vary between subject areas. The CoBRA study group concluded that the results of this initial study were sufficiently promising to make a general recommendation to continue research a stage further. However, the analysis and discussion of the results and the process followed by the study group led them to make a number of specific suggestions on the way in which further research should be taken forward.

1. The study had focussed on proving the existence of adequate correspondence between *LCSH*, RAMEAU and the SWD/RSWK. The editorial process established for the identification and confirmation of links was labour intensive. In order to maximise the impact of such work it would be critical for any real process to focus on the most-used headings in the SHLs. This would impact on access to more bibliographic records and it would capitalise on the finding that these headings were likely to prove the most "matchable."

2. For the same reason further research should give attention to developing an efficient operational process for selection and matching of headings, perhaps by the use of automatic generation of headings and potential matches in the first instance. Possible mechanisms might involve associated classification numbers, or the use of RAMEAU/ *LCSH* links already established on the RAMEAU authority files of the BNF.

3. A mechanism to carry the links would need to be developed. The study had established the intellectual feasibility of matching terms between the three SHLs, but the method for applying and exploiting these links in the catalogues of the participating institutions remains to be defined. The two main options considered were the maintenance of reference links in the separate authority files of each participating institution or the creation of a separate *metathesaurus* for recording and managing links. The study group proposed the creation of a metathesaurus which

stands outside all three systems. This would concentrate editorial activity in one database, but access to it could be available to any participant. It would also provide a readily extensible mechanism for adding headings from other Subject Heading Languages. A heading in the individual SHL would be able to link to the metathesaurus by holding a reference to the identifier in the appropriate metathesaurus authority record. Consideration would need to be given to the best carrier for the metathesaurus record: UNIMARC authority format or Classification authority records were suggested among the possibilities.

4. Another editorial issue for the further development of this work was also identified. The study had shown that comparison between the systems for purposes of matching terms also exposed opportunities for local improvement to the individual SHLs. For the British Library this would mean proposing changes to *LCSH* through SACO, and in some cases with only vicarious literary warrant (for instance, in matching *LCSH* with the application of RAMEAU to an item held in the BNF).

5. Finally, the searching and use of the links in the catalogues of the participating institutions would need to be defined, and consideration given to the presentation of headings in subject indexes (separate indexes or interfiled?), record display, default languages, and the visibility or invisibility of switching from one language to another.

The above recommendations and questions are being taken forward in a further demonstrator project which will develop a prototype system that can be used to examine and evaluate the linking references in a real, online environment. By delivering a test product, Project MACS (Multilingual Access to Subjects) will address all the questions raised by the initial study. This next phase of the project is due to report in the second half of the year 2000.

NOTES

1. CoBRA+ Working Group on Multilingual Subject Access. *Final report*, Bern, March 1999. <http://www.bl.uk/information/finrap.html>.

2. RAMEAU is the acronym for *Répertoire d'Autorité-Matière Encyclopédique et Alphabétique Unifié*.

3. SWD is the abbreviation used for *Schlagwortnormdatei*, the German language list of subject headings. (Ed. note: At other points in this paper, the author refers to the system as "SWD/RSWK." The second initialism stands for the *Regeln für den Schlagwortkatalog*, or, Rules for the Subject Catalogue.)

4. Working Group on Principles Underlying Subject Heading Languages, IFLA Section on Classification and Indexing, *Principles Underlying Subject Heading Languages (SHLs), Final Draft*. Maria Inês Lopes and Julianne Beall, eds., March 1997.

Automated Authority Files
of Spanish-Language Subject Headings

Alvaro Quijano-Solís
Pilar María Moreno-Jiménex
Reynaldo Figueroa-Servín

SUMMARY. Authority control of Spanish-language subject headings is described, with a special focus on Mexico. Efforts currently underway in Colombia, Chile, Spain and Mexico, although they share the same language, are somewhat lacking in standardization and cooperation among countries. In the absence of a national authority for bibliographic control in Mexico, a group of university libraries has initiated a cooperative project to build in the near future a national file of Spanish subject headings for the Social Sciences. The project, based upon the experience and rich collections of El Colegio de México, has attracted support from the U.S. Library of Congress and is being partially financed by the U.S.-Mexican Fund for Culture (sponsored by the Rockefeller and Bancomer Foundations). The paper mentions some of the difficul-

Alvaro Quijano-Solís, BSc, MS, is currently a PhD student (Systems Engineering), National University of Mexico, and is Director, Daniel Cosío Villegas Library, El Colegio de México, Camino al Ajusco # 20,01000 México, D. F. México (E-mail: quijano@colmex.mx). Pilar María Moreno-Jiménex, BA, MLS, is Bibliographer (currently on sabbatical leave), Daniel Cosío Villegas Library, El Colegio de México, Instituto Tecnológico y de Estudios Superiores de Monterrey, Campus Querétaro, Av. Epigmenio González #500, 76130 Querétero, Qro. México (E-mail: pmoreno@campus.qro.itesm.mx). Reynaldo Figueroa-Servín, BA, is Bibliographer and Leader of the Subject Headings Project, Daniel Cosio Villegas Library, El Colegio de México, Camino al Ajusco # 20, 01000 México, D.F. México (E-mail: rfiguero@colmex.mx).

[Haworth co-indexing entry note]: "Automated Authority Files of Spanish-Language Subject Headings." Quijano-Solís, Alvaro, Pilar María Moreno-Jiménex, and Reynaldo Figueroa-Servín. Co-published simultaneously in *Cataloging & Classification Quarterly* (The Haworth Information Press, an imprint of The Haworth Press, Inc.) Vol. 29, No. 1/2, 2000, pp. 209-223; and: *The LCSH Century: One Hundred Years with the Library of Congress Subject Headings System* (ed: Alva T. Stone) The Haworth Press, Inc., 2000, pp. 209-223. Single or multiple copies of this article are available for a fee from The Haworth Document Delivery Service [1-800-342-9678, 9:00 a.m. - 5:00 p.m. (EST). E-mail address: getinfo@haworthpress inc.com].

ties found in translating *LCSH*, which is the main resource for the project. These difficulties can include semantics, syndetic structure, or
pragmatic problems; most have been solved by supplementing the
LCSH with Spanish-language subject heading lists or thesauri. *[Article
copies available for a fee from The Haworth Document Delivery Service:
1-800-342-9678. E-mail address: <getinfo@haworthpressinc.com Website:
<http://www.haworthpressinc.com>]*

KEYWORDS. Subject authority files, Spanish language, *LCSH*, Mexican libraries, Latin America, NACO

BACKGROUND

It was in the early 1960's when a project to provide a systematic list of
subject headings for Latin American libraries was envisioned by some
librarians from the Pan American Union.[1] As a result of this project, the *Lista
de encabezamientos de materia para bibliotecas* (Subject Headings List for
Libraries), compiled by Carmen Rovira and Jorge Aguayo, was published in
1967.[2] That list was used by many public, national, academic, and special
Latin American libraries. Supplements were issued by the Organization of
American States in 1969 and 1970. A new edition was published by the
Instituto Colombiano para el Fomento de la Educación Superior (ICFES)
(Colombian Institute for the Promotion of Higher Education) in 1985.[3] By
then, the list was generated from a database in MARC format. It is to be noted
that from the beginning, the main source for the subject headings list was the
LCSH, along with some other sources in Spanish. A third edition of this list,
also known as LEMB, was published by the Luis Angel Arango Library of
the Bank of the Republic of Colombia in 1998.[4]

Recently, an automated authority file of Spanish-language subject headings that many libraries could share has been envisioned as extremely useful
to the libraries of the Latin American countries and to those American libraries that serve Hispanic communities. That file should cover scientific,
social, and humanities fields, and include terms related to Latin American
history and culture. The information in the records of that database should
include the established heading in Spanish together with the equivalent *LCSH*
heading, as well as synonyms, broader, narrower, and related terms, scope
notes, sources of the heading, subdivisions, etc. A condition for the records to
be exchangable is the use of a compatible USMARC format. The enormity
and complexity of the creation and maintenance of such an authority file,
beyond the financial resources necessary to accomplish it, makes it a likely
project for inter-institutional cooperation.

In the Spanish-language arena some libraries have undertaken large-scale projects to automate their subject authority files. Following are some experiences which can be considered illustrative.

SPAIN

Efforts toward establishing a national authority file in Spain have culminated in a product entitled *Autoridades de la Biblioteca Nacional,* available in print or compact disk.[5] The CD contains personal, corporate and meeting name authorities as well as uniform titles, series and subject authorities. More than 156,000 records of the latter are included in the CD in IBERMARC authorities[6] format (based on the U.S. equivalent USMARC Authorities)[7] which will be expanded as successive editions are published.[8] These headings cover a broad spectrum of subjects from scientific to social disciplines. The subject authority records include related headings, occasionally indicating the hierarchical relationship between them. There are also hypertext links that make it possible to navigate from some records to others by following these related headings. Another interesting feature included in the subject authority records of *Autoridades de la Biblioteca Nacional* are the equivalents in other systems for the heading established in a record, particularly the equivalent in English from the *LCSH* list. Furthermore, the CD makes it possible to download records in various formats such as IBERMARC and ISO-2709 formats, facilitating transfer of authority records to local databases. It should be noted that the limitations to this CD include:

a. IBERMARC format has not been updated to the most recent edition of its USMARC equivalent;
b. it does not include the complete variety of words characteristic of Latin America; and,
c. it does not allow searches by the English term.

COLOMBIA

The Library of the Bank of the Republic of Colombia maintains a subject authority file based on a list of subject headings prepared by the Instituto Colombiano para el Fomento de la Educación Superior (ICFES)[9] (Colombian Institute for the Promotion of Higher Education), with more than 35,000 records in USMARC format and administered by the NOTIS system. The original ICFES list, also known as LEMB, was published enriched and updated in 1998.[10] A CD edition has been planned but postponed due to the incipient state of automation of most of Colombia's libraries.

Among the characteristics of this database are: (a) it has subject headings for all branches of science and social studies including specifically Latin American subjects; (b) it notes as synonyms the diverse words or expressions for a particular term used in the various countries of Latin America; (c) it provides headings related to the established heading, occasionally specifying hierarchical relationships; and (d) it includes headings with subdivisions. One of the principal authority sources for the database is the *LCSH* list and each record includes the English equivalent for the heading.

CHILE

In Chile, the Libraries System of the Pontificia Universidad Católica has a database including more than 150,000 subject authority records in USMARC format available through Chile's Red Nacional de Información Bibliográfica (National Bibliographic Information Network).[11] This database was constructed from the above-mentioned Colombian list. The subject coverage is broad although adjustments were made for the Chilean context. In this case too, one of the main sources is the *LCSH* list and the database also includes the English equivalents for headings.

MEXICO

Mexico has undertaken serious attempts to create automated authority files. The Universidad Nacional Autónoma de México (DGB-UNAM)[12] Dirección General de Bibliotecas, for example, has a subject authority file including more than 89,500 records covering headings for both scientific and social areas. This catalogue includes English equivalents taken from the *LCSH* list. Some of its greater limitations are that it is not yet available in MARC format, it contains practically no notes, and it fails to establish hierarchical relationships between related terms. The library at El Colegio de México[13] maintains an authority file in MARC format containing approximately 5,000 subject records in the social sciences and humanities. The majority of these records include the English equivalent taken from the *LCSH* list. An updated edition in terms of content and structure of the *Lista de encabezamientos de materia* (List of subject headings) by Gloria Escamilla,[14] unquestionably the most used in Mexico, has not yet been published nor is it available in digitized form. A cooperative project to create an automated subject authority file to serve Mexico's libraries has been initiated within the Mexico-United States Interlibrary Loan Network, to which a number of Mexican university libraries as well as the Benjamin Franklin Library of the United States Embassy belong.[15]

Comparative Table of Experiences

	Spain	Colombia	Chile	Mexico
Number of records	Approximately 156,000	Approximately 35,000	Approximately 150,000	Approximately 89,500/5,000
Coverage	Scientific and social areas	Scientific and social areas; Latin America	Scientific and social areas; Chile	Scientific and social areas/Social Sciences and Humanities
Format	IBERMARC	MARC (USMARC)	MARC (USMARC)	No MARC/MARC (USMARC)
LCSH Equivalents	Yes	Yes	Yes	Yes/Yes
Hierarchies	Few	Yes	Few	No/Yes
Records with subdivisions	Yes	Yes	Yes	Yes/Yes
Subdivision Records	No	No	Yes	No/Yes
Type of Library	National library	Public library	University library	University libraries

In terms of the number of records, the richest database belongs to Spain, followed by Chile and the DGB-UNAM in Mexico. In terms of coverage, practically all aspire to cover all of human knowledge; however, some emphasize or go deeper into Latin American subjects, as in the case of Colombia.

With respect to format, the rule is the USMARC format for authorities, though with minimal local adaptations.

An element common to all is the use of *LCSH*, which is not surprising in view of the size, coverage, structure and content that list. The Library of Congress authority database contains approximately 250,000 records covering scientific, social and humanist areas. The database is in USMARC format for authorities, a complex format produced and updated by specialists at the Library of Congress. The records contain complete information on headings, including hierarchical relationships and subdivisions. This great library's technical and human resources make it possible for its database to grow quickly and solidly. The mass of scientific production in English and the great quantity of material catalogued in the Library of Congress enhances the *LCSH* list as an optimal resource.

The poverty of hierarchical relationships and absence of clear linkage between headings and subdivisions in most of the Spanish-language systems considered constitute aspects that should be taken into account for their improvement. Finally, with the exception of the Biblioteca Nacional de España, efforts in the rest of the countries considered come from libraries lacking legitimacy and resources to undertake a project of the scope and dimensions implicit in the creation and maintenance of a national authority database. It is true that there are rules imposed by usage without the need of legal foundation. However, the fact that the activities undertaken are part of those characteristic of an institution (like a national library) warrants that it justifiably seek financing, whereas it is difficult for other libraries (academic and public) to justify expenditures and activities that outstrip the scope of their own mission.

THE PROJECT' S ENVIRONMENT

Library science is relatively recent in Mexico. Although in the 19th century there was a rich bibliographical tradition inherited from Mexican and Spanish tradition, it was not until the second decade of the 20th century that a well-defined profession began to appear. Its pioneers in Mexico were for the most part trained in the United States. Even today it may be said that those who seek postgraduate instruction prefer the U.S. Even so, graduates from Mexico's National University are now in the majority; thus the immense majority of professionals hold a BA which in Mexico dates from 1945. The extensive influence of U.S. library science is therefore not to be wondered at. In the Latin American context, Mexico is the first port of call of the U.S. library science tendencies. The vast majority of Mexican libraries use the LCC or DDC, AACR2, and base their subject headings on *LCSH* or an adaptation of it.

In light of the advantages this standardization represents in an increasingly integrated information world, Mexican library science has neglected two aspects that compromise its ability to participate in such integration. First, and most visible at the international level, is the lack of a national bibliographical authority.[16] The insertion of the National Library into the structure of the National University of Mexico in the 19th century has been more of a hindrance than a help, preventing it from playing a leading role in Mexican library science, particularly in its standardization. Thus, Mexico does not have a national headings list for any kind of library, nor are there national norms equivalent to AACR2 or MARC, although the latter have become *de facto* norms due to their wide usage, particularly in the larger university libraries of Mexico.

A second aspect is that there is little culture of interlibrary cooperation, with the exception of the U.S.-Mexican border It was in the 1970's that the American Library Association's Interlibrary Loan Code was adopted as the basis for cooperation in this region. There are more or less solid groups in areas of knowledge among medical and agricultural libraries arising out of specific needs of documentary exchange, although experience with union catalogues has been very limited. The earliest efforts toward union catalogues date from 1949 for the areas of health, and 1968 saw the first serials catalogue which was continued until 1976. More recently, the UNAM, the largest university in Mexico, annexed the collections of other libraries to its own in order to publish SERIUNAM, the serials catalogue that enjoys the largest coverage in Mexico.[17]

Robert Seal, librarian at the University of Texas at El Paso, proposed in 1989 that a group of university libraries, as well as the USIS Benjamin Franklin Library, start a project for university libraries belonging to the AMIGOS network to promote interlibrary loan between the two countries. The mechanism was based on a line of communication between the Benjamin Franklin Library and the University of Texas at El Paso whereby the two institutions would be responsible respectively for acquiring books and photocopies in Mexico and the United States. The Benjamin Franklin Library Diplomatic Pouch would be used as courier to guarantee that the materials arrive at their destination safely and on time. Seal records this experience in another place.[18] On the basis of this project a consortium of 10 university libraries known as the Network of Mexican Institutions for Library Cooperation was created and has been the embryo of other cooperative projects that have laid the groundwork for efforts of this kind and generated products such as the Ancient Mexican Bibliography (ABIMEX Antigua Bibliografía Mexicana), while negotiating more advantageously with some suppliers at the same time. This group will celebrate its first ten years of existence with a Congress on Digital Libraries in the year 2000.

Under the aegis of the U.S.-Mexican Fund for Culture sponsored by the Rockefeller and Bancomer Foundations, the consortium has obtained funding for ABIMEX and, more recently, for the creation of databases for a machine-readable union subject catalogue. This project was born within the consortium supported by its members. At the present time, however, this project has become the sole responsibility of the Daniel Cosío Villegas Library of El Colegio de Mexico.

THE PROJECT

El Colegio de México is a research and teaching institution that originated in the Casa de España en Mexico created in 1938 as a haven for distinguished Spanish intellectuals fleeing the Spanish Civil War. In 1940, the institution became El Colegio de México, defining its areas of research as the social sciences and humanities. The institution promotes research in Linguistic and Literary Studies, History, International Studies, Asian and African Studies, Demography and Urban Development, Sociology and Economics. It grants a

BA in Public Administration and in International Studies, while the rest of the student body (usually no more than 300) pursue graduate studies in those fields. Both research and teaching at El Colegio de México enjoy worldwide recognition for their high level of excellence. The Daniel Cosío Villegas Library reflects this tradition and is in itself a solid institution enjoying high professional prestige and housing the largest social science collection in Mexico, particularly sources on Latin America and Spain, the United States and Middle East, East and South Asia.

The Library's proximity to its readers assures that its processes of selection, cataloging and classification are carried out at the highest level and pursuant to the rules of bibliographical control.[19] It should also be noted that the Library's administration is committed to guaranteeing that the process of creation and maintenance of catalogue files will generate products whose quality and content contain a high level of documentary value, thereby adding value to the collections by optimizing access to them. It is in this context of optimizing products for the reader, that the Authority Control Project becomes particularly significant:

1. Creation of uniform heading (access points) to ensure collocation of all closely related works;
2. Creation of links (usually in the form of cross-references) to lead the searcher from variant forms of the heading to the established form; and,
3. Provision of adequate information to distinguish the established heading from another similar heading.[20]

From the services perspective, the project seeks to provide users with efficient tools to retrieve information, with its principal focus on authority control. The project's goals are specifically:

a. To increase the supply of subject headings that reflect the subjects of study and research of the Colegio de Mexico's academic community in a way that is current, specific, consistent, uniform and pertinent to our linguistic context;
b. To maintain authority control files up-to-date in keeping with MARC Authority format conventions;
c. To actively create authority and bibliographical files of the online catalogue, as useful to readers for search and retrieval relevant and pertinent to their needs; and,
d. To disseminate and share the results of the program with similar institutions both in print and online, particularly normative documents and authority control files.

Strategies

Strategic planning implies carrying out more precise analysis of the elements involved in the creation and maintenance of new tasks and of procedures. Subject analysis acquires particular relevance as part of the tasks related to the creation of information products with added value. The development of a database of authorized selected subject headings, as well as research aimed at establishing authorities in an original way, constitute part of the library's information policies that represent standardized points of access and assistance to readers in their searches. The consolidation of strategic lines of action from the authorities project has brought about the establishment of the following areas of operative and functional infrastructure.

Automation

- Installation of equipment required to insure complete and integral functionality of ALEPH System version 500.
- Establishment of online and network means of access to Library of Congress authority sources on compact disk, in our case it is ITS presentation.
- Design of workforms, parameter tables, and help screens for capturing authority records in the corresponding ALEPH module.

Standardization and Bibliographical Control

The Daniel Cosío Villegas Library's concept of authority control represents the axis of a more general project that might be divided into logical sub-programs as follows:

- Revision of MARCOLMEX formats for bibliographical and authority records.
- Establishment of policies, procedures, routines and specifications for the creation and maintenance of computer readable authority records.[21]
- Validation of thematic structures based mainly on the indications and principles of the Library of Congress's *Subject Cataloging Manual: Subject Headings* (1993) and their tacit expression in the *Library of Congress Subject Headings*, 21st ed., 1998; or in any of its forms, such as the ITS Authorities compact disk version (Inwood, West Virginia: The Library Corporation, summer 1997).
- Use of sources for the translation of subjects into Spanish, mentioned further on in the usage of field 670.[22] Besides the lists of most up-to-date subject headings in Spanish, a collection of bilingual dictionaries

specialized in the social sciences and the humanities has been selected.

- Definition of the MARCOLMEX authorities format in strict conformity with the USMARC-Authorities format, with specification of all codifying components contained in authority records corresponding subject headings.
- Design of electronic workforms for the creation of original subject authority records.
- Determination of quality control mechanisms by means of:

1. Automatic and manual detecting and correction of spacing, punctuation, spelling, coding errors and invalid forms of headings.[23]
2. Morphological, syntactical and semantic validation of the structures of thematic headings and of the hierarchical networks composed by their associative relationships.
3. Control of the structures of subject headings with subdivisions.

Personnel

Authority control implies reliance on librarians with professional skills in expert cataloguing and classifying, with special emphasis on understanding a system of subject analysis, knowledge of the MARC format as well as normative structures of subject headings and tasks pertaining to documentary languages. Advice, coordination and direction in authority control are part of the process. Thus, staff assigned to the Authority Control Project attended a training course given at Library of Congress for potential NACO contributors. The Program for Cooperative Cataloging (PCC) of the Library of Congress decided as an exception to facilitate a mechanism for the contribution of files via e-mail so that the Daniel Cosío Villegas Library could send its proposals for new entries and headings, even though it was not a member of the either the OCLC or RLIN bibliographical utilities. The Library's designated institutional identification code is: MxMxEMC.

Products

Besides training professional personnel of the Bibliographic Control Department as mentioned above, Ageo García, with the support of the Daniel Cosío Villegas Library, has offered a "workshop in bibliographic authority control with MARC format" at the national level available to technical process personnel of the following institutions: ITAM, ITESM-Mexico State campus and Monterrey campus, University of the Americas, Puebla, Anahuac University-South and North, National Indigenous Affairs Institute, Dr. José Ma. Luis Mora Institute, Autonomous University of San Luis Potosí, Autonomous University of Ciudad Juárez, CIDE, El Colegio de la Frontera

Sur, National Autonomous University of Mexico: National Periodicals Library. A manual entitled "Formato MARC de Autoridades"[24] has been drawn up among the products of the project, as well as a website where authority files can already be consulted.[25] Here some examples of Spanish-language subject authority records in MARC format. (The English equivalence comes in field 750, and in subfield 0 there is the control number of the corresponding LC record.)

```
LDR      - - - - -nz- - - - - - - - - - -n- - - - - -
008      - - - - - - -e-acznnaaan||||||||- -a-bna&&- -d
040      |a COLMEX |b spa |c COLMEX
150      |a Cielo (Religión)
550      |w g |a Paraíso (Islam)
550      |w g |a Vida futura
550      |w h |a Empíreo
550      |w h |a Reconocimiento celestial
550      |w h |a Takamagahara
550      |w h |a Vida intermedia
750 0    |a Heaven |0 sh 85059839
902      |a rfs
670      |a LEMB, 1998: |b p. 200 (Cielo (Religión))
SYS      0001847
```

```
LDR      - - - - -nz- - - - - - - - - -n- - - - - -
008      - - - - - - -e-acznnaaan||||||||- -a-bna&&- -d
040      |a COLMEX |b spa |c COLMEX
150      |a Cielo
550      |w g |a Astronomía
550      |w g |a Atmósfera
550      |w h |a Constelaciones
750 0    |a Sky |0 sh 85123252
902      |a rfs
670      |a Lista CSIC, 1995: |b p. 162 (Cielo)
SYS      0001848
```

For the subjects of "heaven" and "sky," we have two words in English and only one in Spanish; thus in Spanish we need another word to specify the meaning. Notice that the terms in fields 550 are also translated from *LCSH*, and they can be used as new terms to be developed as well if needed. These next examples show terms with no equivalence in English and hence not found in *LCSH*. Sometimes they refer to Mexican culture:

```
LDR        - - - - -nz- - - - - - - - - -n- - - - - -
008        - - - - - - -e-acznnaaan||||||||- -a-bna&&- -d
040        |a COLMEX |b spa |c COLMEX
150        |a Compadrazgo
450        |a Compadres
450        |a Comadres
450        |a Compaternidad
550        |w g |a Parentesco
550        |w g |a Bautismo
550        |w g |a Confirmación
550        |a Tutores
902        |a rfs/RFS/BEC/OAN
670        |a Enciclopedia Internacional de las Ciencias Sociales, D.L. Sills ed., 1979:
           |b vol. 7, p. 599 (Compadrazgo)
670        |a Enciclopedia de México, 1987: |b p. 1715 (Compadrazgo. Institución
           religiosa de origen cristiano establecida en México por los
           conquistadores españoles. La palabra significa "participar por la
           paternidad" y en el caso de la comadre, de la maternidad)
```

```
LDR        - - - - -nz- - - - - - - - - -n- - - - - -
CAT        |a YOHANAN |b 20 |c 19991027 |/ ECM12 |h 0826
008        - - - - - - -e-acznnaaan||||||||- -a-bna&&- -d
040        |a COLMEX |b spa |c COLMEX
150        |a Día de los muertos
450        |a Día de muertos
450        |w nne |a Muerte (en religión, folklore, etc.)
550        |w g |a Muerte |x Folklore
550        |w g |a Muerte |x Mitología
902        |a rfs/OAN
SYS        0001846
```

It could happen that, if field 150 has no English equivalent, some of them do have it in fields 450 and 550. So the construction in English would be as follows:

```
LDR        - - - - -nz- - - - - - - - - -n- - - - - -
008        - - - - - - -e-acznnaaan||||||||- -a-bna&&- -d
040        |a COLMEX |b spa |c COLMEX
150        |a Compadrazgo
450        |a Godparenthood
450        |a Coparenthood

450        |a Pseudo-kinship
550        |w g |a Kinship
550        |w g |a Baptism
550        |w g |a Confirmation
550        |a Sponsors
902        |a rfs/RFS/BEC/OAN
670        |a Parson, Roger. Anthropological glossary, 1985: |b p. 54 (Compadrazgo,
           a system of ritual kinship or godparenthood practised in Latin America)
670        |a Uribe Wod, Elena. The patterning of compadrazgo in Latin America,
           1978: |b p. [1] (Compadrazgo is Catholic in origin and the institution is
           supported by metaphysical sanctions, the secular uses to which
           godparental ties are put, both in Europe and Latin America)
670        |a International Encyclopedia of the Social Sciences. D.L. Sills ed., 1968: |b
           vol. 8, p. 410 (Compadrazgo)
SYS        0001844
```

```
LDR       - - - - -nz- - - - - - - - - - -n- - - - - -
008       - - - - - - -e-acznnaaan||||||||- -a-bna&&- -d
040       |a COLMEX |b spa |c COLMEX
150       |a Day of the dead
450       |a Dead's day
450       |w nne |a Dead (in religion, folklore, etc.)
550       |w g |a Dead |x Folklore
550       |w g |a Dead |x Mythology
902       |a rfs
670       |a Encyclopedia of Mexico : history, society & Culture. Ed. Michael S.
          Werner, 1997 |b vol. 1, p. 391 (Day of the dead)
SYS       0001846
```

Mexico as well as other Latin American countries, could contribute and enrich *LCSH* list with local geographic name records. For example:

```
LDR       - - - - -nz- - - - - - - - - -n- - - - - -
003       DLC
040       |a COLMEX |b spa |c COLMEX
151       |a Tierra Blanca (Guanajuato: Municipio)
902       |a VCC/tph/OAN
670       |a Cuaderno estadístico municipal : Tierra Blanca, 1997: |b port. (Tierra
          Blanca, Estado de Guanajuato)
670       |a Dicc. Porrúa, 1995: |b p. 3496 (Tierra Blanca, Gto., Mun.)
670       |a Los municipios de Guanajuato, 1988: |b p. 204 (Tierra Blanca; f. 1536 ; la
          cabecera municipal es Tierra Blanca, 21°06'09"N. 100°04'44"0.)
SYS       0001374
```

Opportunities

Currently the database has close to 5,000 authority records including authors, subjects, and Mexican local and municipal geographic names. We are presently in the process of review, seeking consistency and uniformity in hierarchical relations, and coherence in notes, with particular attention to the standardization represented by each subject. Among the challenges worth noting is the fact that a project of this kind requires highly trained personnel, costly computer resources and a mature group of libraries to establish a consortium. Were a small group of libraries with similar resources to exist, it would indeed be possible to outline procedures for shared cataloguing among a group of academic libraries imbued with the spirit of cooperation.

The Future

The potential scope of the products generated in the context of the Daniel Cosío Villegas Library's Authority Program, both in its normative aspects and its functional principles, could extend the benefits from the availability of machine-readable authority files, representing in an updated and standardized form the names of authors and subject headings required for the efficient retrieval of information, to those libraries which, having the required basic infrastructure, share common subject areas with El Colegio de México in the social sciences and the humanities. The project is unquestionably the source from which it might be possible to generate a national list of subject headings based on the experience acquired in methodology of development of each heading in El Colegio and, particularly, in vocabulary control based on the opinion of its library's users.

As agreed with the US-Mexico Fund for Culture which supported this project, by the end of the year 2000, libraries on both sides of the border will be supplied with a database of Spanish-language subject headings in MARC format that will cover the areas of Mexican social sciences.

NOTES

1. Marietta Daniels, *Encabezamientos de materia para América Latina.* (Washington: Unión Panamericana, 1965).

2. Carmen Rovira and Jorge Aguayo, eds. *Lista de encabezamientos para bibliotecas.* (Washington: Unión Panamericana, 1967).

3. Instituto Colombiano para el Fomento de la Educación Superior and Organización de los Estados Americanos. *Lista de encabezamientos de materias para bibliotecas.* 2. ed. (Bogotá: Procultura, 1985).

4. Colombia. Banco de la República. Biblioteca Luis Angel Arango. *Lista de encabezamientos de materia para bibliotecas.* (Bogotá: Rojas Eberhard, 1998).

5. Spain. Biblioteca Nacional. *Autoridades de la Biblioteca Nacional,* (Madrid: Ministerio de Educación y Cultura/Chadwyck-Healy, 1996-).

6. The IBERMARC format for authority records has been used in Spain since 1991 but has not yet been published as of this date.

7. *USMARC Format for Authority Data,* Cum. vol. (Washington, D.C., Library of Congress Network Development and MARC Standards Office), 1989; update 3, 1990; ed. 1993, update 1, 1995.

8. The National Library of Spain plans two updates per year. Six disks have appeared so far, the first in November 1996 and the last in June 1999.

9. Instituto Colombiano para el Fomento de la Educación Superior and Organización de Estados Americanos. *Lista de encabezamientos de materia para bibliotecas.* 2. ed. (Bogotá, Procultura, 1985).

10. Colombia. Banco de la República. Biblioteca Luis Angel Arango. *Lista de encabezamientos de materia para bibliotecas.* 3rd ed. (Bogotá, Rojas Eberhard Editores, 1998). 2 v.

11. Pontificia Universidad Católica de Chile. Dirección del Sistema de Bibliotecas. *Proyecto "Implementación de una Base de Datos de Autoridades para un sistema de catalogación automatizada, Chile": Informe final.* (Santiago de Chile, 1986); and: Pontificia Universidad Católica de Chile. Sistema de Bibliotecas, Depto. de Catalogación. *Tratamiento de las Autoridades* (Unpublished document). (Santiago de Chile, 1996).

12. Carlos García López, "Catálogo de Autoridad de Temas de la Dirección General de Bibliotecas," *Biblioteca Universitaria,* vol. 9, n.4, (1994), pp.5-13.

13. Pilar María Moreno, *Control de autoridad y catálogos de autoridad de materia con sistemas automatizados: aplicación a la Biblioteca Daniel Cosío Villegas de El Colegio de México* (Mexico, Universidad Nacional Autónoma de México, 1996), Thesis (Masters' Degree in Library Science).

14. Gloria Escamilla González, *Lista de encabezamientos de materia*. 2. ed. (México, Universidad Nacional Autónoma de México, Instituto de Investigaciones Bibliográficas, 1978).

15. Proyecto Nacional de Autoridades en Español en México (Unpublished paper) (México, 1997).

16. Robert A. Seal, "Mexican and U.S. Library Relations," *Advances in Librarianship*, vol. 20 (1986), p. 74

17. The UNAM has been working for the last 5 years toward repeating this model in maps and BA, Masters and Doctoral theses.

18. Seal, "Mexican and U.S. Library Relations," op.cit.

19. Alvaro Quijano Solís y Oscar Arriola Navarrete, "Medidas de calidad en la creación de catálogos de bibliotecas," *Investigación Bibiotecológica*, vol. 12, n.14 (enero-junio 1998), pp. 49-56.

20. Jean Dickson and Patricia Zadner, "Authority Control and the Authority File: A Functional Evaluation of LCNAF on RLIN," *Cataloging & Classification Quarterly*, vol. 9, n.3 (1989), pp. 57-58.

21. A document is already in print detailing aspects related to administrative routines, procedures and rules, obtainable from Reynaldo D. Figueroa Servín: <rfiguero@colmex.mx>.

22. The sources mentioned here are only those in Spanish most frequently cited in field 670:

• Escamilla González, Gloria. **Lista de encabezamientos de materia**. 2' ed. México: UNAM, 1978.
• **Lista de encabezamientos de materia de la Red de Bibliotecas del CSIC**. Madrid: Consejo Superior de Investigaciones Científicas, 1995.
• Instituto Colombiano para el Fomento de la Educación Superior. **Lista de encabezamientos de materia para bibliotecas**. 2ª ed. Bogotá: ICFES, 1985.
• **Lista de encabezamientos de materia para bibliotecas**. 3ª ed. Bogotá: Rojas Ebernard, 1998.
• **Lista de encabezamientos de materia utilizados en la Biblioteca de la U.C.V.** Caracas: Universidad Central de Venezuela, 1974.
• **Bilindex: una lista bilingüe en español e inglés de encabezamientos de materia**. Berkeley, Calif.: Floricanto, 1984- .
• **Encabezamientos de la Biblioteca Nacional**. Madrid: Chadwyck Healy España, Diciembre, 1996- .
• Naciones Unidas. **UNBIS tesauro: edición española**. Nueva York: ONU, 1996.
• **Tesauro de la UNESCO**. Paris: UNESCO, 1995.

23. James Tilio Maccaferri, "Managing Authority Control in a Retrospective Conversion Project," *Cataloging & Classification Quarterly*, vol. 14, nos. 3-4 (1992), pp. 148.

24. *MARC de Autoridades*. Adaptación por Ageo García Barbabosa. México, 1999. [internal working paper]

25. <http://200.12.161.172:4505/ALEPH/SESSION-29403/start/ecm12>.

FUTURE PROSPECTS

Entering the Millennium:
A New Century for *LCSH*

Lois Mai Chan
Theodora Hodges

SUMMARY. *Library of Congress Subject Headings* (*LCSH*), a system originally designed as a tool for subject access to the Library's own collection in the late nineteenth century, has become, in the course of the last century, the main subject retrieval tool in library catalogs throughout the United States and in many other countries. It is one of the largest non-specialized controlled vocabularies in the world. As *LCSH* enters a new century, it faces an information environment that has undergone vast changes from what had prevailed when *LCSH* began, or, indeed, from its state in the early days of the online age. In order to continue its mission and to be useful in spheres outside library catalogs as well, *LCSH* must adapt to the multifarious environment.

Lois Mai Chan, PhD, is Professor, School of Library and Information Science, University of Kentucky, Lexington, KY 40506-0039. Theodora Hodges, PhD, is Lecturer and Assistant Professor, 1968-1972, School of Librarianship (now School of Information Systems and Management), University of California at Berkeley, and is a freelance editor and indexer.

[Haworth co-indexing entry note]: "Entering the Millennium: A New Century for *LCSH*." Chan, Lois Mai and Theodora Hodges. Co-published simultaneously in *Cataloging & Classification Quarterly* (The Haworth Information Press, an imprint of The Haworth Press, Inc.) Vol. 29, No. 1/2, 2000, pp. 225-234; and: *The LCSH Century: One Hundred Years with the Library of Congress Subject Headings System* (ed: Alva T. Stone) The Haworth Information Press, an imprint of The Haworth Press, Inc., 2000, pp. 225-234. Single or multiple copies of this article are available for a fee from The Haworth Document Delivery Service [1-800-342-9678, 9:00 a.m. - 5:00 p.m. (EST). E-mail address: getinfo@haworthpressinc.com].

One possible approach is to adopt a series of scalable and flexible syntax and application rules to meet the needs of different user communities. *[Article copies available for a fee from The Haworth Document Delivery Service: 1-800-342-9678. E-mail address: <getinfo@haworthpressinc.com> Website: <http://www.haworthpressinc.com>]*

KEYWORDS. *Library of Congress Subject Headings*, Library of Congress, controlled vocabulary, subject access

LCSH TO DATE

In the course of the twentieth century, *Library of Congress Subject Headings (LCSH)* grew from a subject access system designed for a single library to become the main subject retrieval tool for libraries throughout the United States and in many other countries around the world. With its current size at approximately a quarter million terms, it is now the most comprehensive non-specialized controlled vocabulary in the English language, and, in addition, has become the *de facto* standard for subject cataloging and indexing in circumstances far beyond those for which it was originally designed. At the present time, it continues to fulfill its original function as a subject cataloging tool for the Library of Congress. But with increasing outside use of the system–and with easy access to it through the Internet and other online vehicles–its role continues to grow.

Within the United States, it is the predominant tool for subject access to online library catalogs. Furthermore, many commercial retrieval services such as WILSONLINE and DIALOG carry databases with MARC records, thus providing subject access through LC subject headings, and, as well, many other commercial databases use adaptations of *LCSH* as the vocabulary on which they base their subject indexing. More widely, as libraries and other information agencies around the world have been moving toward the use of controlled vocabularies, many have been turning to *LCSH* as a model–perhaps because it is one of the largest non-specialized controlled vocabularies in the world. Libraries that have adopted, translated, or adapted *LCSH* as the basis for their controlled vocabularies include those in Belgium, Brazil, Canada, the Czech Republic, France, Great Britain, Lithuania, Malaysia, and Portugal.

LCSH springs from modest beginnings. Towards the end of the nineteenth century, Library of Congress officials decided to adopt the dictionary form for the main catalog. At that time Charles A. Cutter's *Rules for a Dictionary Catalog* was in its third edition and the dictionary arrangement was well on its way to becoming the predominant catalog form in American libraries.

Furthermore, the American Library Association had published a list of sub-ject headings, which was "calculated for small and medium sized libraries of a generally popular character" (Hanson 1909). It was this list that was chosen as a basis for the LC list, with the understanding that considerable modifica-tion and specialization would be needed. In retrospect, J. C. M. Hanson, the first chief of the Catalogue Division, recounted how work on the list began:

> As a first step preliminary to the real work of compilation, a number of copies of the List were accordingly provided, a number of blank leaves sufficient to treble the size of the original volume were added, and the copies thereupon bound in flexible leather. . . . New subjects as they came up for discussion and decision were noted on slips and filed. If the subject had already been adopted by the A.L.A. committee, i.e., had appeared as a regular printed heading on the List, a check mark was added to indicate regular adoption by the Library of Congress. (Hanson 1909)

In the same account, Hanson noted that many other catalogs, encyclopedias, and dictionaries were consulted; these included the Harvard list of subjects, the New South Wales subject index, and Forescue's subject index.

The question may be asked, as the system passes its century mark, how a subject access tool, conceived for use in a limited milieu, could have achieved such impressive acceptance and growth? Two factors, neither intrin-sic to the system itself, have undoubtedly been operative in this regard.

One is that, throughout the twentieth century, the Library of Congress has made its cataloging records available to other institutions. For most of the century, of course, distribution was through the Library's printed card ser-vice, which began in 1902. More recently, with the advent of the online age, MARC records have been distributed electronically. And, since 1993, LC cataloging data and *LCSH* itself have also been accessible online through the Internet; under these latter conditions, there was a steep rise in the use of LC cataloging information.

The second factor is that, almost from the beginning, the Library took responsibility for giving other libraries an account of its own cataloging policies and practices. Indeed, according to Hanson, one of the Library's reasons for adopting the dictionary catalog form was "a desire to be in a position to cooperate with the largest possible number of American libraries" (Hanson 1909). One example was the publication of the list itself with ongo-ing accounts of additions and changes; early on, as use of LC printed cards increased, participating libraries wanted access to LC's subject headings list, and the Library responded with the continuing series of editions and supple-ments which we now know as *LCSH*. (The 10th [1986] edition saw the completion of its conversion to machine-readable form, and the file is now available on the Internet, through bibliographic utilities, and, in combination with LC Classification, on a CD-ROM product called Classification Plus.) Furthermore, to assist catalogers in the application of the system, in 1984 the Library of Congress began publishing *Subject Cataloging Manual: Subject Headings*. In addition, a steady effort was made throughout the century to render the system responsive to societal changes and evolving language usage, an effort that accelerated in recent decades. A measure toward this end is that since the mid-1980s, as a way to increase the usefulness of *LCSH* to the library community at large, the Library of Congress has invited outside libraries to contribute headings to the system; over seventy-five libraries worldwide now do this through SACO, the Subject Authority Cooperative Program.

In the end, however, it must be concluded that the primary reason for the long dominance of *LCSH* is that it has been, at bottom, a reasonably effective retrieval tool. On the one hand, information professionals have long acknowledged that *LCSH* is far from an ideal system; it exhibits considerable internal inconsistency, and retains certain characteristics that still cater more to manual than to online systems. On the other hand, over the years, *LCSH* has proved preferable to other available alternatives. One reason may be that it has dependable authority control, with a generous lead-in vocabulary–factors which increase the chance for high retrieval recall. Another reason may be that it is, for the most part, a precoordinated system, a factor for high retrieval precision. And in structure it is dynamic, with the capacity to expand and accommodate new topics easily and promptly–though in practice the Library of Congress has been forced to balance the advantages of updating existing headings (and their syndetics) against implementation costs, which are substantial. Overall, *LCSH* has clearly demonstrated its versatility in response to changed external circumstances, offering subject access to a wide range of audiences in a wide range of environments, from book and card catalogs to the electronic and online environment, from libraries to other venues of information providers. (Indeed, it has been almost surprisingly effective in the OPAC (online public access catalog) environment.) The question for us now is, can it continue to do as well in the future?

Even as the twentieth century was approaching its end, it was clear that the information environment had undergone vast changes from what had prevailed when it began, or, indeed, from its state in the early days of the online age. As online resources proliferated, the situation even within the library or OPAC environment was no longer monolithic. For instance, the same bibliographic record might contain subject data from different schemes. Later, access to the rapidly growing Internet and web resources became a significant part of the services provided by libraries to their users. But the World Wide Web environment differs in many respects from that of a traditional library. Its store of resources is vast, and access to those resources is apparently easy even though retrieval results are not always satisfactory; as a result, information seekers have changed not only their behavior but their expectations. However, while the web offers an enormous store of information, its resources vary not only in type, source, and provenance, but in the search devices through which they can be accessed. Furthermore, they also present the challenge of multiple subject access provisions. Thus, in spite of its richness of content, the web's size and range are often overwhelming to those searching for information. As a result, with the need to access such a wide variety of disparate resources both within their walls and at remote sites, and with users so often falling short in their searches, librarians began finding themselves facing the need to adjust the traditional methods of providing information to the new environment.

LCSH IN THE FUTURE

In the new information circumstances just described, what might be the role of the LC subject headings system? Will *LCSH* continue to be useful, even viable, in the years ahead? No one can predict the future. Still, one thing seems certain: the Library of Congress can continue to be a player in the information-access world of the future, even in respect to resources quite different from those for which its systems have been used in the past, resources that are primarily available within an increasingly heterogenous digital environment. Something else can be stated with conviction: if *LCSH* is to play an important role in subject access to information, it must adapt to the new environment.

What direction might needed changes take? For a subject access system to become adaptable in the current and future environment, three qualities warrant serious consideration: simplicity, interoperability, and scalability. In fact, the first two have been adopted by the Dublin Core Metadata Initiative as two of its primary characteristics (The Dublin Core, 1998). Traditionally, subject data have been typically provided by trained catalogers and indexers. In the web environment, increasingly, more and more people not necessarily trained in intricate methods of information storage and retrieval are engaged in providing subject data for information resources. For this reason, simplicity becomes a requisite for efficient organization and retrieval of information. A system can be judged sufficiently simple if it can be used by non-catalogers to tag whatever material is covered by the system—if, in other words, records can be created by personnel not trained in sophisticated standards of bibliographic control. In the multifarious environment, information systems no longer function alone; interoperability is important. A system can be judged interoperable if it provides the ability to search across discipline boundaries and, desirably, also across information retrieval and storage systems. The third criterion for an adaptable system is scalability; a system can be considered scalable if it has provisions for use in circumstances that vary considerably in depth and sophistication. An example of the scalability of application rules is the different degrees of depth and exhaustivity in assigning headings. At different times in the past, the average number of subject headings assigned by the Library of Congress to each item has varied, with the current instruction being "Generally a maximum of six is appropriate" and "Do not assign more than ten headings to a work" (Library of Congress, 1996-). In the recently implemented core level records, the number of subject headings assigned to each record has been scaled down.

Thus, somewhat expanded from the above, it can be held that the functional requirements of a subject vocabulary suitable for the web environment include at least the following:

1. it should be simple in structure (i.e., easy to assign and use) and easy to maintain;
2. it should provide optimal access points; and,
3. it should be flexible (that is, scalable) and interoperable across disciplines and in various discovery and access environments, not the least among which are OPACs.

In light of the above, as those charged with the responsibility of choosing a general subject indexing vocabulary to be used in the broader sphere as well as in the OPAC, it would appear that there are three options:

1. creating a totally new controlled vocabulary covering all subject areas for subject access on the web; or,
2. applying *LCSH* as it is currently done, and accepting the fact that its usefulness and effectiveness will be limited largely to the OPAC environment; or,
3. retaining *LCSH* and applying it with a flexible and scalable syntax.

Adopting the first option, though attractive, would require a larger investment in time and effort than appears practical either at the present time or in the foreseeable future. Adopting the second option would amount in some degree to backing away from the responsibility to the larger information-seeking world. It seems, however, that adopting the third option offers real promise.

On the criteria listed earlier, the LC subject headings system as currently applied comes up somewhat short as an efficient tool for subject access in the web environment. Its particular disadvantages include:

1. the LC system is so complex, in syntax and current application rules, that assigning subject headings as currently constructed requires trained personnel;
2. it is very costly to maintain subject heading strings in bibliographic or metadata records;
3. in its present form and application, *LCSH* is not compatible in syntax with most other controlled vocabularies;
4. its subject heading strings do not lend themselves to mapping onto other controlled vocabularies; and,
5. it is not amenable to search engines outside of the OPAC environment, particularly those that operate on the web.

On the other hand, *LCSH* has many advantages as the possible basis for a web-friendly indexing tool. These include:

1. it is a rich vocabulary covering all subject areas, easily the largest general indexing vocabulary in the English language;
2. it provides synonym and homograph control;
3. it contains rich links (cross-references) among terms;
4. it is a *de facto* universal controlled vocabulary, having been translated or adapted as a model for developing subject headings systems by many countries around the world; and,
5. it is compatible with subject data in MARC records.

To adapt to the broader information community and particularly the web environment, what would be required would be to separate *LCSH* terminology from its current syntax, and to devise a simplified syntax (perhaps a series of syntaxes with varying degrees of complexity) according to which *LCSH* terminology would be applied. Such a step would result in a flexible and scalable scheme, based on the vocabulary and relationships already established in *LCSH* but applied with different policies and procedures. Within the OPAC environment, where trained personnel is available for the creation and maintenance of complex subject headings strings and the on-line system is capable of handling such, the current rules and policies for complex syntax can continue to function. For situations which require the handling of large quantities of information resources for which trained personnel and financial resources are not abundantly available and in online systems that are not equipped to take full advantage of the subject strings, *LCSH* may be applied with simpler syntaxes. In other words, *LCSH* would offer a source vocabulary with, in application, options for varying degrees of complexity in syntax and in application rules. An advantage of such an approach would be that the richness of *LCSH* vocabulary and syndetics could be retained at the same time that the system would become relatively easy to apply and maintain–and easier and more effective on the searching end as well.

A possible step towards simplifying the *LCSH* string is to adopt a more faceted, postcoordinate approach. Although *LCSH* began as an enumerative system, in recent decades it has become a system where precoordination is preferred, but with postcoordination allowed and used in many instances, i.e., when a single subject heading string cannot cover the overall content. A move towards greater use of postcoordination is to break non-topical elements (geographic, chronological, and form data) out of the string. A proposal to that effect was put forth at the Subject Subdivisions Conference (also known as the Airlie Conference), held in May 1991 (Chan 1992). In response, there were arguments for and against such an approach; at the end, perhaps because of the particular OPAC environment at the time and an overwhelming desire to retain the advantages of achieving precision through full subject heading strings, no recommendation towards implementation of the proposal was put forth. Now, almost a decade later, in the totally different web environment which imposes different functional requirements on subject indexing systems, there appears to be renewed interest in this particular approach. Furthermore, LC's recent efforts to distinguish form subdivisions from topical subdivisions represent yet another important step toward more rigorous faceting that offers the possibility for a greater degree of postcoordination.

In the web environment, the notion of providing a postcoordinate approach to subject data in metadata records is particularly tantalizing. The advantages of a simplified, postcoordinate approach to subject data in metadata records include:

1. A postcoordinate approach is more adaptable and amenable to changes in the web environment. It will not require the extensive training necessary to apply *LCSH* according to current policies and procedures;
2. An online thesaurus based on faceted principles is easier to display and for non-catalogers or non-librarians to use;
3. A postcoordinate subject vocabulary is compatible in structure and syntax with most other controlled vocabularies; and,
4. A postcoordinate single-term approach is more amenable than full subject strings for mapping to other controlled vocabularies, to other languages, or to classification schemes such as DDC.

Furthermore, a postcoordinated controlled vocabulary based on or compatible with *LCSH* would be a factor for interoperability between MARC and other resource description models. The content richness of the MARC database makes it desirable to maintain MARC records even in the digital environment and to make them interoperable with other types of metadata records; even more desirable would be to provide the potential for integrating various types of metadata records and MARC records into a single system. Being able to do so would extend the returns on the enormous investments that have gone into preparing MARC records in the past.

Of course, separating non-topical elements from the subject heading is not without drawbacks. A major one is the loss of precision in instances where false or cross coordination may occur. The advantage of achieving precision through full heading strings in the OPAC is well recognized. In systems that do not provide subject heading browsing and full string indexing, this advantage cannot be realized. A more faceted *LCSH* with a less rigid syntax as applied now would allow users flexibility in application. Each implementation would be able to adopt the approach most compatible with its priority with regard to subject access, taking into consideration its systems design and available personnel and resources.

In view of the factors considered above, the ALA Subject Analysis Committee's Subcommittee on Metadata and Subject Analysis has been considering endorsing the use of flexible syntax with the *LCSH* vocabulary for different applications, particularly with regard to a more faceted, postcoordinate approach for metadata systems such as the Dublin Core. Currently, OCLC is also studying the feasibility of adopting a faceted approach to the application of *LCSH* in its CORC (Cooperative Online Resources Catalog) project.

CONCLUSION

LCSH was born as the Library of Congress prepared to meet the challenges of the approaching twentieth century. Its history supports the prediction that in another new century, *LCSH* will continue–with vigilance, flexibility, and adaptability–to evolve as needed to accommodate changing information resources and changing demands on and for information. Only this time, it will do so not as a newborn but as a mature system that has stood the test of many changing environments. *LCSH* contains an enormously rich vocabulary and it offers great potential for successful adaptation to the electronic environment. It is up to the information profession to determine whether it can fulfill that potential, and, if chances are judged good, what measures should be adopted toward that end.

REFERENCES

Chan, Lois Mai. "Alternatives to Subject Strings in the Library of Congress Subject Headings System," In *The Future of Subdivisions in the Library of Congress Subject Headings System: Report from the Subject Subdivisions Conference, Sponsored by the Library of Congress, May 9-12, 1991*, ed. Martha O'Hara

Conway, 46-54. Washington, DC: Library of Congress, Cataloging Distribution Service, 1992.

The Dublin Core: A Simple Content Description Model for Electronic Resources. c1998. URL: <http://purl.oclc.org/dc/>.

Hanson, J. C. M. "The Subject Catalogs of the Library of Congress," *Bulletin of the American Library Association* 3 (1909): 385-97.

Library of Congress. Cataloging Policy and Support Office. *Subject Cataloging Manual: Subject Headings.* 5th ed. Washington, D.C.: Cataloging Distribution Service, Library of Congress, 1996- .

Index

FORTHCOMING AND NEW BOOKS
FROM HAWORTH LIBRARY & INFORMATION SCIENCE

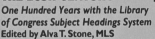

Take 20% Off Each Book! Special Sale

PUBLISHING AND THE LAW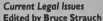

Current Legal Issues
Edited by Bruce Strauch
This unique book includes a history of copyright law up
through current international treaties so you will have a
better understanding of how copyright law and the
electronic environment intertwine.
(A monograph published simultaneously as
The Acquisitions Librarian, Vol. 13, No. 26.
$49.95 hard. ISBN: 0-7890-0777-0.
$24.95 soft. ISBN: 0-7890-0812-2.
Available Summer/Fall 2001. Approx. 195 pp. with Index.

NEW TECHNOLOGIES AND REFERENCE SERVICES

Edited by Bill Katz, PhD
This book explores developing trends in publishing,
information literacy in the reference environment,
reference provision in adult basic and community
education, searching sessions, outreach programs, locating
moving image materials for multimedia development.
(A monograph published simultaneously as
The Reference Librarian, Vol. 34, No. 71)
$39.95 hard. ISBN: 0-7890-1180-8.
$24.95 soft. ISBN: 0-7890-1181-6.
Available Winter 2000/2001. Approx. 112 pp. with Index.

CATALOGING AND CLASSIFICATION FOR LIBRARY TECHNICIANS, Second Edition

NEW EDITION!

Mary L. Kao, MLS, PhD
Among the concepts in this **Second Edition** are
bibliobgraphic records and library catalogs, descriptive
cataloging, subject headings, classification systems, original
and copy cataloging, online cataloging (the MARC format),
routines for a cataloging department, and issues and trends
in the field.
$39.95 hard. ISBN: 0-7890-1062-3.
$19.95 soft. ISBN: 0-7890-1063-1.
Available Winter 2000/2001. Approx. 142 pp. with Index.

The Haworth Information Press
An imprint of the Haworth Press, Inc.
10 Alice Street
Binghamton, New York 13904–1580 USA

REFERENCE SERVICES FOR THE ADULT LEARNER

Over 400 Pages!

*Challenging Issues for the
Traditional and Technological Era*
Edited by Kwasi Sarkodie-Mensah, PhD
Addresses issues such as technophobia, technostress,
and information literacy, this guide provides you with
learning theories and suggestions from adult learners
to help you understand what these clients need to know
about finding information.
(A monograph published simultaneously as
The Reference Librarian, Vol. 33, Nos. 69/70).
$89.95 hard. ISBN: 0-7890-0972-2.
$49.95 soft. ISBN: 0-7890-0990-0.
Available Fall 2000. Approx. 431 pp. with Index.

ACQUIRING ONLINE MANAGEMENT REPORTS

Edited by William E. Jarvis
Provides discussions and suggestions on several topics,
including working with vendors, developing cost-effective
collection development methods to suit your library,
assessing collection growth, and choosing the best electronic
resources to help meet your goals.
(A monograph published simultaneously as the
Journal of Interlibrary Loan, Document Delivery &
Information Supply, Vol. 10, No. 4)
$49.95 hard. ISBN: 0-7890-1041-0.
$32.95 soft. ISBN: 0-7890-1042-9.
Available Summer 2000. Approx. 134 pp. with Index.

READERS, READING, AND LIBRARIANS

Over 200 Pages!

Edited by Bill Katz, PhD
Explores whether the focus on electronic wonders
has really shifted the basic mission of the librarian by taking
away from such services as the readers' advisory service
in favor of maintaining technological services.
(A monograph published simultaneously as
The Acquisitions Librarian, Vol. 13, No. 25.)
$49.95 hard. ISBN: 0-7890-0699-5.
Text price (5+ copies): $24.95.
Available Summer 2000. Approx 235 pp.

THE LCSH CENTURY

Over 250 Pages!

*One Hundred Years with the Library
of Congress Subject Headings System*
Edited by Alva T. Stone, MLS
Explore the most significant changes in **LCSH** policies and
practices, including a summary of other contributions
celebrating the centennial of the world's most popular
library subject heading language.
(A monograph published simultaneously as the
Cataloging & Classification Quarterly, Vol. 29, Nos. 1/2.)
$69.95 hard. ISBN: 0-7890-1168-9.
$34.95 soft. ISBN: 0-7890-1169-7.
Available Summer 2000. Approx. 264 pp. with Index.